FREUD
and the Critic

FREUD

and the CRITIC

The Early Use of Depth Psychology in Literary Criticism

by Claudia C. Morrison

The University of North Carolina Press · Chapel Hill

Quotations from *A Reviewer's ABC*, *The Ordeal of Mark Twain*, and *Edgar Allan Poe: A Study in Genius* used by permission of the following:

From *Collected Criticism* (formerly *A Reviewer's ABC*)
Oxford University Press
Copyright © 1935, 1929, 1940, 1942, 1951, 1958 by Conrad Aiken
Reprinted by the permission of Brandt & Brandt.

From the book *The Ordeal of Mark Twain* by Van Wyck Brooks.
Copyright, 1920, by E. P. Dutton & Co., Inc. Renewal, 1948, by
Van Wyck Brooks. Reprinted by permission of the publishers.

From *Edgar Allan Poe: A Study in Genius* by Joseph Wood Krutch
(New York: Alfred A. Knopf, Inc., 1926; Russell & Russell, Inc.,
1965). Reprinted by permission of Joseph Wood Krutch.

To Faith Ogden

Preface

At the present time, the use of psychoanalytic concepts in literary criticism is quite common. Archetypes and Oedipus complexes, psychic wounds and primordial symbols abound in the literary essays appearing in critical journals, and in even the most conservative of them a certain Freudian flavor can be discerned. Few contemporary literary biographers would neglect to mention their subject's relationship with his parents and siblings. If the hero of a novel dreams of being chased by a horse, it is a rare critic who will leave the dream uninterpreted and not pursue it into the depths of the hero's, and the author's, unconscious. Almost all of the major figures in American and English literature, and many of the minor ones as well, have been subjected to post-mortem analyses, and in some cases—Edgar Allan Poe comes immediately to mind—we are so familiar with the unconscious "meaning" of his works that the current critical problem is to point out the author's conscious preoccupations in order to redress the balance.

This, of course, was not always the case. The origins of this critical approach—when and how Freudian and Jungian ideas entered the discipline of literary criticism, and the original impact these ideas had on the theory of literature—has yet to be examined in detail. Frederick J. Hoffman, in *Freudianism and the Literary Mind*, has presented an excellent study of the use of psychoanalytic material by twentieth century writers and poets; and, more recently, Louis Fraiberg has examined six American literary critics who have used the psychoanalytic approach, but a historical treatment of the origin and development of such criticism does not yet exist. To fill in this gap in the history of English and American literary criticism is the aim of this book. In it I have attempted to trace the introduction of Freudian ideas into the literary world and to study the reaction to them among literary critics of the first quarter of this century.

Although much of this early criticism is now primarily an object of curiosity or, in some cases, amusement, several of these early attempts to apply Freud's ideas to literature and literary biography still possess merit. Moreover, a review of such criticism in its early phases has the virtue of revealing the issues which depth psychology posed for the literary critic in basic outline, unobscured by the qualifications and subtleties which later, more sophisticated scholars and students of literature tended to display when using the Freudian approach. This new body of information which "science" held out as a promising method for examining literature was attractive to a surprising number of critics; it seemed to shed new light on age-old critical problems: the mystery of the creative process, the nature of the aesthetic response, the problem of the "universality" of great art, the problem of the extent to which form or content contributes to aesthetic enjoyment. Freud and his followers claimed to have discovered and charted a new area of consciousness, to have unlocked the mysterious phenomenon of dreams, and this new knowledge, if valid, was of immediate relevance to literary theory, or at least this was the feeling at the time. The actual grasp of the principles of depth psychology in these early years was frequently somewhat hazy, but the stimulus that Freudian and Jungian hypotheses gave to students of literature and the creative process led to a widespread and serious reconsideration of basic concepts in criticism and resulted in a fruitful discussion of the theory of literature, as well as in some challenging interpretations of specific literary works.

Although my original intention was to deal only with American literary criticism, I soon realized that the study could not be limited in this way. Several of the most important Freudian analyses done at this time were by British critics, such as Ernest Jones, Her-

bert Read, and D. H. Lawrence. These studies, which were widely read on this side of the Atlantic, exercised considerable influence
and stimulated much discussion. My survey was therefore extended to include psychoanalytic criticism in England as well as
in the United States, although the first chapter deals only with the
reception of Freud's thought in this country. In assessing the
material, I have attempted to place it in its historical context and
to judge these critical works on the basis of the psychoanalytic information available at that time, without censuring a psychoanalytic naïvete that was unavoidable during those years.

This survey attempts completeness, particularly insofar as
American literary criticism is concerned, one purpose being to
document the extensiveness as well as the quality of the criticism
influenced by concepts of depth psychology in the first quarter of
this century. In my researches I have relied on the standard in-
dices to periodicals, the bibliographies published in *Literature and
Psychology*, and the recent (1963) work by Norman Kiell, *Psychoanalysis, Psychology and Literature: A Bibliography*, as well
as on my own examination of major American and British literary
journals between 1910 and 1926 and all major psychology journals between these dates. I am sure, however, that there are still
a few articles or books which have escaped my notice; I can only
hope that these do not represent a significant omission.

I am, of course, indebted to many people for the help and
stimulation they have provided in the course of writing this book.
The studies of Hoffman and Fraiberg were of considerable value
in enabling me to understand more thoroughly the impact of
Freudian thought on the intellectual milieu of early twentieth century America, and there are many articles, too numerous to cite,
on aspects of the influence of psychoanalytic concepts on our culture which have in one way or another affected my treatment of
the material here. More specifically, I am grateful to friends and
associates at the University of North Carolina, where this work
was originally conceived, and particularly to O. B. Hardison, Jr.,
whose excellent course in literary criticism first aroused my interest in the subject.

Claudia C. Morrison

Youngstown, Ohio
January, 1968

Contents

Preface   vii

1. The American Reaction to Freud   3

2. Freudian Criticism: The Theorists   37

3. Freudian Criticism: The Practitioners   99

4. The Criticism of Conrad Aiken   142

5. Ernest Jones, Hamlet, and the Oedipus Complex   161

6. Van Wyck Brooks's Analysis of Mark Twain   176

7. Joseph Wood Krutch and Edgar Allan Poe   192

8. D. H. Lawrence and American Literature   203

9. Retrospect   226

Appendix A: *233*

*A chronology of events relevant to the
acceptance of Freud's Ideas in the United States*

Appendix B: *237*

*An annotated list of selected early works on
psychoanalysis and the application of psychoanalysis to literature*

Index   *245*

FREUD
and the Critic

1. The American Reaction to Freud

Although the validity of the concepts of Sigmund Freud is still a source of wide dispute, the stature of the man in the history of modern western thought is not. The influence of Freud's theory of the dynamics of human personality extends far beyond the discipline of the behavioral sciences, reaching out into major areas of the humanities, in philosophy, history, and literature. A bibliography of current books and articles treating various aspects of Freudian thought would probably entail several volumes, and the list is constantly growing. Explications of Freud's theories are plentiful, even superabundant, as are analyses of Freud as a personality and studies of the influences which helped to shape his thought.

Curiously enough, however, there has not yet been any comprehensive treatment of the initial reception of Freudian theory in America, although Ernest Jones's three-volume biography of Freud has provided a fairly thorough history of the adoption of Freud's concepts in continental Europe.[1] At present it is difficult to imag-

1. Ernest Jones, *The Life and Work of Sigmund Freud* (New York: Basic Books, 1955), II, 27-66. Other studies which treat aspects of the growth of Freud's American reputation include Clarence P. Oberndorf, *A History of Psychoanalysis in America* (New York: Grune and Stratton, 1953); Celia B. Stendler, "New Ideas for Old: How Freudianism Was Received in the United States from 1900 to 1925," *The Journal of Educational Psychology*, XXXVIII (April, 1947), 193-206; Ernest Jones, "Early History of Psychoanalysis in English-Speaking Countries," *The International Journal of Psychoanalysis*, XXVI (1945), 8-10; Frederick J. Hoffman, *Freudianism and the Literary Mind* (Baton Rouge: Louisiana State

ine a time when Sigmund Freud's basic premises were unknown, when childhood was viewed as a period of purity and innocence and the infant seen as trailing clouds of glory rather than all the unmentionable instincts of the id. The impact of Freud's theory of man was such as to cause a major revolution in American cultural attitudes, attitudes which we now largely take for granted. Tracing the early reaction to these theories in the scientific and popular press in the early part of this century is a fascinating by-path in the history of ideas.

Freud's thought modestly entered the American intellectual world through a few highly specialized journals. Credit for the first article on psychoanalysis in America is generally given to Boris Sidis, a student and friend of William James, for his brief abstract of Freud's *Psychopathology of Everyday Life* in *The Journal of Abnormal Psychology* in 1906.[2] Sidis' article was the first substantive treatment of Freud's ideas, but there had been earlier references to Freud, indicating some familiarity with his thought, in various technical journals during the last decade of the nineteenth century. It is a rather remarkable fact that Freud's name was first mentioned in America even before the *Studien Über Hysterie* appeared in Vienna in 1895. In the *Proceedings of the Society for Psychical Research* in 1893-94, F. W. H. Myers devoted several pages of his article on the "subliminal consciousness" to Freud's ideas, emphasizing particularly the carthartic method of treatment and the concept of an unconscious memory of a trauma as the cause of hysteria. Although brief, Myers' essay contained several quotations from an article by Breuer and Freud published in 1893.[3]

University Press, 1957); A. A. Brill, "The Introduction and Development of Freud's Work in the United States," *The American Journal of Sociology*, XLV (1939), 318-25; and F. H. Matthews, "The Americanization of Sigmund Freud," *Journal of American Studies*, I (April, 1967), 39-62.

2. Hoffman, *Freudianism*, p. 47; Oberndorf, *History of Psychoanalysis*, p. 52.

3. Frederick W. H. Myers, "The Subliminal Consciousness: The Mechanism of Hysteria," *Proceedings of the Society for Psychical Research*, IX (1893-94), 3-128 (especially 12-15). Jones, in his "Early History" (p. 8), reports that Myers delivered an address before the Society in March, 1897, on "Hysteria and Genius" in which he gave an account of the *Studien*; this was published at greater length in his *Human Personality and Its Bodily Survival After Death* (1903).

Two years later, Dr. Robert Edes referred favorably in a lecture to "Breuer and Freud's hypothesis about hysteria";[4] and in 1896, in one of his Lowell lectures on psychopathology, William James stated that "in the relief of certain hysterics, by handling the buried ideas, whether as in Freud or in Janet, we see a portent of the possible usefulness of these new discoveries."[5] Shortly after this, in England, Dr. Mitchell Clarke reviewed the *Studies in Hysteria* in the journal, *Brain*; the review was noted by Havelock Ellis and apparently led to his reading of the *Studies*. In 1898 Ellis published "Hysteria in Relation to the Sexual Emotions" in *The Alienist and Neurologist*,[6] and reprinted it in his popular *Studies in the Psychology of Sex* in 1904, in which he devoted several pages to Freud's "fascinating and really important" researches.[7]

Thus, by 1898, there had been at least five references to Freud's *Studies in Hysteria* in English, made largely by men who had a considerable professional reputation. This does not, of course, indicate that Freud's ideas were by any means widespread at the time, even in psychology circles, but the American professional community's awareness of Freud compares very favorably with the scant recognition accorded him in Europe at the same time.

Until about 1909, however, a knowledge of Freudian theory was the possession of only a few. That the majority of American psychologists were unfamiliar with Freud's ideas is demonstrated by the volumes of *The American Journal of Psychology* from 1900 to 1906, in which articles appeared on both hysteria and dreams by authors obviously ignorant of the new theories that were slowly gaining acceptance on the other side of the Atlantic. Occasionally the journal carried reviews of books by Freud's followers, but in general the texts of the feature articles show no evidence of an acquaintance with Freud himself. When in 1906 Joseph Jastrow published a book entitled *The Subconscious*, which presented a theory of the "subliminal self" that took no cognizance of Freudian thought, neither John B. Watson nor James R. Angell,

4. Oberndorf, *History of Psychoanalysis*, p. 41.
5. *Ibid.* Oberndorf quotes here from *The James Family*, ed. F. O. Matthiessen (New York: Alfred A. Knopf, 1947), p. 226.
6. IX (1898), 599-615.
7. Jones, "Early History," pp. 8-9.

prominent psychologists of the time, who reviewed the work, criticized it in the light of Freud's concepts.[8]

Many psychologists during this period, however, had discovered Freud independently and had communicated this knowledge to their students. Ernest Jones encountered him through Wilfrid Trotter, an English physician who had read the *Brain* article and Myers' book, *Human Personality*. An early convert, Jones began practicing psychoanalysis in London as early as 1905.[9] A. A. Brill, the man mainly responsible for the spread of psychoanalysis in America, was advised in 1907 to do his post-graduate work in psychiatry at the Bergholzi clinic in Switzerland, where Jung and others were applying Freud's theories; his adviser in this instance was Professor Fred Peterson of Columbia University. Brill returned to the United States in 1908 to become the first practicing analyst in America.[10] While doing post-graduate work in Europe, Clarence P. Oberndorf, another early analyst, had heard of Freud through a Dr. Louis Casamajor, another neurology professor at Columbia.[11] On his return to America, Oberndorf became connected with the Manhattan State Hospital, which, under the direction of Adolf Meyer and August Hoch, became the first state hospital to use psychoanalysis regularly for diagnosis and treatment.[12] An awareness of Freud's theories, then, was spreading slowly but steadily among psychologists and neurologists, although up until the time of the founding of *The Journal of Abnormal Psychology* in 1906, Freud received no significant public recognition.

The real turning point in the growth of Freud's American reputation came in 1909, the year he was invited by G. Stanley Hall to lecture at Clark University in Worcester, Massachusetts, to celebrate the twentieth anniversary of the university's founding. How Hall, a prominent psychologist and the author of a book on adolescence that had already become a classic, had discovered Freud's ideas is unknown, but it is something of a paradox that a one-time President of the New England Watch and Ward Society should be responsible for the first official recognition of

8. Stendler, "New Ideas for Old," p. 196.

9. Jones, "Early History," p. 10: "Psychoanalysis was first practiced in London in 1905, in New York in 1908 and in Boston in 1910."

10. Oberndorf, *History of Psychoanalysis*, p. 55.

11. *Ibid.*, p. 78.   12. *Ibid.*, p. 83.

Freud in the United States.[13] Freud himself was very pleased with the invitation and with his reception in America: "It is one of the pleasantest phantasies to imagine that somewhere . . . there are decent people finding their way into our thoughts and efforts, who after all suddenly make their appearance. That is what happened to me with Stanley Hall. Who could have thought that over there in America, only an hour away from Boston, there was a respectable old gentleman waiting impatiently for the next number of the Jahrbuch, reading and understanding it all, and who would then, as he expressed it himself, 'ring the bells for us'?"[14]

At Worcester, Freud delivered five lectures in German on the basic theory of psychoanalysis, and Jung and Sandor Ferenczi lectured on "The Association Method" and "The Psychological Analysis of Dreams." Among the audience were such influential men in the field of the social sciences as Franz Boas, E. B. Titchener, Ernest Jones, Adolf Meyer, Joseph Jastrow, William James, A. A. Brill, E. B. Holt, and James J. Putnam, the majority of whom were already familiar, in varying degrees, with Freud's work. According to Jones, the reaction to the lectures was mixed, but the net effect was very favorable. In a letter to his wife on September 8, Jung wrote: "Yesterday Freud began the lectures and received great applause. We are gaining ground here, and

13. Hall was not a full-fledged advocate of Freud's ideas—his reaction was always somewhat mixed—but while he was editor of *The American Journal of Psychology*, he published many articles on psychoanalysis. In his autobiography, *Life and Confessions of a Psychologist* (New York: D. Appleton and Company, 1923), Hall speaks of the advent of Freudianism as marking "the greatest epoch in the history of our science. Not only did it bring the elements of feeling . . . into the foreground of attention but it made it the prime determinant of human development. If the Freudian claims of the all-dominance of sex were excessive, as they certainly seem to me to be, it was only a natural reaction to the long taboo and prudery that would not look facts in the face" (p. 409). Hall remained dubious about some of Freud's tenets: "My sense of its [psychoanalysis'] importance . . . has steadily grown. This is despite the fact, too, that I cannot believe that normal children show to any marked extent the infantile aberrations which are postulated; that I especially balk at the *Analerotik* . . . ; that I am convinced from years of study of my own dreams and those of my pupils that while there is a class of them which pretty strictly conforms to Freud's rubrics there are others that cannot possibly be explained by them. . . ." (*ibid.*, p. 410).
14. Jones, *Life and Work*, II, 57-58.

our following is growing slowly but surely. Today I had a talk about psychoanalysis with two highly cultivated elderly ladies who proved to be very well informed and free-thinking. I was greatly surprised, since I had prepared myself for opposition . . . . It is said that we shall be awarded honorary doctorates by the university next Saturday, with a great deal of pomp and circumstance . . . . We have also been interviewed by the *Boston Evening Transcript*. In fact we are the men of the hour here."[15] The lectures had apparently been awaited with eager anticipation, for there had been several colloquiums on Freud's thought held in New England by Jones and others in the previous year.[16] In addition, *The Journal of Abnormal Psychology* had published several articles making use of Freudian concepts in the early issues of 1909,[17] so that the audience which came to hear Freud had some knowledge of what he was going to say.

Newspaper coverage of these lectures, however, was slight. The celebration at Clark University involved speeches by many famous scientists; Freud was therefore treated merely as another specialist in his field, and as of no more importance than any of the other psychologists attending the meeting. Indeed, the *Boston Evening Transcript* of September 9 gave more space to the non-psychoanalytic papers read by E. B. Titchener and Adolf Meyer than it did to Freud's. The news accounts of the following two days, however were more detailed. Jung's paper on the association test and its ability to detect criminals—a subject which seems to have attracted immediate popular interest—was described, and the *Transcript* outlined briefly Freud's concept of repression and mentioned that he had abandoned the use of hypnotism because many people were incapable of being hypnotized. Freud's dream theories were said to include the hypotheses that "dreams preserve infantile inclinations, give 'the inside of the unconscious life,' and may frequently, if not always, be interpreted." On September 12, the *Tran-*

15. C. G. Jung, *Memories, Dreams, Reflections* (New York: Pantheon Books, 1963), p. 276.

16. Jones, *Life and Work*, II, 56.

17. Ernest Jones, "Psychoanalysis in Psychotherapy," *The Journal of Abnormal Psychology*, IV (June-July, 1909), 140-50; and B. Onuf, "Dreams and Their Interpretation As Diagnostic and Therapeutic Aids in Psychopathology," *The Journal of Abnormal Psychology*, IV (February-March, 1909), 339-50.

script carried an interview with Freud which constitutes one of the first lengthy discussions of the man and his work to appear in the popular press. Under the heading "The Eminent Vienna Psychotherapist Now in America," the article, which comprised two full columns, opened with some highly flattering remarks: "It was certainly an excellent idea of President Stanley Hall's to invite Professor Sigmund Freud of Vienna to Clark University as a guest of honor. Professor Freud needs no further introduction to physicians, but for the lay public it may be said that Professor Freud is not only the most eminent neurologist of Europe, but also that he is recognized as one of the greatest, if not the very greatest, of psychotherapists." In a description of Freud's character, the author of the article. Adelbert Albrecht, made use of terms derived from phrenology, an interesting instance of the encounter between an old system of ideas and the new which was soon to replace it: "[Dr. Freud] is a man of great refinement of intellect and of many-sided education. His sharp, yet kind, clear eyes suggest at once the doctor. His high forehead with the large bumbs of observation and his beautiful, energetic hands are very striking. He speaks clearly . . . but unfortunately never of himself." Albrecht discussed Freud's views on psychotherapy, his strong disapproval of hypnosis (on the grounds that it was not only useless but demoralizing), and, perhaps most interesting, Freud's own critique of his "analytic" method. During the interview, Freud alluded to Hamlet's speech to Rosencrantz and Guildenstern and added, "The instrument of the soul is not so easy to play and my technique is very painstaking and tedious. Any amateur attempt may have the most evil consequences." He further emphasized that patients suffering from a nervous ailment must sincerely desire a cure if the analytic method were to succeed: "Everything depends on whether the patient can be trained to subject himself to the method. Even if that has been done with success, the number of cases where it can be employed is limited." The modesty of this comment is in striking contrast to remarks made on the efficacy of psychoanalysis by many of Freud's followers only a few years later.

Albrecht's interview provided an opportunity for an American, or at least a Boston, audience to be given a personal glimpse of

Freud. Although the article itself was highly laudatory, and thus served as a piece of positive propaganda for Freud's ideas, its effect was slight; the other Boston newspapers did not consider Freud's presence in the United States to be worthy of notice. The significance of the Clark University lectures lies not in the recognition Freud received in the press, but rather in the number of friends Freud made in America who were later to spread his ideas throughout the country.

One of these was William James, who, as has been mentioned, was among the first to have encountered Freud's work. In a letter written shortly after the Worcester meeting, James described his own somewhat mixed reaction:

Speaking of "functional" psychology, Clark University had a little international congress the other day in honor of the twentieth year of its existence. I went there for one day in order to see what Freud was like. I hope that Freud and his pupils will push their ideas to their utmost limits, so that we may learn what they are. They can't fail to throw light on human nature; but I confess that he made on me personally the impression of a man obsessed with fixed ideas. I can make nothing in my own case with his dream theories; and obviously "symbolism" is a most dangerous method. A newspaper report of the congress said that Freud had condemned the American religious therapy (which has such extensive results) as very "dangerous" because so "unscientific." Bah![18]

Whatever initial respect James may have had for psychoanalysis had steadily diminished; but his parting words to Freud—"The future of psychology belongs to your work"—were very encouraging.[19]

A more important contact was James J. Putnam, a neurology professor at Harvard, the past president of the American Neurological Association, and the future first president of the American Psychoanalytic Association. Putnam had published in 1906 the first paper to deal specifically with psychoanalysis, although his conclusion at that time was, in general, adverse.[20] He originally distrusted Freud's ideas, and was skeptical of the whole Freudian

18. Henry James (ed.), *The Letters of William James* (Boston: The Atlantic Monthly Press, 1920), II, 328.
19. Quoted in Jones, *Life and Work*, II, 57.
20. Jones, "Early History," p. 9. The article appeared in *The Journal of Abnormal Psychology* in February of 1906.

approach before attending the Clark lectures. His meeting with Freud led him to reconsider, and in the December and January issues of *The Journal of Abnormal Psychology* Putnam published a highly influential article entitled "Personal Impressions of Sigmund Freud and His Work," which praised Freud highly and devoted considerable space to overcoming possible prejudice against his emphasis on sexuality. Since Putnam's reputation as a psychologist was firmly established, his conversion was of considerable importance. In the following year, according to Oberndorf, "he had the temerity to present a laudatory paper on Freud at the meeting of the entirely unsympathetic American Neurologican Association, of which he had been president."[21] It was actions such as these which led Freud to consider Putnam the man most responsible for the spread of psychoanalysis in America.

The Clark University lectures on psychology were translated into English and published in the April, 1910, issue of *The American Journal of Psychology*, along with two articles by Jones and Ferenczi on Freud's dream theories. These articles were widely read by psychologists and also, apparently, by many laymen, and for several years they remained the main single source of Freud's ideas in English. Before Freud's appearance at Worcester, there had been almost no mention of him; after 1909, the number of articles and books on his ideas steadily increased until by the 1920's there were, according to one source, "more than two hundren books dealing with Freudianism."[22]

Specifically Freudian concepts only gradually began to receive publicity. At the same time, however, an awareness of the concept of the unconscious, and—more vaguely—of Freud's and Charcot's new views on hysteria, began to circulate. *Scribner's*, for example, carried an article in September, 1909, entitled "Dreams and the Subconscious," which argued that the best way to know "that subconscious self of which we hear so much" was to know it through dreams. Its author, however, had apparently never heard of Freud. His concept of the "unconscious," which was somewhat hazy, derived probably from such American psychologists as F. W. H. Myers and Morton Prince, who used the

21. Oberndorf, *History of Psychoanalysis*, p. 59.
22. Mark Sullivan, *Our Times: The United States, 1900-1925* (New York: Charles Scribner's Sons, 1926-35), IV, 171.

term in a different sense than did Freud. Another 1909 article, "Psychologist's Denial of the Existence of the Subconscious Mind," appearing in *Current Literature*,[23] triumphantly announced that according to Dr. Hugo Münsterberg, the "greatest of contemporary psychologists," there was no such thing as the subconscious and that the results obtained from hypnosis and hysteria cases could be explained strictly on physiological grounds. The editors' apparent delight in this "defeat" of the theory of the unconscious was due to their belief that "it is in the realm of the conscious where alone lie our duty and our morality." Even before Freud's ideas were understood, the unconscious was suspect on moral grounds.

In the following year, H. Addington Bruce published in *The American Magazine* "Masters of the Mind: Remarkable Cures Effected by Four Great Experts Without the Aid of Drugs or Surgeons' Tools,"[24] one of the first explicit introductions to Freud as a medical man to appear in popular periodicals. Freud was here treated not as a revolutionary thinker, but merely as one of several physicians experimenting with a new concept. The four men discussed—Pierre Janet, Morton Prince, Boris Sidis, and Freud—had all achieved cures by using the new wonder methods of hypnosis, "hypnoidization," and, with Freud, "psycho-analysis." Bruce's section on Freud mentioned his "audacious theory" that repressed incidents were always of a sexual nature, and that this idea was being "pressed vigorously by Freud and his disciples": "By some Freud is regarded as having delved deeper than any other man into the mechanism of mentally caused diseases; by

23. XLVII (August, 1909), 206. *Current Literature* was a reprint magazine which "digested" articles from other periodicals. It did not always, however, cite the original article or bother to use quotation marks when making direct quotations. A comparison of the reprint article with its original frequently shows a bizarre mixture of misquotations, editorial interpolations, and "quoted" material, tied together with eye-catching subtitles. On the whole, *Current Literature* seems to have combined the appeal of *The Reader's Digest* with that of a scandal sheet. Its circulation in 1910 was 77,000; by 1918, it had declined to 40,000. Its name was changed in 1913 to *Current Opinion*. See Frank L. Mott, *A History of American Magazines* (Cambridge: Harvard University Press, 1938), IV, 509.

24. LXXI (1910), 71-81. Bruce had an earlier article, "Psychology and Daily Life," in *The Outlook* for June 25, 1910, which mentioned Jung and the association test but did not refer to Freud by name.

others he is condemned as an extremist who is 'riding a hobby to death.' "[25] The author himself was not qualified to judge.

A more extensive article on Freud appeared in *Popular Science Monthly*, a review of current dream theories by Havelock Ellis, with particular emphasis on *The Interpretation of Dreams*. This was a more scholarly article which assumed a knowledge of Freud among psychologists, if not among laymen. Although it was largely an attack on Freud's dream theories, Ellis was quite sympathetic to many of Freud's ideas: "It is due to the genius of Professor Sigmund Freud of Vienna—today the most daring and original psychologist in the field of morbid psychic phenomena— that we owe the long-neglected recognition of the large place of symbolism in dreaming."[26] After outlining briefly Freud's basic propositions on dreams and referring to Freud's major works, to English expositions of his theories,[27] and to German critiques of his system, Ellis presented his main argument against Freudian interpretation—namely that it was "too narrow and exclusive": "The wish-dream of the kind elaborately investigated by Freud may be accepted as . . . extremely common, and . . . a real and not rare phenomenon. But it is impossible to follow Freud when he declares that the wish-dream is the one and only type of dream. The world of psychic life . . . is rich and varied; it cannot be covered by a single formula. Freud's subtle and searching analytic genius has greatly contributed to enlarge our knowledge of this world of sleep. We may recognize the value of this contribution to the psychology of dreams while refusing to accept a premature and narrow generalization."[28]

Ellis' critique of the theory was comparatively sound, uninfluenced by an emotional bias which so frequently obscured the issue in later criticisms of Freud. Although many of his arguments were to be repeated, with variations, by others, the influence of

25. *Ibid.*, p. 21.
26. Havelock Ellis, "The Symbolism of Dreams," *Popular Science Monthly*, LXXVII (July, 1910), 42-55. This journal, before it changed hands in 1915, was a much more respectable magazine than it is today. See Mott, *History of American Magazines*, III, 495-99.
27. Specifically, the Clark lectures, published in the April, 1910, issue of *The American Journal of Psychology*, particularly Jones's article on dreams.
28. Ellis, "Symbolism," p. 55.

this essay itself was probably negligible, few of his readers being prepared at this time to follow his arguments.

In 1911 several significant articles appeared, testifying to the growth of Freud's recognition in the United States. One of the best of these is H. W. Chase's "Freud's Theories of the Unconscious," also appearing in *Popular Science Monthly*.[29] Chase, a psychology professor at the University of North Carolina, presented a brief but lucid account of the basic concept of the unconscious (and how Freud's conception of it differed from others using the term) and of Freud's system of dream interpretation. Freud was referred to as one "who is just beginning to be known in this country" but whose importance was becoming more and more obvious: "Psychologists are beginning to recognize that, right or wrong, he must be reckoned with. He has given a stimulus to work . . . that may go a long way toward the ultimate solution of some of our baffling psychological problems."[30] Chase's article, although early, is excellent. He did not have to defend Freud, since the latter was not as yet controversial; he could, therefore, like Ellis, calmly examine the new theory on its merits, something which later writers were more or less unable to do.

Attacks on Freud were already appearing, although generally not in the popular press. A critique of the Freudians and the psychoanalytic method in *The Journal of Abnormal Psychology* in 1911 scored several points: Freud and Jung were too dogmatic in their approach; the usefulness of psychoanalysis was still highly theoretical; many of Freud's "cures" themselves had relapsed after treatment; many of the Freudian results could be a product of the method—i.e., a product of autosuggestion; and dream symbolism might be in the mind of the beholder.[31] Articles similar to this appeared rather frequently in psychology journals from

29. LXXVIII (April, 1911), 355-63. It is interesting that even in this early discussion of Freud's ideas, application of the theory to the world of art is made. "What, says Freud, are the symbols of the artist and the poet but just such disguises [as dreams], a product of the conflict in his own soul between the primitive and the civilized ways of thought? Other observers have already shown that the root of art is in sex; here we see that it is through the symbolism of a sex-conflict that it develops" (p. 362).

30. *Ibid.*, p. 363.

31. A. Friedländer, "Hysteria and Modern Psychoanalysis," *The Journal of Abnormal Psychology*, V (February-March, 1911), 279-319.

1910 on, although those responding favorably to Freudian theory seem to outweigh those in opposition to it.

The establishment in 1911 of a laboratory at the Johns Hopkins University to study functional nervous disorders using Freudian methods was the occasion of a highly laudatory article on Freud in *Harper's Weekly*. The tone of the essay suggests that the author did not expect his audience to be familiar with Freud's name. He described the theory briefly:

> Freud, who has done the most important investigation of modern times in the field of neuroses, lays great stress on the probable underlying neurotic reaction. He believes the condition to be a mechanism of defense. Some idea pertaining to the sphere of the biological instincts and tending to the satisfaction of an inherent need is repressed by an extraneous edict and there sets in at once the condition of psychic conflict . . . . Freud's method of investigation is concerned largely with dreams . . . . What the subconscious self desires frequently expresses itself in the dream life . . . . Many of his conclusions from dreams are highly interesting, and the story of the faint clues which he follows through so many intricate windings is as enthralling as the most highly wrought melodrama.[32]

Psychoanalysis was seen as essentially humane, its purpose being to "teach the patient to understand the underlying causes of his sufferings and to control and unify them himself." It is surprising how few writers viewed Freud's concepts in this light.

Edward M. Weyer's "The New Art of Interpreting Dreams," appearing in *Forum*,[33] was another highly laudatory article on Freud. This brief essay was intended primarily as a stimulus to other readers, and as such the author did not attempt a full-length explanation of the dream theories. Weyer's enthusiasm is evident: "Freud's theories have illuminated dreams, day-dreams, mental disease, crime, wit and humor, the growth of myths and superstitions; [the principles governing dreams] are found to operate throughout broad ranges of mental phenomena extending

32. "New Views on Hysteria," *Harper's Weekly*, LV (June, 1911), 6.
33. XLV (1911), 589-600. Weyer had apparently been influenced by the Clark lectures, which had led him to read *The Interpretation of Dreams* in the original: "Little was known in this country concerning this entire scientific movement before the coming of Professor Freud and some of his co-workers to participate in the meetings held in September of 1909 to celebrate the twentieth anniversary of the founding of Clark University."

from the practical affairs of everyday life in health and disease to the rare manifestations of genius in literature and art."[34] In short, a new science had been born, and a new hero had appeared—Sigmund Freud.

The published comments on Freud in 1911 were on the whole extremely favorable. Even *Current Literature*, which stood squarely on the side of piety and "morality," reprinted two articles on Freud with no adverse comment.[35] To be sure, their impression of him seems to have been rather confused—"psychanalysis" (*sic*) seems to be equated in the editors' minds with Jung's association test in one article—but the concept of infantile sexuality was presented forthrightly without the editors' addition of a scurrilous sub-heading, a practice common in this magazine's later reprints of articles on psychoanalysis.

By 1912, the image of Freud as a significant but controversial figure in the world of psychology had become fairly well established. Edwin T. Brewster referred to him in *McClure's* as "probably today the most discussed man in his field in the entire scientific world."[36] Brewster discussed the new "scientific" theory that dreams were meaningful, and outlined briefly the concept of the dream as a protective device, the wish-fulfillment hypothesis, and the idea of the censor. Two dream analyses were presented as examples, taken from an unnamed book by Ernest Jones.[37] No reference was made, however, to Freud's concept of sexuality or to the Oedipus complex; the psychological significance of memory lapses was discussed in a paragraph. Despite its flippant tone, Brewster's article was in general favorable to Freud, although the author's personal doubts about these strange new ideas are be-

34. *Ibid.*, p. 600.

35. "Freud's Discovery of the Lowest Chamber of the Soul," *Current Literature*, L (May, 1911), 512-14; and "Medical Report from a New Psychological World," *Current Literature*, L (February, 1911), 167-69. The first of these is based on Chase's article in *Popular Science Monthly*, already discussed; the second on a column in the *New York Medical Record* by Dr. E. Scripture. For *Current Literature*'s editorial practice, see n. 23 above.

36. "Dreams and Forgetting: New Discoveries in Dream Psychology," *McClure's*, XXXIV (1912), 715.

37. This is probably Jones's *Papers on Psychoanalysis*, published in 1912. These same two dreams are related by Max Eastman in his two articles in *Everybody's* for 1915. They originally appeared in Jones's essay in the April, 1910, issue of *The American Journal of Psychology*.

trayed by his concluding statement: "Perhaps as the Freudians maintain, every person's conjugal fate turns on his parent of the opposite sex. Perhaps the whole thing is only a crazy dream of Dr. Sigmund Freud."[38]

Like Brewster's, these early articles generally tended to soft-pedal the concept of sexuality in Freud's system, although the majority of the writers were themselves aware of the importance Freud placed on it. The Reverend Samuel McComb, writing in *The Century Magazine* in 1912, mentioned it only to state that some doctors disputed the point. *The Interpretation of Dreams* was said to be "epoch-making";[39] despite this judgment, the Reverend Mr. McComb refused to believe that *all* dreams represented a fulfillment of a wish and cited as proof the nightmare (as if Freud had never considered this point). On the whole, it seems to have been the dream theories rather than the theory of neurosis which attracted the most attention among the lay public.

Periodical essays were not the only source of Freud's ideas available to Americans in 1912. The "Freudians" had begun publishing books on the subject,[40] theatres were beginning to capitalize on the concept of the unconscious (if not on Freud's ideas specifically),[41] and Freud's name was in general circulation. Newspapers also occasionally found the controversy over psychoanalysis newsworthy. The *New York Times* on April 5 reported extensively on a speech made by Dr. Allen Starr before the New York Academy of Medicine, in which he denounced Freud. Starr's attack, and his reasoning, indicate the emotional fervor that Freud's ideas were capable of arousing. Denying the validity of

38. Brewster, "Dreams and Forgetting," p. 719.
39. Samuel McComb, "The New Interpretation of Dreams," *The Century Magazine*, LXXXIV (1912), 665.
40. For an annotated bibliography of some of these full-length books, see Appendix B.
41. See W. David Sievers, *Freud on Broadway* (New York: Heritage House, 1955). Sievers gives many plots of plays which he feels were influenced by Freud, but many of these seem to be drawing on general conceptions of the unconscious rather than on Freud's. *Good Gracious, Annabelle* (1915) makes use of Jung's association test, the "lie detector" properties of which attracted considerable interest. Susan Glaspell's *Suppressed Desires*, produced at the Provincetown Playhouse in 1915, was probably the first drama in America to capitalize specifically on Freudian concepts. The use of these concepts by later playwrights, particularly Eugene O'Neill, was mainly a post-war phenomenom.

psychoanalytic theory (specifically, the idea that the sex instinct was the main determinant of man's behavior), Starr protested that Freud's ideas were a consequence of his environment: " 'I knew Dr. Freud well . . .' Dr. Starr said. 'Vienna is not a particularly moral city, and working side by side with Freud . . . I learned that he enjoyed Viennese life thoroughly. Freud was not a man who lived on a particularly high plane. He was not self-repressed. He was not an ascetic. I think his scientific theory is largely the result of his environment and of the peculiar life he led.' "[42] Considerable confusion followed Starr's attack. Present at the meeting, among others, were William A. White, A. A. Brill, James J. Putnam, and Smith Ely Jelliffe. "All of these physicians," the *Times* reported, "had stated that Freud's theory . . . was absolutely correct according to their experience. Professor Putnam had gone so far indeed as to state that he had always found that persons who denied the accuracy of Freud's theory were generally the best example of its absolute truth. Although these and other Freudians in the crowded room seemed to be considerably startled by Dr. Starr's remonstrances, other physicians in the room applauded Dr. Starr warmly."[43]

Freud's image as a figure of controversy in the medical world was probably the dominant one in the mind of the average American before World War I. Increasingly, articles found it necessary to refer to the disagreement between the followers of Freud and his opponents, while at the same time urging their readers to consider Freud's ideas on their own merits: "The persistent courage and indefatigable ingenuity of Freud no less than the zeal, number, and talents of his followers, merit that his teachings be judiciously considered. If the foolish and merely prurient of the writings of the ignorant Freudians be set aside, and if Freud's doctrines, as enunciated by himself, and by the many distinguished scientists among his adherents be studied, one tithe of the energy spent now in vituperation would settle for ever the value of the whole Freudian system."[44]

42. *New York Times*, April 5, 1912, Sec. 1, p. 8. According to Ernest Jones, in his biography of Freud, Starr's claim to have "known Freud" well was simply not true.
43. *Ibid.*
44. J. M. A. Maloney, "Modern Means of Investigating Mental Pro-

Some of these attacks on Freud came from sophisticated, intellectual corners. Early in 1913 *The Monist* published an article by Paul Carus, "Wrong Generalizations in Philosophy: Schopenhauer and Freud." Carus, the journal's editor, attacked the generalization that all psychic phenomena could be explained on the basis of the erotic instinct as a philosophic over-simplification, and predicted that Freud's hypothesis would soon die—a prophecy made hopefully by several writers of the time: "Freud's theory has become quite prominent but we predict that it will not last. In his various investigations he has made many valuable comments but on the whole his explanations do not explain; they leave the problem where it was before.[45]

Despite the fact that he disagreed with Freud's views, the editor printed in the same issue an interesting article by Albert R. Chandler, "Tragic Effect in Sophocles Analyzed According to the Freudian Method." This essay, written by a graduate student at Harvard, was awarded a Bowdoin prize in May, 1911. That a student would have been acquainted with Freud's thought this early is rather surprising, and suggests that a knowledge of Freud in this country even before an English translation of his major works was more widespread than has been previously supposed. The essay itself[46] indicates that the author was familiar not only with *The Interpretation of Dreams* but with Freud's other works as well. His explanations of the mechanisms of dream formation and the concept of sublimation show a good grasp of the theory, even though its application to tragedy is somewhat naïve.

In 1913 A. A. Brill published his translation of *The Interpretation of Dreams.* The book was widely reviewed, and the reviewers' common assumption of an acquaintance with Freud's ideas on the part of their public strongly suggests that by this date the average educated layman was aware of his basic concepts, although the extent of this knowledge, of course, varied greatly.

cesses," *Scientific American Supplement,* LXXIV (November 9, 1912), 290.

45. Paul Carus, "Wrong Generalizations in Philosophy: Schopenhauer and Freud," *The Monist,* XXIII (January, 1913), 151.

46. Albert R. Chandler, "Tragic Effect in Sophocles Analyzed According to the Freudian Method," *The Monist,* XXIII (January, 1913). Chandler's application of Freud's concepts to the drama is discussed in Chapter 2.

The book reviews were in general unfavorable, but the subject was handled with great respect; Freud's stature was such that he could not be treated as a quack, even though to several reviewers his conclusions were obviously bizarre. In almost all cases the reviewers had to admit that the book was "worthy of serious consideration," but they cautioned against an uncritical acceptance of what was, after all, only a theory.

The least favorable of these reviews appeared in *The Nation* and in *The Athanaeum*; other periodicals were more moderate in their conclusions. The anonymous reviewer in *The Athanaeum* resorted to an *ad hominem* attack: "Professor Freud writes with a degree of introspection which betrays his Oriental heredity and often leads him into pure mysticism. His conclusions are sometimes far-fetched, and fit the premises incompletely, whilst an atmosphere of sex pervades many parts of the book and renders it unpleasant reading. The results he reaches are hardly commensurate with the labor expended, and reveal a seamy side of life in Vienna which might well have been left alone."[47] The review indicates a fairly widespread misconception of Freud's method, namely that he drew his conclusions about the nature of dreams solely from abnormal specimens. This misconception represents either a hasty reading of the book or, more probably, a strong desire to avoid the conclusion that one's own dreams betrayed the same dynamics that Freud analyzed in the dreams of neurotics: "Fortunately for our estimate of human nature," stated this reviewer, "he deals with the morbid rather than the healthy dreamer." *The Nation's* reviewer attacked the book on the basis of its unscientific method and its use of false logic, claiming that this misuse of scientific method cast doubt on the reliability of Freud's earlier work on hysteria. Although he attempted a rational critique, the author's emotional revulsion seems to have prompted his conclusion: "In his other writings our author has given evidence of a morbid tendency to over-emphasize the potency of erotic influences in all of experience and in the field here considered the results of this preconception are conspicuous, leading him to revolting and improbable explanations."[48]

47. *The Athanaeum* (April 9, 1913), p. 424.
48. Review of *The Interpretation of Dreams*, *The Nation*, XCVI (May 15, 1913), 504. *The Nation* was at this time under the editorship of Paul

A more temperate review was Horace Kallen's in *The Dial*, a journal which was quick to recognize the literary potential of Freud's theories. Kallen, however, had some reservations about Freud's logic: "Exposition and proof of this theory of dreams is offered as the outcome of the method [i.e., psychoanalysis] and the method, conversely, is justified by the theory, in terms of numerous analyzed dreams. The circularity is patent . . . ."[49] He also maintained, erroneously, that since Freud based his conclusions on studies of abnormal people, the theory could not be applied to dreams in general. He reminded his readers that although Freud's hypotheses were vulnerable to criticism on logical grounds, so had Darwin's been; and that although this "interpretation of dreams" was "quite acceptable in principle," it was "inconclusive in concrete detail."

The reviewer in the *New York Times* also hesitated to give *The Interpretation of Dreams* unqualified approval. Admitting that "it is a work that has made for its author a world-wide reputation" and that Freud's "system of 'psychoanalysis' now [is] widely employed by psychiatrists," the reviewer pointed out that the theory had been "strongly combatted by Dr. Morton Prince and others in this country" and that "the general Freudian conception has not been generally accepted, although its value as an original contribution to the subject is recognized."[50] F. L. Wells, in *The Journal of Philosophy*, also had reservations. More sophisticated in his knowledge of Freud's works, Wells neither accepted nor rejected the new theories but counseled a "wait and see" policy: "Let us not lose sight of the fact that psychoanalysis has not carried its theories to the ultimate test . . . ."[51] He concluded with a warning, one which several of the reviewers could have profitably heeded: "He is the most fortunate who is not prevented

---

Elmer More, one of the Humanists who opposed Freud's thought because of its determinism.

49. Horace Kallen, "The Mystery of Dreams," *The Dial*, LV (1913), 79. This reviewer, like several others, had read the book in the original and criticized the Brill translation.

50. "The Interpretation of Dreams," *New York Times*, June 1, 1913, Sec. 6, p. 328.

51. F. L. Wells, "The Interpretation of Dreams," *The Journal of Philosophy*, X (September 25, 1913), 555.

by factors of personal affect from seeing and using what is advantageous in all."[52]

The most favorable review of *The Interpretation of Dreams* appeared in *Science*. The author, C. M. Campbell, was familiar with the arguments made against the dream theory, and although he could not accept it in its entirety, his critique and conclusion were quite sensible: "Any person who has had to deal seriously with the psychoneuroses . . . will look upon this book as a serious contribution to a most important field. The more knowledge he has of the actual facts the slower will he be in dogmatically rejecting even those statements of the author which are unconvincing and apparently rather extreme."[53]

After the appearance of the English version of *The Interpretation of Dreams*, any reputable discussion of dreams had at least to make reference to Freud's theories. Henri Bergson, for example, published two articles on dream theory in *The Independent*, revised versions of an address made in 1901. Although Bergson's own theories differed significantly from Freud's, the following footnote was now felt to be necessary: "Author's note (1913). This would be the place where especially will intervene those 'repressed desires' which Freud . . . [has] studied with such penetration and ingenuity . . . . When the above address was delivered (1901) the work of Freud on dreams . . . had been published, but 'psychoanalysis' was far from having the development that it has today."[54] By 1913, then, Freud's ideas had a fairly wide currency. They were well enough established to allow a

52. *Ibid.*
53. C. M. Campbell, "The Interpretation of Dreams," *Science*, n.s. XXXVIII (September 5, 1913), 344. This view is reminiscent of A. A. Brill's statement that the theories of psychoanalysis generally were rejected until the individual became convinced of them through his own experience. In "The Introduction and Development of Freud's Work in the United States," Brill says, "It was not until I found the Freudian mechanisms in my own dreams with the help of my more experienced colleagues that I became, as it were, a Freudian by conviction." According to Brill, this experience was common to all psychoanalytic converts (p. 349).
54. Henri Bergson, "Such Stuff as Dreams Are Made On: A Study of the Mechanisms of Dreaming," *The Independent*, LXXXVI (October 23, 1913), 163. In the second article, "The Birth of the Dream," Bergson refers to Freud merely as "Freud" rather than "Dr. Sigmund Freud of Vienna," which again suggests that writers in 1913 assumed that their readers knew something of the man and his ideas.

magazine like *Current Opinion* to capitalize on them with articles bearing such titles as "How Psychoanalysis Has Obsessed the World With Sex" (reprinted from an article in the *British Medical Journal* attacking vehemently Freud's "belief" that life was "one long sex-pursuit.[55] Freudian theory was said to be a "travesty of life": I eat a meal and am satisfied; does this mean that there is something sexual in it? Obviously not, declared the author with a flourish. The controversy over the sexual emphasis in Freud's work was patently relished by *Current Opinion,* which seized every opportunity to reprint articles on the subject, complete with lurid headings.[56]

Before 1913, many of the popularizations of Freudian thought appearing in non-professional journals were written by medical men or by those connected with psychology such as Havelock Ellis and Henri Bergson. After 1913, the field was more open to educated laymen who were thoroughly acquainted with Freud's works. Three such men were of particular importance in presenting simplifications of Freud's ideas to the American public: Max Eastman, Alfred Booth Kuttner, and Walter Lippmann. The ways in which these three, and others like them, became acquainted with Freud's thought reflects its growing diffusion among intellectuals in the pre-war period. The Greenwich Village influence on the intellectual milieu of America is of primary importance here. All three of these writers were at one time or another residents of the Village, and probably received their first impression of Freud

55. "How Psychoanalysis Has Obsessed the World with Sex," *Current Opinion,* LVI (June, 1914), 441.

56. For example, "American Expert's Indictment of American Dream Analysis as Psychological Humbug," *Current Opinion,* LX (January, 1916), 34-35; "Is the Psychoanalyzed Self a Libel on the Human Race?" *Current Opinion,* LXIII (August, 1917), 105; "Secret of Psychoanalysis as Havelock Ellis Reveals It," *Current Opinion,* LXIII (October, 1917), 265-66; "Novelists Who Have Succumbed to the Lure of Psychoanalysis," *Current Opinion,* LXIII (December, 1917), 413. The magazine's attitude toward Freud is illustrated in such remarks as "We must hold the entire 'sex' theory with its many ramifications as standing upon the same ground as the green cheese hypothesis of the composition of the moon" ("American Expert's Indictment," p. 35). Even when the article itself was favorable (e.g., the reprint of the Havelock Ellis essay), the editor would give the picture of Freud a derogatory caption ("The High Priest of the Psychoanalytic Cult"). By the fourth article (December, 1917), the words "psychoanalysis" and "sex" had become synonymous.

there. By 1913, according to Floyd Dell, the Village was quite familiar with psychoanalytic theory. Dell himself had come across Freud through an interest in Burton's *Anatomy of Melancholy* while he was still living in Chicago: "Burton had led me to the reading of Freud and his disciples, though I did not understand many of these writings, and misunderstood much that I thought I grasped. Everybody in the Village had been talking the jargon of psychoanalysis ever since I came. We had played the parlor games of 'associating' to lists of words, and had tried to unravel dreams by what we supposed to be the Freudian formula."[57] Alfred Booth Kuttner was already a post-graduate of psychotherapy by 1912, having completed his analysis under A. A. Brill. During the summer of 1912, he shared a cabin with his friend, Walter Lippmann. Kuttner had in his possession the manuscript of Brill's translation of *The Interpretation of Dreams* and gave it to Lippmann, who was immediately impressed by it.[58] Max Eastman, like Kuttner, had also been analyzed—or was being analyzed—at this time, one of his therapists being Smith Ely Jelliffe.[59]

Both Eastman and Lippmann were friends of Mable Dodge Luhan, a remarkable woman then at the center of many major artistic movements, who was also an analysand.[60] Her Thursday evening "salon," which was organized to encourage a free play of ideas among New York intellectuals, was extremely popular. According to Lincoln Steffens, hers was "the only successful salon

57. Floyd Dell, *Homecoming* (New York: Farrar & Rinehart, 1933), p. 291. Dell arrived in New York in the summer of 1913.

58. Hoffman, *Freudianism*, p. 54.

59. In *Heroes I Have Known* (New York: Simon and Schuster, 1942), Eastman says, "Freud was not only my teacher, but by proxy at least, my Father Confessor. More than one of his American apostles had given me psychoanalytic help in times of trouble. . . . As a result of one of my sessions with Dr. Jelliffe, I had studied Freud's works very thoroughly and published in *Everybody's* magazine in 1915, the first popular American exposition of his theories and methods of healing" (p. 263). The last statement is somewhat exaggerated.

60. See Mable Dodge Luhan, *Intimate Memories* (New York: Harcourt Brace & Co., 1933-1937), III. It is obvious from these last remarks that being analyzed was very much in vogue during the 1913-18 period. According to Floyd Dell, who began his own analysis in 1917, "Most of my friends were presently being psychoanalyzed, and we could talk together without being thought mad" (*Homecoming*, p. 294).

I have ever seen in America."[61] Several of the Thursday evenings were given over to a discussion of psychoanalysis and its implications. On one occasion, A. A. Brill was invited to lecture; he later recalled the incident: "Another interesting group before whom I spoke during the winter of 1913 was at Mable Dodge's salon. The person who invited me to speak there was a young man named Walter Lippmann, a recent Harvard graduate working with Lincoln Steffens. There I met radicals, litterateurs, artists, and philosophers, some of whom have influenced the trends of our times in no small way . . . . My talk aroused a very interesting and lively discussion, and the questions I was asked there by such people as John Collier, Sam Lewissohn, Bill Haywood, and others equally distinguished, were quite different from those posed by medical men."[62] The influence of Mrs. Dodge's salon has also been attested to by Lincoln Steffens: "It was there that some of us first heard of psychoanalysis and the new psychology of Freud and Jung, which in several discussions, one led by Walter Lippmann, introduced us to the idea that the minds of men were distorted by unconscious suppressions, often quite irresponsible and incapable of reasoning or learning. The young writers saw a new opening for their fiction, the practical men a new profession . . . . There were no warmer, quieter, more intensely thoughtful conversations at Mable Dodge's than those on Freud and his implica-tions."[63]

During 1914 and 1915, Alfred Booth Kuttner wrote four articles popularizing and defending Freud. The first of these reviewed Brill's translation of *The Psychopathology of Everyday Life*. An entire page of the *New York Times* was devoted to this review, with an impressive three-column, half-page picture of the sage himself. Written to popularize Freud's concepts, the essay greatly over-simplified the subject, but included copious amusing examples to demonstrate Freud's thesis that "we forget things which we want to forget" and that "we mean what we say." As if

61. Lincoln Steffens, *The Autobiography of Lincoln Steffens* (New York: Harcourt, Brace & Co., 1931), p. 665.

62. Brill, "Introduction and Development of Freud's Work," pp. 322-23. Later in this article Brill stated: "I feel that my contacts with the non-medical groups . . . have done at least as much to popularize and establish Freud in this country as my work in medical groups" (p. 325).

63. Steffens, *Autobiography*, pp. 665-66.

to forestall criticism, Kuttner continually assured the reader that "of course," Freud did not mean to explain *all* cases of forgetting and *all* slips of the tongue by his theory. Aware that the book's thesis might seem implausible, Kuttner advised his readers to examine their own slips candidly, assuring them that such self-study was frequently "one of the best proofs of the existence of an unconscious mind."[64]

Kuttner's three other articles appeared in *The New Republic*. His "Note on Forgetting: Theories of Freud" treated *The Psychopathology of Everyday Life* on a more sophisticated level, directed to an audience which could be assumed to know more about Freud than did the readers of the *Times*. In 1915 he reviewed Edwin B. Holt's *The Freudian Wish and Its Place in Ethics*,[65] an odd book that attempted to graft Freud's concept of the "wish" (which Holt took to be the "basic unit" of psychology, replacing the older unit of sensation) on to an ethic of "truth." Despite the vagueness of Holt's thesis, Kuttner's review was quite sympathetic.[66] His most extensive article was a response to Pearce Bailey's essay on Otto Rank's *The Myth of the Birth of the Hero*.[67] Bailey's review, although generally favorable, had criticized the Freudians on several points: for their "sweeping generalizations," their belief in the Oedipus complex, and for their idiosyncratic approach to dream symbols. Kuttner, in reply, began by pointing out that because "gross abuse of Freud is no longer considered altogether good form," critics like Bailey gave the appearance of accepting Freud while at the same time rejecting his most basic propositions. If such concepts as the Oedipus complex were rejected, Kuttner argued, what was left to "accept" was commonplace: "The theory of the interpretation of dreams and symbols, the theory of unconscious psychic mechanisms, and the psycho-sexual theory, are

64. Alfred Booth Kuttner, "The Psychopathology of Everyday Life," *New York Times*, October 18, 1914, Sec. 5, p. 10.

65. *The New Republic*, V (November 27, 1915), 101-3.

66. Holt's book was apparently fairly widely read and approved of. Ashley Brown, in "An Interview with Conrad Aiken," *Shenandoah*, XV (Autumn, 1963), says that Aiken recalled the book very favorably: "By the way, have you read E. B. Holt's *The Freudian Wish*? It develops a kind of potential *ethics* of the whole Freudian concept. A brilliant little book. It should be reprinted" (p. 36).

67. Pearce Bailey, "Hero Myths According to Freud," *The New Republic*, II (March 13, 1915), 160-61.

fundamental in the Freudian psychology. Take them away and there is nothing left of Freud except a few happy accidents of truth on which even the most fantastic theorists sometimes stumble."[68] Max Eastman's two articles in *Everybody's* magazine in 1915 were not, as he later claimed, "the first popular American exposition of [Freud's] theories,"[69] but they were among the first to present an extended account of Freud's basic theories to a middle-class, rather than to an intellectual, audience. "Exploring the Soul and Healing the Body" discussed the "new method" of curing mental illness, gave a short history of psychoanalysis, and emphasized that it was a "preeminently established method of treatment."[70] Eastman took pains to discuss psychoanalysis as an already established science, presenting facts to substantiate its authoritativeness; he mentioned, for instance, that there were in America at that time five medical journals devoted exclusively to its development. In this highly sympathetic essay, Eastman selected as the cornerstone of the Freudian doctrine the idea that nervous disorders and dreams were both the result of suppressed desires. The second article, dealing mainly with *The Psychopathology of Everyday Life*, presented Freud's explanation for the slips of the tongue, indecisions, and other "mistakes" made in the ordinary course of living. Numerous examples and brief case histories were given, and the article was plentifully illustrated. Although obviously simplified, Eastman's essays were highly entertaining and served to awaken further a curiosity about the "new psychology" on the part of the average reader. Similar popularizations were to appear in *Good Housekeeping* in 1915 and *The Ladies Home Journal* in 1917.

Walter Lippmann, writing for *The New Republic*, contributed several excellent essays on Freudian psychology in 1915 and 1916.[71] "Freud and the Layman" took up the problem of the

68. Alfred Booth Kuttner, "The Freudian Theory," *The New Republic*, II (March 20, 1915), 183. Kuttner's articles on psychoanalysis and the artist for *The Seven Arts* in 1917 are discussed in Chapter 2.

69. Eastman, *Heroes*, p. 203. Eastman later met Freud in Vienna in 1926. During the early twenties he had written a book on Marxism which contained a chapter on "Marx and Freud." Freud had read the book and had written him a letter about it, so that Eastman called on him when he was in Europe.

70. *Everybody's Magazine*, XXXII (June, 1915), 744.

71. Lippmann also aided the spread of Freudianism through his books,

layman's reaction to the new theories. Lippman implied here that Freud and *The Interpretation of Dreams* had become popular subjects of dinner-party conversations, despite the fact that an accurate knowledge of Freudian psychology was quite rare. Objecting to the commonly heard criticism that "Freud exaggerated" when the would-be critic did not know wherein and to what extent he exaggerated, Lippmann advised that Freud be read thoroughly and dispassionately. He admitted the difficulty in doing this: "Because Freud is discussing the very nature of interest it becomes very difficult to consider Freud disinterestedly."[72] Lippmann suggested that the reader "get the sense of his method and the quality of his mind" and then judge his ideas. In Lippmann's own view, "there has rarely been a great theory worked out so close to actual practice, a hypothesis that has been so genuinely pragmatic in origin . . . . He has formulated no immutable doctrine; the history of his career is the history of opinion bending and modifying before experience."[73] He concluded this intelligent essay, which can still be read with profit, with a word of praise and a prophecy: "I cannot help feeling that for his illumination, for his steadiness and brilliancy of mind, he may rank with the greatest who have contributed to thought . . . . From anthropology through education to social organization, from literary criticism to the studies of religions and philosophies, the effect of Freud is already felt. He has set up a reverberation in human thought and conduct of which few as yet dare to predict the consequences."[74]

In his review of the English translation of Jung's *Psychology of the Unconscious*, Lippmann was fairly generous to Jung's ideas, although the major part of the review outlined the Freudians' objections to them and thus, by implication, discussed the differences between Freud and Jung: "Jung has taken some of the prepossessions of the psychoanalyst to make a moral world for himself. He has introduced into the empirical labors and tentative inductions of Freud a series of grandiose generalizations about human

---

particularly *A Preface to Politics* in 1914, which is discussed in Appendix B.

72. "Freud and the Layman," *The New Republic*, II (April 17, 1915), Part II, 9.

73. *Ibid.*, pp. 9-10.

74. *Ibid.*, p. 10. It is interesting to note how many of these early articles refer to the application of psychology to literary criticism.

destiny."⁷⁵ Jung's procedure—using Miss Miller's visions, which could not be checked for accuracy, and then psychoanalyzing them in terms of psychoanalytically interpreted myths—was, according to Lippmann, bad scientific method; Jung was interpreting "one unknown factor in terms of another." Moreover, he had weakened Freud's concept of the libido by expanding it to embrace Bergson's *élan vital*. Despite its fascination, Lippmann concluded, Jung's work was "a personal adventure in search of a philosophy, far more than a contribution to psychoanalytic understanding."

The translation of Jung's *Psychology of the Unconscious* was another significant event in the history of American reception of psychoanalytic theory. This long and complex book was widely reviewed and caused considerable controversy. James Oppenheim replied to Lippmann's essay the following week in "What Jung Has Done," where he defended Jung, citing as an authority G. Stanley Hall's remark that "in his opinion this book is without doubt a most important contribution in the whole realm of psychoanalytic literature."⁷⁶ Lippmann, in an appended explanatory note, pointed out that Oppenheim was a great follower of Jung and his "religion." However that may be, it is apparent that Oppenheim was thoroughly familiar with the Jung-Freud split, a quarrel which must have confused the average reader.

The New York *Times*, reviewing the *Psychology of the Unconscious*, mentioned Jung's differences with Freud but found them basically unimportant. Like most of the reviews of the book, this one was guarded in its praise: "It is better to acknowledge frankly that Jung's book has deep interest, even when it does not convince, and that it has great value for all of the already large, and steadily increasing, number of people who have accepted the Freudian psychology as a long step, probably the longest ever taken, toward an understanding of mental mysteries hitherto in-

75. Walter Lippmann, Review of Jung's *Psychology of the Unconscious*, *The New Republic*, VII (May 6, 1916), 22. For a brief discussion of this book, see Appendix B.

76. James Oppenheim, "What Jung Has Done," *The New Republic*, VII (May 20, 1916), 68. Oppenheim's knowledge of the new psychology was fairly wide. The editor of *The Seven Arts* in 1917, he took issue with Alfred Booth Kuttner for "following after Otto Rank." See his "Editorial," *The Seven Arts*, I (February, 1917), 390-94.

soluble."[77] The attitude of *The Dial's* reviewer was also ambivalent. Although admiring the book as a whole, he seems to have been somewhat bewildered by its intricacies: "That the 'Song of Hiawatha' and the myths of Brahma, the Christian mysteries and the classic wonder-tales, are likewise products of the Freudian activities of the psyche is rather a difficult and comprehensive thesis. The courage to maintain it and the erudition to carry through the exposition are the notable qualities of this remarkable book."[78]

An interesting facet of these reviews is the respect accorded Freudian works even when their conclusions seemed untenable to the reviewers. As Lippmann pointed out, "the evidence for the existence of the Oedipus complex is too overwhelming to permit anyone the pleasure of rejecting it out of hand."[79] By 1916, it seems, it was past the time when Freud could be rejected as a crank; and those who seriously objected to Freudian theory were hard put to it to voice their objections in a level tone. The ones who tried were in a difficult position, for if they protested against Freud's concepts, their opponents responded with a bland smile and the implication that their arguments were only a defense against their repressed complexes, a neurotic resistance to comprehending the "true" nature of their own unconscious. The frustration resulting from this type of "well-poisoning" argument can be seen in Warner Fite's essay on the *Psychology of the Unconscious* and the resulting controversy it aroused.

Reviewing the book for the *Nation*, Fite took the opportunity to write a long, vituperative critique of the entire system of Freudian psychology. He opened with an attack on Jung: "In this book Dr. Carl Jung . . . presents some 500 odd pages of incoherence and obscenity in the form of a psychoanalytic interpretation of the experiences of a sentimental young woman . . . who wrote verses and believed herself to be inspired. From these seemingly harmless confessions as a point of departure, Jung develops a theory of myth and poetry, with illustrations extending from Homer . . . to Anatole France, according to which . . .

77. *New York Times*, May 21, 1916, Sec. 6, p. 217.
78. *The Dial*, LX (June 8, 1916), 556.
79. *The New Republic*, VII (May 6, 1916), 22.

every statement not strictly of the order of 'the day is warm' or 'this is a chair' . . . is the expression of a motive not merely sexual, but incestuous."[80] The *Nation* had previously published a review of Franz Ricklin's *Wishfulfillment and Symbolism in Fairy Tales*, in which the reviewer, while criticising Ricklin's application of psychoanalytic theory to literature, had conceded that Jung and other Freudians were reliable in their own field. Referring to this, Fite stated categorically, "I shall treat Jung's book as an excuse for questioning that concession," and devoted the rest of his article to an attack on psychoanalysis itself. With heavy sarcasm, Fite denounced all Freudians as obscene sensationalists. That he seriously misunderstood Freud's basic ideas is apparent from even a casual reading of his article, although a charitable argument could be made that he was directing his attack against certain followers of Freud rather than against Freud himself.[81]

"Psychoanalysis and Sex Psychology" caused a flurry of letters to the editor. Samuel A. Tannenbaum, an analyst, protested against Fite's "misrepresentations," to which Fite replied with a defense of his position.[82] Another letter arguing for the validity of Freud's theories was signed by "one who has been psychoanalyzed." Still another, by Robert S. Woodworth, was angry but sensible. Woodworth's argument, supported by a lengthy example from his own experience, was that with the free association method, one could eventually cover *all* possible subjects; the Freudians' choice to stop when a sexual topic was "uncovered" was quite arbitrary.[83] The last letter, also defending Fite, resorted to a personal attack on Freud as a German, an example of the anti-German feeling prevalent during the first World War.

80. Warner Fite, "Psychoanalysis and Sex Psychology," *The Nation*, CIII (August 10, 1916), 127. Some of Fite's sarcastic jibes at Jung are rather clever, such as his reference to the book as "the new Dr. Casubon's 'Key to All Mythologies.'"

81. Eduard Hitschmann, for example, the author of *Freud's Theory of the Neuroses*, is much more categorical about the role of sexuality in human behavior than was Freud himself. See Appendix B for a discussion of this book.

82. "Psychoanalysis Debated," *The Nation*, CIII (September 7, 1916), 218-20.

83. Robert S. Woodworth, "Followers of Freud and Jung," *The Nation*, CIII (October 26, 1916), 396.

Accusing Freud of being both unscientific and immoral, he reminded the reader that "the German mind is (as has been often
pointed out) to a certain extent undeveloped when contrasted with
the logical and moral sanity of the non-German civilized nations."[84]
Nietzsche's corruption of German youth was being continued by
Freud; consequently, Freudianism was a threat to civilization
itself.

The controversy over Jung's *Psychology of the Unconscious*
was part of a minor war waged against psychoanalysis that gained
in momentum as Freudian theory became increasingly widespread.
By and large, however, Freud's ideas were favorably received.
Between 1916 and 1918, there were frequent extended book reviews of his works and those of his disciples, reviews which were
basically intelligent and objective. The sensational side of Freudianism, of course, still attracted attention, as his ideas were distorted to suggest a new "scientific" approval of sexual license. The
New York Times on February 4, 1916, carried an editorial about
a case then in the courts in which a child had been taken from
its parents because of the demoralizing situation in the home. The
father claimed that the "irregular conditions he had established
with the boy's mother" were a result of his "having studied psychoanalysis under the eminent Jung, that he and the woman both
'believed' in its 'doctrines,' and that they scorned their critics and
demanded to be let alone as the exponents of a higher and nobler
knowledge."[85] Commenting on this, the editorial writer reminded
the *Times'* readers that psychoanalysis was a method of curing
mental abnormalities, not a "philosophy of morals": "Expert
opinion is not yet unanimous as to the correctness of Freud's
theory . . . or as to the merits and worth of psychoanalytic treatment, but the well-informed antagonists of Freud would not be
less ready to assert the utter irrelevance of psychoanalysis to either
the observance or violation of social conventions on the part of
its practitioners or their students." Incidents such as this no doubt
tended to strengthen the association between Freud and sensation-

84. C. L. Franklin, "Freudian Doctrines," *The Nation*, CIII (October
19, 1916), 373.
85. "Never Was a Larger Non-Sequitur," *New York Times*, February
14, 1916, Sec. 12, p. 5.

al sexuality, an association well established by the end of World War I.

A new tone began to appear in articles on Freud written during the war, exemplified by Wilfrid Lay's essay, "John Barleycorn Under Psychoanalysis," in *The Bookman* in 1917, a cavalier application of psychoanalytic concepts to the works of Jack London. Here psychoanalysis was treated as a magic science, capable of revealing, to the initiate, the final truth about man. If the Freudians were much more dogmatic and doctrinaire than Freud himself, the layman who had received his knowledge of Freud at third had was even more so. Were an analyst to look into London's works, claimed Mr. Lay, "he would find clearly indicated the traits of Sadism-Masochism, homosexuality, and extraversion in a high degree, all of these being features of the infantility which is the main trouble with us all."[86] Absurd and confused, the essay is indicative of the sophisticated Freudian chatter that was beginning to be popular among self-styled intellectuals. Its self-conscious, "in-group" tone, as well as its implication that Freud had revealed the last word on man, was no doubt irritating both to Freud's opponents and to his more well-informed followers.

As has been suggested previously, the application of Freud's ideas to literature was attempted quite early. By 1916, the practice had become frequent enough for the reviewer of Ricklin's *Wishfulfillment and Symbolism in Fairy Tales* to protest strongly against it. Ricklin's use of a preconceived idea to analyze works of literature, he complained, resulted in his discovering a Freudian symbol under every bush: "That he finds what he is looking for is not surprising. The only rivals of the Freudian hypothesis in the art of seeing what one brings are the Baconian cyphers."[87] The reviewer's quarrel was not solely with Dr. Ricklin who, he granted, occasionally presented valid insights, but with the many psychologists blithely practicing literary criticism: "If Dr. Ricklin's monograph stood alone, it would not, probably, be especial-

---

86. Wilfred Lay, "John Barleycorn Under Psychoanalysis," *The Bookman*, XLV (May, 1917), 54. The absurdity of the article, together with the author's name, suggests the possibility that the essay was intended as a parody rather than a serious treatment. Irony, sixty years later, is sometimes difficult to detect.

87. "Freudian Fairy Tales," *The Nation*, CIII (July 6, 1916), 12. For a brief discussion of Ricklin's book, see Appendix B.

ly significant. But it typifies, as it happens, a growing tendency on the part of the Freudians to enter other fields . . . with [an] airy disregard of the fact that these departments of knowledge have developed methods of investigation at least as rigid as the technique of psychoanalysis itself . . . . Literature is interpreted in the technical journals of psychopathology in accordance with a system as fearful as it is wonderful."[88] Both Jung and Freud were cited as sinners in this regard, and the author concluded by suggesting that "folklore and literature may well be treasure-troves for the practitioners of psychoanalysis, and results of value may conceivably be obtained from such research. But they will not be obtained until the Freudians pay to the other sciences the tribute of a preliminary understanding which they rightly exact of those who approach their own."[89]

The dominant attitude toward Freud on the part of the educated American by 1918 is reflected in several reviews in *The Dial, The Bookman,* and *The New Republic*—of Oscar Pfister's *The Psychoanalytic Method,* Jung's *Analytical Psychology,* Freud's *Wit and Its Relation to the Unconscious,* and *Totem and Taboo.* In each case, psychoanalytic theory was treated with great respect, although the Oedipus complex and infantile sexuality in general were not wholeheartedly accepted. While maintaining some skepticism on details of the theory, the reviewers acknowledged Freud's greatness as an innovator: "In the end the knowledge of man's psyche may no more resemble Freud's than our present knowledge of the circulation of the blood resembles the Greeks'. But the age opened out by Freud is beyond doubt a supreme adventure . . . ."[90] The attitude of Havelock Ellis, writing in *The Bookman,* is typical. Although critical of Freud's theory on several points, Ellis concluded: "We do not demand of a Columbus that he shall be a reliable surveyor of the new world he discovers. Freud has enlarged our horizon . . . . He has revealed the possibility of new depths, new subtleties, new complexities, new psychic mechanisms. That is the great and outstanding fact."[91]

88. *Ibid.,* p. 13.
89. *Ibid.*
90. Francis Hackett, "Totem and Taboo," *The New Republic,* XV (July 20, 1918), 348.
91. Havelock Ellis, "Psychoanalysts," *The Bookman,* XLVI (September, 1917), 60.

Freud's American reputation as the author of an important new philosophy of man emerged slowly from its beginnings in 1895, where it was confined to a small group of specialists, through the pre-war period of recognition first in professional journals and then increasingly in the popular press, to its status of having become common intellectual currency in the post-war years. The steady growth of this recognition was aided by the publication of the Brill translations, which began appearing in 1910,[92] and by books on Freudian psychology published by the Nervous and Mental Disease Monograph Series, Moffat, Yard and Company, and others. The 1913 publication of the translation of *The Interpretation of Dreams* was of great importance in this growth, both because it made Freud's major work available in English and because of the attention it received. By World War I, the Greenwich Village intellectuals had made psychoanalysis a fad, and although during the war, interest in Freud may have diminished slightly, his ideas continued to gain followers. Journalists discussing Freud's thought treated him respectfully, despite the reservations they may privately have had about specific psychoanalytic tenets. As might be expected, there was considerable reticence in handling such tabooed concepts as infantile sexuality; no journalists discussed outright Freud's unmentionable views on castration fears and penis envy, and they treated infantile incestuous desires, if at all, in the vaguest and most desexualized terms possible. It was at least partly because of this cautious treatment that Freud was so infrequently attacked in the popular press. Freudian theory was not without critics in this country, and there were occasional vituperative and semi-hysterical attacks on it, but on the whole the amount of opposition to Freud's ideas, even from the clergy, was surprisingly small.[93] Freud as a figure of real con-

92. A. A. Brill received Freud's permission to translate his works in 1908. In "The Introduction and Development of Freud's Work in the United States," Brill discusses the difficulties he had in publishing the translations: "Dr. Smith Ely Jelliffe readily accepted the small volumes on the neuroses and sex for his new monograph series, but it took a few years before I finally found English publishers for *The Psychopathology of Everyday Life* and *The Interpretation of Dreams*. No American publisher was willing to take the risk of putting them out in this country" (p. 324).

93. This same surprising lack of concerted opposition to ideas threatening to religion is also apparent in the nineteenth century, when the Darwinian hypothesis was absorbed into Protestant thought with comparative

troversy was a phenomenon of the early twenties, and by that time his reputation was already secure.

The application of psychoanalysis to literary criticism was made almost from the beginning, in Ernest Jones's study of *Hamlet* in 1910, Albert Chandler's interpretation of Greek drama, and F. C. Prescott's use of Freud's dream theory in *Poetry and Dreams*. The appeal of Freudian psychology to the literary artist and critic was almost immediate. By the end of the first World War, the general public was sufficiently informed about Freud's ideas to make psychoanalytic literary criticism both comprehensible and marketable. The introduction of a new "scientific" theory which purported to hold a key to the mysteries of the creative process opened up a rich field of investigation into artists and their works which both psychologist and non-psychologist alike proceeded to mine with great enthusiasm.

---

ease. See Richard Hofstadter, *Social Darwinism in American Thought* (Philadelphia: University of Pennsylvania Press, 1944), Chapter I. For European and American attacks on Freud and his followers, see the chapter, "Opposition," in Jones's biography of Freud.

2. Freudian Criticism: The Theorists

The widespread currency of Freudian theory after the first World War was centered largely in the big cities of the East. Alfred Booth Kuttner claimed that in 1916 there were about five hundred individuals willing to psychoanalyze patients in New York City alone: "Advertisements offered to teach psychoanalytic technique by mail and instructors in chiropractic included it in their curriculum."[1] Publishers' blurbs announcing the publication of new books promised that the new psychoanalytic techniques would yield rich dividends of psychic strength. The following Harper and Brothers advertisement, which appeared under the heading "Getting What We Want," is typical: "Are you 'getting what you want' in health, happiness, money? If not, it's probably because you are not doing the sort of work you are fitted for by mental and physical heritage. Dr. Edison's new book will show you how to psychoanalyze yourself." The "little magazines" of the period, mostly published in New York, reveal the popularity of Freud's ideas among the litterateurs.[2] The advertisements for the Gothic Book Mart in *The Little Review* for November, 1915, had a special heading for "Sexology" books, under which were listed Eduard Hitschmann's *Freud's Theory of the Neuroses*, Jung's *Theory of Psychoanalysis*, and Freud's *Studies in*

1. Alfred Booth Kuttner, "Nerves," in *Civilization in the United States*, ed. Harold E. Stearns (New York: Harcourt, Brace & Co., 1922), p. 435.
2. See Frederick J. Hoffman *et al.*, *The Little Magazine* (Princeton: Princeton University Press, 1947).

37

Hysteria and *Three Contributions to the Theory of Sex*.³ By 1917 there had been added Oscar Pfister's *The Psychoanalytical Method*, Adler's *The Neurotic Constitution*, and Freud's *Wit and Its Relation to the Unconscious*. It is apparent from these advertisements that the appeal of Freudianism, both to middle-brow and high-brow, was varied, incorporating both the desire for commercial success and latent prurient interests, as well as the impulse toward self-understanding.

To the aspiring literary artist, the theories of Freud and his followers possessed a further attraction. In 1916 *The Little Review* carried an article by Florence K. Frank entitled "Psychoanalysis: Some Random Thoughts Thereon," which reveals both the interest in Freudian theory on the part of would-be artists, and the emergence of the psychoanalyst as a new hero. Wrote Miss Frank: "The Freudian searching into motives is the accredited material of the novelist; the use of dream symbols the very stuff of the poet. The successful psychoanalytic physician ought to combine the adroitness of the fictionist with the imagination of the versifier."⁴ An interesting facet of this article is its demonstration of the extent to which the ideas of Jung as well as Freud had been assimilated, and of a noticeable preference for Jung. Freud, Miss Frank suggested, was of interest primarily to the physician, whereas the ideas of Jung "open up a realm of speculation and discovery more fascinating than that of Darwinism."⁵ Enthusiastically portraying the wonders of the new world revealed by the psychoanalysts, Miss Frank speculated that it would take perhaps five more years for this knowledge to penetrate the consciousness of the average man in the streets, who was as yet unaware of its import. She was, however, quite aware of the implications of the new theories, and was delighted to discover that "we are more wonderful than we thought": the man on the street quite unexpectedly turned out to be not a dull clod but at one with the "ancient Hindus and the dancing sun-worshippers," and the mind of the woman shopping on Fifth Avenue

3. Jung's *Psychology of the Unconscious*, Abraham's *Dreams and Myths*, and Freud's *On Dreams* were listed under the heading, "Science."
4. Florence K. Frank, "Psychoanalysis: Some Random Thoughts Thereon," *The Little Review*, III (June-July, 1916), 16.
5. *Ibid*.

was suddenly found to contain "the symbolism of the Elusinian mysteries."[6]

The enthusiasm that psychoanalytic theory was capable of generating in some of its converts even reached so skeptical a mind as H. L. Mencken. In an article in *The Smart Set* for 1918, Mencken admitted somewhat reluctantly to having been won over to the new psychology. After a rather flip introduction describing his initial aversion to psychoanalytic theory, he added more seriously: "But the further I proceeded through the fat tomes of the psychoanalysts the more I am convinced that . . . there must be something in it. The early announcements of Professor Sigmund Freud, the founder, had an appearance of extravagance . . . and, in point of fact, some of them *were* extravagant, but the more his fundamental ideas have been put to the test the more plain it has become that they are essentially sound."[7] Mencken found particularly appealing the concept of unconscious causality, and essayed an explanation of the Freudian unconscious as a sort of "cold-storage warehouse" for old memories where "the more you try to hold down the lid, the more these quasi-corpses pick at their grave-cloths, and poke their heads out of their tombs, and whisper into the inner ear, and fill you with disquiet."[8] He concluded his article with a selected list of books on Freud which he highly recommended as "a literature of singular interest. There is in it all the horror of theology and all the fascination of fiction."[9]

The early issues of *The Criterion* carried several lively articles discussing Freud and his theories. One of these, Jacques Rivière's "Notes on a Possible Generalization of the Theories of Freud," indicates the same sort of enthusiasm for psychoanalysis found in Miss Frank's essay. In this still readable article, the author proposed not to analyze Freud's doctrine in detail, but "supposing it to be known to all my readers," to "bring out . . . its potentialities."[10] He discussed at some length three of the implications of Freudian theory. The first of these "sublimities" was Freud's

6. *Ibid.*, p. 17.
7. H. L. Mencken, "Rattling the Subconscious," *The Smart Set*, LVI (September, 1918), 138.
8. *Ibid.*, p. 139.
9. *Ibid.*
10. Jacques Rivière, "Notes on a Possible Generalization of the Theories of Freud," *The Criterion*, I (July 19, 1923), 332.

concept of the unconscious; the second was the implication of a "deceptive principle" inherent in the mind, with the resulting corollary that "hypocrisy is inherent in consciousness";[11] and the third was the explanation of the aesthetic emotion Freud's theory offered. To Rivière, the concept of the libido had revealed the "sensual element the work [of art] always possesses when it is sincere," and suggested that the critic should look at the work of art not for its surface story but for "the current of desire, the impulse in which it was born."[12] If criticism were to apply itself to this task, "a sort of vague aesthetic criterion might be established, which would enable us to distinguish works born of an inclination from those manufactured by the will, the aesthetic quality being, of course, reserved to the former."[13] As for the effect of Freudian theory on fiction, the author foresaw a new scope in the fictional interpretation of character, and almost unlimited possibilities for new themes.

The early issues of *Broom*, another avant-garde magazine of the time, also reflected the literary artist's interest in Freud. Malcolm Cowley satirically portrayed a bohemian's paradise, where the works of Freud and D. H. Lawrence would be openly sold at newstands,[14] and Matthew Josephson severely attacked the popular Freudian novels of Waldo Frank for portraying a character's subconscious to the exclusion of his consciousness: "Prepared by years of journalistic warfare, one fails to be revolted by the simple-mindedness of the psychoanalytic novel proper . . . . Its interest lies chiefly in the application of the Freudian tactic: we shall hearken only to the subconscious strata of the brain, observing only instinctive behavior, and speak only in the shadowy dictum of dreams."[15] In attempting to portray the "real" elements of character (an attempt to "catapult himself, through Freudian formula, into the ultimate sappy core of reality," according to Josephson), Waldo Frank had rendered his characters tedious and unsympathetic. Rather than human beings, they were merely "slack balloons appended to bulbous genitals."[16]

11. *Ibid.*, p. 339.　　12. *Ibid.*, p. 343.　　13. *Ibid.*, p. 340.

14. Malcolm Cowley, "Young Mr. Elkins," *Broom*, IV (December, 1922), 55.

15. Matthew Josephson, "Instant Note on Waldo Frank," *Broom*, IV (December, 1922), 57.

16. *Ibid.*, p. 59.

A good deal of the discussion of Freud in the literary magazines, both "little" and big, arose in response to the flood of Freudian fiction immediately after the war. Not only Waldo Frank, but D. H. Lawrence, Sherwood Anderson, May Sinclair, and many lesser known figures, now forgotten, came under attack by critics for writing according to a Freudian formula. *The Dial*, for example, took Sherwood Anderson to task, comparing him unfavorably with Theodore Dreiser: "Where Mr. Dreiser like a giant mole with strong flat hands tore up the soil and prepared the ground for a more liberal treatment of sex in American literature, Mr. Anderson, nervous and mystical, follows along like the anxious white rabbit . . . clasping instead of a watch the latest edition of Sigmund Freud."[17] Of all the novelists influenced by Freud, however, it was Waldo Frank who came in for the most abuse and was chosen as the symbol of the writer's "obsession" with psychoanalysis that had become "at once the craze and the curse of the modern novelist."[18] Maxwell Bodenheim, in an angry article in *The Nation*, denounced Frank and others for having twisted Freud's "modest claim" that dreams were veiled allusions to sexual desire into the contention that "sex underlies and dominates all human motives and is the basis of all creations."[19] The "enticing claim" of the psychoanalysts that "nothing exists in human beings except sex," had resulted in a mass of bad fiction with "sensuality at the core." The same charge was leveled at American writers by Raoul Reed in *The Freeman*. Novels were being written to a formula, he complained, and it was a false formula at that. "The good writer studies closely and sees clearly not psychoanalysis but life," Mr. Reed somewhat obviously pointed out, and added, "It is the business of the novelist to describe life as he sees it . . . , not to explain it."[20] J. D. Beresford, also writing in *The Freeman*, argued that a self-conscious use of any scien-

17. Alyse Gregory, "Sherwood Anderson," *The Dial*, LXXV (September, 1923), 246.

18. J. D. Beresford, "Psychoanalysis and the Novel," *The Freeman*, I (March 24, 1920), 35.

19. Maxwell Bodenheim, "Psychoanalysis and American Fiction," *The Nation*, CXIV (June 7, 1922), 683. It is interesting that Bodenheim absolved Freud himself of any such idea.

20. Raoul Reed, "Psychoanalysis in Literature," *The Freeman*, V (1922), 490.

tific knowledge inevitably resulted in meretricious writing, and expressed his annoyance at the monotonous series of heroes suffering from Oedipus complexes.[21] He maintained, however, that the use of Freudian material by novelists was inevitable and would ultimately result in a better literature once the material had been "so assimilated and transmuted as to become a personal experience and conviction."[22]

John Crowe Ransom took a somewhat similar position in the *Saturday Review*, pointing out that had James and Conrad known of Freud, they might have probed their characters in even greater depth than was possible in their time. A knowledge of psychoanalytic theory, if used well, as Ransom felt it was by Anderson, D. H. Lawrence, and Rebecca West, could result in good literature. Further, Ransom pointed out, "psychoanalysis is not at all points a new technique, but rather the systematic or scientific application of technique that poets and artists have generally been aware of."[23]

Perhaps even more extensive than the quarrel over the effect of psychoanalysis on fiction were the heated debates over the effect of psychoanalysis on literary criticism. Even by 1919 psychoanalytic criticism had become so widespread that it had called forth a satire entitled *Euclid's Outline of Sex* by one Wilbur P. Birdwood. There was an amusing review of this piece in *The Atlantic* called "The Scandal of Euclid: A Freudian Analysis." Although broad, the satire did manage to capture the studious air of much Freudian criticism: "In no field . . . has the search after new meanings and values by the light of the Freudian principle been carried on with such painstaking labor and such ex-

21. Beresford, "Psychoanalysis and the Novel," p. 35.
22. *Ibid.*, p. 37.
23. John Crowe Ransom, "Freud and Literature," *The Saturday Review of Literature*, I (October 4, 1924), 161. This article is a dual review of Freud's *Group Psychology and the Analysis of the Ego* and *Beyond the Pleasure Principle*. Ransom's attitude toward Freud was one of great admiration: "As for psychoanalysis, it is quite becoming that doctors should still disagree about it, but the poets . . . find much less difficulty in accepting it as gospel truth" (*ibid.*). He even accepted the tenets of *Beyond the Pleasure Principle*, remarking that "nothing of his has so teased the imagination as the vast and brilliant speculations in his last two small volumes" (*ibid.*, p. 162). For another favorable review of *Beyond the Pleasure Principle*, see George Santayana, "A Long Way Round to Nirvana," *The Dial*, LXXV (November, 1923), 435-42).

traordinary restraint as in the sphere of imaginative literature. No disciple of Freud has ventured to interpret an entire literature as the precipitant of the repressed desires of a nation. For that, it is recognized, the time has not come. A great deal of spade work still remains to be done. That work is now being carried on by a rapidly growing band of investigators . . . ."[24] Euclid's works, according to this interpretation, were the result of the geometer's attempt to rid himself of a "haunting Triangle complex," a theme which recurred obsessively throughout his first five books. The "complex" originated in the circumstances of Euclid's early life: " 'Now what do we know of the principal events of Euclid's life?' our author asked himself. The answer was, not a thing . . . . 'With this as a basis,' continues Mr. Birdwood, 'are we not justified in filling in the sketch until the entire career of the great geometer rises vividly before us?' "[25] After this biographical analysis, the reader was treated to a learned discussion of the problem of the "bisexualization of angles," the "deadly parallel," and the "homosexual triangle." The book concluded with a promise of a new study devoted to Euclid's later works: "If . . . in the Euclidian Plane Geometry we find the transfiguration of a child's day dream, in the Solid Geometry we enter the domain of the nightmare."[26] As a parody, the book succeeded in mimicking the frequent thought leaps of the poorer psychoanalytic critics and their habit of enveloping their conjectures with the halo of science; its publication indicates the extent to which psychoanalytic criticism was being practiced, mostly by Freudian psychologists.[27]

The debate over the validity of applying Freudian psychology to literary criticism was quite animated between 1910 and 1926. Freud's views on art had raised several issues which were to be attacked and defended from a variety of standpoints: Was the artist a neurotic individual who found release for his emotional problems in artistic expression, or was he a superior individual endowed with a greater than normal ability to harness unconscious

24. Simeon Strunsky, "The Scandal of Euclid: A Freudian Analysis," *The Atlantic*, CXXIV (September, 1919), 332.
25. *Ibid.*, p. 333.
26. *Ibid.*, p. 337.
27. The book was also reviewed by M. A. Meyer in *The International Journal of Psychoanalysis*, where much of the early psychoanalytic criticism appeared. Mr. Meyer was not amused.

emotional forces and transform them into universally communicable images and themes? To what extent did art represent a "wish-fulfillment" of the artist's unconscious needs and desires? What part did consciousness play in the creative process? If the source of creativity was the unconscious, how were the artist's personal symbols rendered meaningful to his audience? To what degree was the effect of the art work on its audience a result of the unconscious appeal of its content and to what degree was it a result of purely formal qualities? These questions, and others closely related to them, stimulated literary theorists to produce a considerable number of essays and books exploring the implications of the psychoanalytic view of the creative process, an exploration which resulted frequently in a good deal of confusion, and even some nonsense, but one which also contributed genuinely valuable and provocative insights into the nature and effect of art.

Freud's own pronouncements on the artist and the nature of the creative process were available in scattered remarks throughout his major works and in several brief essays pertaining directly to literary criticism.[28] Second in importance to these were the numerous full-length studies by his disciples, particularly those relating directly to the problem of the artist.[29] A third important source for the critic were the various remarks on creativity scat-

28. For example, comments on the nature of the artist were to be found in *The Interpretation of Dreams, Wit and Its Relation to the Unconscious, Three Contributions to the Theory of Sex, Totem and Taboo, A General Introduction to Psychoanalysis,* and *Beyond the Pleasure Principle.* Separate articles included "The Relation of the Poet to Day-Dreaming," "The Occurrence in Dreams of Material from Fairy Tales," "Some Character Types Met With in Psychoanalytic Work," and "The Antithetical Sense of Primal Words." Examples of Freud's application of his ideas to criticism included *Delusion and Dream in Jensen's Gradiva, Leonardo da Vinci,* "The Theme of the Three Caskets," and "The Moses of Michelangelo." The dates of these works, and the dates of their English translations, where available, are listed in Appendix A.

29. Of particular interest here are Jung's "On the Relation of Analytical Psychology to Poetic Art," *The Psychology of the Unconscious,* and *Psychological Types*; Franz Ricklin's *Wishfulfillment and Symbolism in Fairy Tales*; Otto Rank's *The Myth of the Birth of the Hero, Der Künstler,* and *Das Inzesmotiv in Dichtung und Sage* (the latter two untranslated during this period); Karl Abraham's *Dreams and Myths*; and Ernest Jones's *Essays in Applied Psychoanalysis.* For the dates of these works, see Appendix A.

tered thoughout articles in professional journals both by the immediate members of Freud's circle (Karl Abraham, Otto Rank, Wilhelm Stekel, Hanns Sachs, Ernest Jones, Sandor Ferenczi) and by those whose knowledge of Freud was second- or third-hand. There were also redactions of Freud's hypotheses on the artist by non-psychologists, men who approached the problem of creativity as literary critics using Freudian psychology rather than Freudian psychologists trying their hands at literary criticism.

Probably the best example of this latter category is a long essay by Alfred Booth Kuttner published in *The Seven Arts* in 1917. Noting that Freudian psychology owed much to the artist for the hints he had provided, Kuttner examined in his essay the relation of the artist to the normal man, to the neurotic, and to the insane, his thesis being that if mankind could be classified according to its relation to the "reality principle" on the one hand and to the "pleasure principle" on the other, the artist fell somewhere between the two groups and was in a class by himself. The normal man sought to adapt himself to reality and to free himself from the unconscious: the neurotic was "abnormally dominated by his unconscious";[30] and the insane man succumbed to it entirely. In contrast to all of these, the artist "avoids surrender to the unconscious but he cannot adapt himself to reality. He does something in between. He creates an ideal reality."[31] Hovering between the sane and the insane, the artist at times manifested distinctly neurotic traits and might become obsessed with them at the expense of his artistry. The creative impulse itself, however, was essentially healthy rather than unhealthy, and functioned therapeutically. Because of this creative impulse, the artist was saved from a neurosis: "The unconscious which he cannot relinquish in favor of reality threatens to overwhelm him. But he is saved from the blind alley in which the neurotic staggers by a peculiar biological endowment which lies outside the unconscious: the gift of technique."[32] This gift, this "technique," was not used to subdue the external world—the response of the normal man—but was used to harness the unconscious and turn it into a fantasy world which had social value. "Art, therefore, represents a compromise be-

30. Alfred Booth Kuttner, "The Artist," *The Seven Arts* (February, 1917), p. 409.
31. *Ibid.*   32. *Ibid.*

tween the principles of reality and of pleasure and reconciles them in a way which is entirely unique."[33]

The artist served society by allowing men, through their experience of his art, to return temporarily to the pleasure principle and to give expression to their own unconscious needs. Why, then, asked Kuttner, was society ambivalent toward its artists? The answer lay in the artist's "peculiar psycho-sexual constitution," in his closeness to the universal "psychic infantilisms" present in all men. By giving expression to these "infantilisms," the artist disturbed the social order. On the one hand, he "unites us in the realization of our common unconscious heritage," but on the other, "he reminds us how arduous our progress toward reality is, and casts doubts upon the value of the struggle."[34] He was suspect because of his constant reminder that we were not as free from our common infantile impulses and needs as we would like to believe.

James Oppenheim, an editor of *The Seven Arts*, took issue with Kuttner in an editorial appearing during the same month. Oppenheim objected to Kuttner's supposed implication that the artist was neurotic. To Oppenheim, the artist was a superior man "born into the world with that difference in him which made adaptation difficult."[35] The artist's suffering was not the result of a neurotic disposition but of his inability to produce in this world the ideal he envisioned. This was the "wound" which never healed and which furthermore should not heal. To state that the artist was neurotic, implied that he should be "cured" of his art. On the contrary, Oppenheim argued, he should be "cured" only in the direction of making him super-normal: "Normality means repression, with its corollary of conventionality. What should be sought after is not to teach the artist to repress his desires, but to express them . . . in those human, those higher ways that fall under the

33. *Ibid.*, p. 410. Kuttner's ideas here are taken from Freud's essay, "Formulations of the Two Principles of Psychic Activity" (at that time still untranslated). He quotes Freud to the effect that the artist "finds his way back from the world of phantasy to reality by shaping his phantasies into a new form of reality . . . . Thus, he becomes the hero, king, creator, lover, that he aspired to be without making the tremendous detour of really changing the outer world" (p. 411).

34. *Ibid.*, p. 412.

35. James Oppenheim, "Editorial," *The Seven Arts*, I (February, 1917), p. 392.

head of sublimation."[36] Many artists had achieved this "victory" of being both a healthy citizen and an artist—witness Milton, Shakespeare, and Goethe, whose involvement with reality made them greater artists than Poe, Oscar Wilde, or Remy de Gourmont.[37]

Kuttner replied to Oppenheim's editorial in the following issue. He repeated his earlier position and emphasized that Freud himself placed the artist in a special class, adding, "The Freudian psychology has always been keenly aware of its limitations . . . . In such a special study as that of the artist, for instance, it makes no claim to give a full explanation of him or in any sense to explain him away."[38] Clarifying some of his other points, Kuttner enlarged upon his concept of the "gift of technique," which he saw as being a general biological endowment, similar to manual dexterity, that enabled the artist to mould materials into pleasing forms. All men possessed this gift to some degree, and part of the enjoyment of art arose from seeing this gift used more skillfully than our own, more limited, capacities could admit.[39] Technique itself was merely a "brute endowment," which was for the psychologist a "given"; psychoanalysis could contribute no insight into its nature. The artist, however, "does not come into being until he has a conception to express in artistic terms." It is at this point that the psychologist could be of use to the literary critic: ". . . psychoanalysis claims and substantiates its claim that it can tell us something of the genesis of the artistic conception, that it can explain its psychic economy and that it can relate it to psychic mechanisms and impulses that are common to mankind. It can interpret it in universal psychological terms and explain its meaning to the individual artist and its value to the mass. That is all it claims to do."[40] To Kuttner the artist was not, could not be, and should not be normal. Psychoanalysis had no particular desire to "cure" the artist, he argued, only to cure him of a neurosis which might be interfering with his art. Furthermore, since a patient who did not want treatment was incapable of being treated, it would be impossible for analysts to "reduce an artist to normality" even if they desired to do so.

36. *Ibid.*, p. 393.   37. *Ibid.*, p. 394.
38. Alfred Booth Kuttner, "The Artist (A Communication)," *The Seven Arts*, I (March, 1917), p. 549.
39. *Ibid.*, p. 550.   40. *Ibid.*, p. 551.

Kuttner's essay was designed as a "preliminary communication" to "forestall misapprehensions." His plan was to write a series of articles on the nature of the artist viewed in the light of modern psychology. *The Seven Arts*, however, expired with this issue, and apparently the articles were never written. This is unfortunate, for the two essays that did appear were exceptionally clear and well-informed discussions of the subject. They presented a view of the artist which was to become fairly widespread among later psychological critics: that although the artist shared with the neurotic an access to unconscious material, he differed from him in the ability to express this material therapeutically, to give it a form, and by so doing to rescue both himself and his audience from potential neurotic suffering. His art itself was not neurotic, but beneficial; the artist was a special case, differing not only in degree but to a certain extent, in kind, from other men.

Wilhelm Stekel's series of articles entitled "Poetry and Neurosis" exemplifies the approach taken toward the creative process by a practicing psychologist.[41] In contrast to men of letters who used psychology, like Kuttner, the psychologist *qua* literary critic tended to be considerably more dogmatic in his assertions of Freudian theory, and tended toward a more rigid insistence that the artist was fundamentally a neurotic individual who found release from his sufferings through his creations. Stekel's articles, as a series, do not present an entirely coherent picture; his somewhat extravagant style leads him into several inconsistencies, but essentially his view of the artist differed from Kuttner's in that he saw the artist as being always a neurotic.

In this view the artist, like the neurotic, was "under the sway of repression . . . a victim of the dissonance between consciousness and the unconscious which leads to a *psychic conflict*."[42] Quoting a passage from Otto Rank's *Der Künstler* which placed the artist in a category that included the dreamer and the neurotic, Stekel emphatically stated, "Between the artist and the neurotic there is no essential difference. Not every neurotic is an artist.

41. Wilhelm Stekel, "Poetry and Neurosis," trans. James S. Van Teslaar, *The Pscyhoanalytic Review*, X (January, 1923), 73-93; (April, 1923), 190-208; (July, 1923), 316-28; (October, 1923), 457-66; XI (January, 1924), 48-60.
42. Stekel, "Poetry and Neurosis," X (January, 1923), 77.

But every artist is a neurotic."[43] Stekel denied, however, that his theory bore any similarity to those of Nordau and Lombroso, who viewed genius in terms of insanity and degeneration. For one thing, neurosis was a universal trait, a result of the conflict between culture and the instincts; it was "only a result of the progressive cultural level of existence."[44] Furthermore, to be neurotic did not mean to be insane. In partial contradiction to his earlier statement, Stekel suggested that the artist was in some sense actually healthier than the neurotic in that his art had enabled him to come to terms with his neurosis: "Creative activity is virtually a process of healing through auto-analysis."[45] Despite this, Stekel's delineation of the character traits of the poet tended to place the artist more definitely in a category of sickness than of health. Summarized, these traits included "symptoms of hysteria, repression, incest fancies, anxiety states, perversions [i.e., a strong tendency toward homosexuality], feelings of disgust, predisposition to falsehood and to phantasie making, flights to religion, etc."[46] Several of Stekel's articles were devoted to examining these traits, using examples drawn mainly from European writers (Heine, Goethe, Grillparzer, Strindberg, Alfred de Musset, Baudelaire). He concluded from this examination that "all creative artists are neurotics, and the neurosis from which they suffer is hysteria—that old, baffling disorder without which the race would not have attained the cultural level which today appears to us quite natural but which is really the greatest of all wonders."[47]

One of the peculiar and confusing aspects of Stekel's articles is the high value he placed upon neurosis and hysteria. At one point he borrowed an image from Heine and compared poetry to the pearl which is a product of the oyster's disease.[48] The artist himself was neurotic, but, paradoxically, the effect of his art was healthy: "Keenly sensitive to the sway of our passions and at the same time endowed with a conscience finely responsive and far above the rest of mortals . . . the creative artist struggles and suffers for humanity and pays with his agony for the happiness of others."[49] Here the artist is viewed as almost a superman, a

43. *Ibid.,* p. 78.
45. *Ibid.,* p. 84.
47. *Ibid.,* p. 207.
49. *Ibid.,* p. 57.

44. *Ibid.,* p. 80.
46. *Ibid.,* p. 206.
48. *Ibid.,* XI (January, 1924), 56.

Christ-like figure whose sacrifice contributes to the salvation of humanity.

In his final article, Stekel concerned himself with the difference between artist and neurotic, having firmly placed them earlier in the same general class. That there was a difference he admitted. How was this to be explained? Or, as Stekel phrased it, "What is the measure of repression combined with self-knowledge, eroticism and coyness, of religiosity and free thought, what precisely the right combination of submissiveness and rebellion, capable of turning the sufferer into a creative artist? As yet the deeper understanding of this problem is beyond us."[50] Despite this disclaimer, Stekel ventured a few suggestions. For one thing, the neurosis of the artist could not be so intense as to paralyze his joy of work, or he would not be an artist. More important, the artist's peculiar neurosis must contain a tendency toward exhibitionism, the "joy of exposure."[51]

The series concluded rhetorically with a rather strange hymn of praise for the cultural benefits derived from mental imbalance: "A world without hysteria would be a lamentable world. Illness and health belong together, like pleasure and pain, each conditioning and completing the other,—neurosis is the fruit of the tree of progress . . . . Everywhere nature pays for improvement with numberless sacrifices. The rise of a single destructive-creative genius involves 1,000 useless sacrifices; numberless neurotics vainly torment themselves in the attempt to produce something worthwhile before a single masterly creation makes its appearance."[52] The flamboyance of Stekel's style is personal, but the position he took here, and his dogmatic manner of expressing it, is fairly representative of the Freudian psychologist's view of the artist. The roots of creativity were to be found in the unconscious; the impulse to create art, a special fantasy activity, arose from neurotic needs. Despite his own sickness, however, the artist's creations could be an instrument of health, not only for himself but for his

50. *Ibid.*
51. "What do artists do, in the last analysis, but expose themselves and others in all nakedness? . . . Artistry is a form of psychic exhibitionism" (*ibid.*, p. 58).
52. *Ibid.*, p. 59.

audience; his sufferings produced works of value which transcended their original cause.

Early in the series Stekel had stated: "There is essentially no difference between dream and poetry . . . . They are almost identical psychic mechanisms. The dream derives its material from the depths of the unconscious. And does not true artistic talent consist in the ability to draw upon one's unconscious powers?"[53] This analogy between poetry and the dream is perhaps the central doctrine of Freudian theory drawn upon by literary critics. Its fullest exposition is to be found in the works of F. C. Prescott, especially in *Poetry and Dreams* and in *The Poetic Mind*. Because of the importance of these books in the debate over the validity of Freudian criticism, and because of their intrinsic value, they deserve examination in some detail.

Prescott's *Poetry and Dreams* appeared originally as a series of articles in *The Journal of Abnormal Psychology* in 1912,[54] and was later published in book form in the same year. It is surprising that a work of this sophistication should have appeared so early. Prescott's intention was to explore the resemblances between poetry and the dream, and to examine the poetic process with the aid of Freud's theories, using remarks on creativity made by poets themselves. As a layman, he explained, he was forced to accept Freud's theories for purposes of his argument, despite the fact that they were still a subject for debate. His own study, he suggested, might serve to corroborate some of Freud's tenets, if he could present evidence from the poets which agreed with Freud's conclusions.[55]

Prescott's first major premise was that all works of the creative imagination were products of a wish or desire. On the simplest level, "the use of poetry is to afford an escape from reality: to transform the real world, by an effort of the poetic imagination, into an ideal world in accordance with our desires, our hopes, our

53. *Ibid.*, X (January, 1923,) 75.
54. F. C. Prescott, "Poetry and Dreams," *The Journal of Abnormal Psychology*, VII (April-May, 1912), 17-46; (June-July, 1912), 104-43.
55. The extent of Prescott's familiarity with Freud is well attested to. According to A. A. Brill, Prescott conferred with him frequently about his books, checking them with Freudian theory; Prescott in turn helped Brill with his translation of Freud's works. See Frederick J. Hoffman, *Freudianism and the Literary Mind* (Baton Rouge: Louisiana State University Press, 1957), p. 44.

aspirations."[56] At this point Prescott introduced a limitation in his subject matter, dividing poetry into two types: primary poetry, which was "original," and secondary poetry, which merely "copies the forms of inspiration."[57] He restricted his discussion to the first type, to what he called "poetry of inspiration."[58] In judging the principle that the purpose of poetry, like dreams, was to satisfy desire, two considerations, he felt, should be kept in mind: "First, that the gratification of poetry may extend no further than that derived from the idealized expression . . . . Secondly, that in poetry, the poet's desires are not represented openly and literally; they are disguised, conveyed through a medium of fiction, bodied forth in strange forms as a result of the alchemic action, the 'dream-work' of the poet's brain."[59]

The creation of a poem, in this view, was not the result of a voluntary, intellectual act but of an unconscious, involuntary activity which Prescott called the "poetic imagination."[60] If this were true, and since poetry was the expression of desires, "Is it not natural to suppose that the desires of the poet, as of the dreamer, are impeded and consequently repressed—forced back into unconsciousness?"[61] Unconscious desires were for various reasons prevented from serving as a motive for action; they still remained operative, however, and found a "fictional gratification" in the created poem. This consideration of the source of the poem in a repressed desire led Prescott to a discussion of Keble's theory of poetry as an indirect expression of feeling, indirect be-

56. F. C. Prescott, *Poetry and Dreams* (Boston: The Four Seas Company, 1912), p. 17.
57. *Ibid.*
58. This is a rather serious limitation, which tends to vitiate his argument. Aside from ruling out a large body of poetry, Prescott also stated that no one poem was "true poetry" in its entirety. "Some parts of a poem are written with vision; they come from the deep unconscious sources that have been referred to. Others are written with the conscious mind; these are the work of the skillful artificer, not of the true poet" (*ibid.*, p. 49). This distinction between "visionary" and merely "technical" poetry probably owed something to Coleridge's famous distinction between the poetry of imagination and the poetry of fancy. A more direct source was the *Lectures* of the Reverend John Keble, wherein the same distinction between "primary" and "secondary" was made. Cf. M. H. Abrams, *The Mirror and the Lamp* (New York: Oxford University Press, 1953), p. 145.
59. Prescott, *Poetry and Dreams*, p. 18.
60. *Ibid.*, p. 24.
61. *Ibid.*, p. 27.

cause the force of the direct emotion would be too strong to be accepted by any reader, or, indeed, by the writer himself.[62] This indirect expression of an emotion that was unacceptable either because it was "too strong" (Keble) or because of its very nature (Freud) functioned to secure the poet's mental health. It was a "safety-valve, tending to preserve him from mental disease."[63] This theory is similar to Aristotle's concept of catharsis which, as Prescott pointed out, was Freud's own name for his method of curing mental illness. "The conclusion," Prescott stated, "to which this evidence leads is that poetry is the expression of repressed and unconscious desires; and that the function of poetry, biologically considered, like that of dreams, is to secure to us mental repose and hence health and well-being."[64]

In addition to preserving mental balance in the same way that the dream preserved sleep, the poem and the dream were alike in having their source in the emotions and in being concrete in their expression.[65] As the dream was the result of a compromise between two conflicting elements—the repressed wish and the "censor"—so poetry was the result of a conflict between the poet's inspiration and external authority, whether this be some inner mental inhibition or the conscious desire to conform to the poetic conventions of the time. Prescott called the first of these, the unconscious motive of the poem, the "impulse," and the form in which the final poem emerged the "control." Rhythm, however, was apparently a product of the "impulse" rather than the "control." Any strong emotion expressed itself in waves, "which constitutes a natural rhythm"; for this reason, poetry, an emotional expression, was rhythmical.[66] Prescott elaborated on Keble's idea that a directly expressed emotion would be too strong to be accepted by suggesting that the poet's feelings "become comparatively tolerable, not to say interesting to us, when we find them so far under control as to leave those who feel them at liberty to pay attention to measure and rhyme, and the other expedients of metrical composition."[67] Rhythm and rhyme, then, functioned to provide the reader assurance that the poet was not at the mercy of emo-

62. *Ibid.*, p. 28.   63. *Ibid.*, p. 29.
64. *Ibid.*, p. 32.   65. *Ibid.*, p. 42.
66. *Ibid.*, p. 37.   67. *Ibid.*, p. 38.

tions powerful enough to dominate him; thus reassured, the reader could respond to the emotion without anxiety.[68]

Prescott next compared Freud's concept of the "dream-work" to analogous devices in poetry. The conciseness and at the same time the rich suggestiveness of poetry, he suggested, might be due partly to "condensation," that is, "to the fact that each portion of the poetic product is 'over-determined,' and has many roots in the poet's mind."[69] Further, there might be something analogous to Freud's concept of "secondary elaboration" in the creative process. That is, the poet's original vision was instinctively moulded to fit into or harmonize with the waking thoughts and beliefs of both the poet and his readers. Inevitably, therefore, much of the "poem" never achieved expression: "There was more poetry in Shelley's heart than could find expression in the finished lyric."[70]

The concept of the necessity for "secondary elaboration" in order to render the poem acceptable caused Prescott to return to a more extensive discussion of the nature of the unconscious desires which served as a motive for the poem. The primary desires of mankind were "desires which serve the preservation of life and the propagation of the species."[71] Since the sexual desire was the one most frequently in conflict with external authority, it was the one most frequently repressed, and therefore most often relieved in dreams and in poetry.[72] Not only general sexual desires were expressed in poems, however, but more specifically individual desires as well. Prescott, it seems, was uncertain whether or not to follow Freud's dream theory to the extent of finding the origin of poetry (as in the dream) in repressed incidents of the poet's childhood: "It would be difficult to show any direct evidence that poetry generally or often goes back to repressed experiences of childhood. Other considerations, however, suggest that in some respects the parallel holds again here."[73]

68. Although Prescott's psychological approach to the conscious element in the artistic process seems to indicate an under-valuation of the form of poetry at the expense of its "latent content," he was aware that the former was an essential ingredient of any good poem: ". . . in every tolerable literary expression . . . there must be, or will be, not only the element of inspiration but the element of control, which in poetry employs metre as one of its commonest instruments. Art as well as inspiration is essential to poetry" (*ibid.*, p. 39).

69. *Ibid.*, p. 41.   70. *Ibid.*, p. 51.   71. *Ibid.*
72. *Ibid.*, p. 62.   73. *Ibid.*, p. 44.

Up to this point, Prescott's discussion of the origin of poetry was quite in accord with orthodox Freudian interpretation. He was unwilling, however, to accept the idea that poetry was wholly, or even primarily, the result of unconscious desires if these desires were conceived as being always sexual in nature, as they were so conceived by the Freudians. For this reason he broadened his conception of the poet's unconscious desires to include his aspirations toward the ideal and "desires of a universal character." It was the expression of these latter "universal" desires which gave poetry its value: "The poet in his poetry expresses his desires, primarily his own desires, but also, through his well-known universal and representative character, the desires of others—of his class or country, of mankind. Great poets are great for that reason, because their writings give 'some shadow of satisfaction' to the minds of all men."[74] Because of the generalized nature of the desires expressed in a poem, the reader was able to secure his own personal gratification: "He identifies himself with the poet and himself lives through the poem; the poet is only his spokesman, providing him with the needed outlet for his pent emotion; for him, too, the poem expresses what would otherwise remain inexpressible. Thus countless readers find relief and comfort in poetry."[75]

Prescott's position on the question of whether the poet was neurotic was similar to Alfred Booth Kuttner's. "It is not strange," Prescott wrote, "that poets should be, as we have seen, great dreamers, since their mental condition is one approaching a neurosis."[76] That is to say, the poet had many points in common with the neurotic, but was not necessarily himself always neurotic. A little further on, Prescott discounted the problem as being incapable of solution: "It is . . . alike vain and unscientific to discuss the question whether poets are mentally diseased or not, the line between mental health and disease being a vague or imaginary one; and the poet at most only showing in greater degree traits which are common to all men, all men being dreamers, poets, and neurotics in some measure. We can only say that poets are inevitably subject to mental disturbance, which may go so far as to make them 'peculiar' or incapable of discharging the or-

74. *Ibid.*, p. 20.   75. *Ibid.*, p. 30.   76. *Ibid.*, p. 65.

dinary duties of society."[77] Ultimately, however, Prescott saw poetry as an instrument of health rather than illness. "The poet's madness," he argued, "is not, as so many have thought, a sign of weakness, abnormality, or degeneration, but rather of power."[78] Prescott recognized that his discussion of the "poetic madness" was not entirely satisfactory, and that he had not reached a complete understanding of it. "We have made some progress, however, if instead of calling it merely a 'celestial inspiration,' we connect it with other things with which we are familiar, and recognize in this matter also the common character of poetry, dreams, and the manifestations of hysteria."[79]

Poetry and Dreams was much closer to a strict psychoanalytic interpretation than were Prescott's two later books on creativity. He was attempting here to give the explanation of the poetic process a scientific basis, whereas later he was more concerned to restore to poetry the element of mystery and divinity of which it seemed to him to have been robbed by science. His romantic bias, however, was quite apparent even here: "classical" poetry was more or less excluded from discussion as being of the "secondary" type, and the quotations he cited were drawn largely from writers of the romantic school—Emerson and Poe, Shelley, Wordsworth, and Robert Louis Stevenson. Furthermore, Prescott's apparent unwillingness to accept Freud's idea of the unconscious as being the reservoir of basically sexual impulses led him into an inconsistency. On the other hand, poetry, because it expressed instinctual desires, was the individual's safety-valve against madness; on the other hand, poetry, he claimed, involved the expression of desires other than merely individual or sexual ones—it was the prefigurement of an ideal, the expression of wishes which were in the "unconscious of mankind": "Poetry, with its allied mental productions, presents before our eyes a picture, not of the world as it is, but of the world as we wish it to be, or—since surely our desires are not meaningless but like all else in

77. *Ibid.*, p. 66. Because of his belief in the poet as prophet, it is natural that Prescott should dislike the equation of the artist and neurosis. He granted, however, that poets of the romantic school were very close to being neurotics: "It would seem . . . that something in the romantic temper, with its individualism, its passion, its fondness for solitude and hatred of society, were conducive to mental aberration" (p. 61).

78. *Ibid.*, p. 70.   79. *Ibid.*, p. 71.

nature ordered and significant—may we not say, not of present reality but of coming reality . . . . The poet prefigures the world which is to come, and points the path later men are to follow . . . ."[80] It is this last position which is developed at greater length in *The Poetic Mind* and in *Poetry and Myth*. The concept of poetry as prophecy and the concept of poetry as a product of unconscious desires contradict one another unless one postulates some sort of "racial unconscious"—as Carl Jung had already done by 1922—or else redefines the unconscious in such a way as to include both instinctual and "idealistic" desires. The contradiction would have been minimized if Prescott had availed himself of Freud's idea of sublimation, but the word does not appear in any of his books. Through this concept the "higher" purposes of poetry, of which Prescott was firmly convinced, could in some sense be reconciled with the "lower" source of their origin. As it stands, however, Prescott's theory lacks complete coherence. With this qualification, *Poetry and Dreams* is on the whole a stimulating work, particularly the discussion of poetic "dream-work."

The Poetic Mind appeared in 1922. Prescott's reaction against the scientific view of poetry can be seen in his Preface, where he stated that to him "the rigorously scientific method . . . seems inapplicable, and it may be the enemy as well as the friend of progress."[81] His own approach would avail itself of "older and freer methods," mainly citations from the poets themselves. "It is a great gain," he argued, "to be able to form or even state conclusions without proof. If the proofs, which are of only mediate importance, can be dispensed with there is a tremendous saving."[82] Science, for example, might see in the Greek poet's belief in his inspiration as "divine" only a metaphor; but to the non-scientist, it could be taken to embody a truth about man's nature, and might conceal a deeper truth about the mind itself. With this brief justification for his admittedly "unscientific" procedure, Prescott announced his purpose, which was "to attempt some further explanation of poetic vision, of the poetic imagination and poetic

---

80. *Ibid.*, p. 72.

81. Frederick Clarke Prescott, *The Poetic Mind* (New York: The Macmillan Company, 1922), p. x.

82. *Ibid.*, p. xi.

creation, of the poetic madness, and of the prophetic nature and function of poetry."[83]

He began by distinguishing between the poetic inspiration and the poetic product or the expressed poem. It was the former, he argued, which presented difficulties; if the process of inspiration could be understood, we should be able to undertsand the poem.[84] He repeated the distinction made in *Poetry and Dreams* between "primary" and "secondary" poems, adding, however, that the distinction was "not final as to the permanent value of the product," for a good "secondary" poem would be better than a poor "primary" one.[85] The test of "inspiration" in poetry was "the presence of imagination in the substance and of rhythm in the form . . . ."[86]

Discussing the nature of imaginative, as contrasted with ordinary, thought, Prescott again put forward the "striking analogy" between the poetic vision and the vision of dreams. His view here, however, represented a distinct departure from his earlier Freudian position: "From the earliest times men have believed that dreams . . . draw from the deeper portions of the mind which are the sources of wisdom . . . . If we take this older view, we may believe that dreams not only reveal to us our own deeper character, but draw from these deeper sources moral wisdom, truth not ascertainable by our conscious waking minds, even truths touching the life of the spirit and immortality."[87] Imaginative thought drew on the unconscious as a source and was therefore

83. *Ibid.*, p. 5.

84. This assumption is an arbitrary one, and leaves out the actual process of poetic composition. This position led Prescott eventually to consider the "real poem" as existing in the mind of the poet before it was written. It can be argued that if this were true, literary criticism would be more or less pointless, since the "real" poem could never be subject to examination. Prescott's concern with the poetic *process* rather than the poetic *work* places him clearly in the main line of nineteenth century Romantic criticism; this approach to poetry M. H. Abrams has called "the expressive theory of art." See Abrams, *The Mirror and the Lamp*, pp. 21-26.

85. *The Poetic Mind*, p. 7.

86. It can be objected here that this definition must result in arbitrary and subjective value-judgments of literature. What constitutes "imagination" to one may be banality to another. Beyond these few remarks, Prescott did not pursue the problem further.

87. *The Poetic Mind*, pp. 26-27.

similar to the thought processes of primitive man and of the mystics. The similarity between the dream and myth prompted Prescott to quote Karl Abraham's dictum in *Dreams and Myths* that myth was the dream of a people, and the dream the myth of the individual. Prescott commented, "This is essentially true; the parallel is perfect,"[88] adding, "the myths are dreams and they are poetry: all three come to the same thing."[89] The primitive mode of thinking had been under-valued by modern science, according to Prescott, since it viewed "associative" thought as having been superceded by rationality. This was to Prescott a fallacy, and he criticized William James and, oddly enough, Jung,[90] for taking this position: "the heart still sees further than the head; the poet still sees more deeply and more quickly than the reasoner; poetry still shows the way in which science must follow."[91] If primitive thought was older, he argued, it might also be deeper.[92]

Poetry was capable of discovering truth, but the resulting insight would be "poetic truth" rather than the truth of the reason. "There is a disposition in this age of science to doubt the mystic's vision," he wrote, "as a source of truth, as there is to doubt the dream as such a source, which the ancients believed in . . . . Truth in the sphere of reason becomes in the sphere of imagination beauty: the two are analagous."[93] The truths of vision, however, were not separable from the vision itself.[94] It was true that "for purposes of instruction," the poet's vision could be interpreted and

88. *Ibid.*, p. 66.   89. *Ibid.*, p. 67.
90. *Ibid.*, p. 68, n. 2. The reference here was to Jung's *Psychology of the Unconscious*, which Prescott felt "depreciates the phantasy and its products" (*ibid.*, p. 68, n. 2).
91. *Ibid.*, p. 69.
92. *Ibid.* This belief led Prescott to conjecture that all great poetry had been written early in the history of the race; it followed from this also that the best poetry had already been written.
93. *Ibid.*, p. 83.
94. The idea here is similar to what Cleanth Brooks called "the heresy of paraphrase." Prescott criticized Freud for extracting from the dream the abstract latent content and translating it into concrete terms: "This is surely the error of those who suppose that the Greek contrived his moral and then invented a myth to embody it. The dream content is the actuality; the dream thought is the fiction of the psychologist . . . ." (*ibid.*, p. 71). This concept is also similar to Jung's definition, in "On the Relation of Analytical Psychology to Poetic Art," of the symbol as "the expression of an intuitive perception which can . . . neither be apprehended better, nor expressed differently."

the meaning abstracted from the concrete images, but we must beware, he argued, of supposing "that the poet's intuitive thought can always be rationalized. Some deeper portions of poetic truth, particularly those arising from the unconscious mind . . . may be entirely incapable of such rationalization . . . ."⁹⁵

To say that any poem deriving from unconscious sources was a good poem would be an error, according to Prescott, for unconscious thought might result in weak thinking as well as conscious thought. The quality of the unconscious varied with the individual, and depended upon the stored experiences of the individual.⁹⁶ However, "on the whole, the unconscious mind is superior in insight and wisdom, to the conscious one; and this must be insisted upon because it will demonstrate the superiority of poetry drawing upon this source to any merely intellectual product."⁹⁷ All products of the unconscious, by definition, were original. Prescott's high valuation of the unconscious led him to object specifically to the Freudian conception that in dreams we "lead to the full the individual life" and "give our animal impulses unbridled license."⁹⁸ Since this view would argue the moral inferiority of the unconscious in comparison to the conscious, Prescott felt it must be false, for the unconscious mind, in general, represented a "deeper wisdom and morality."⁹⁹ The unconscious must be in some sense racial rather than individual; and it was in this racial unconscious that poetry had its source.¹⁰⁰ The mind could be compared to an island; if the waters were removed we would see that the foundations of the individual merged with other land bodies. "The visible mind is individual, even its submerged base is partly so, but the deeper foundations—the unconscious part of the mind—may not be so isolated as they first appear."¹⁰¹

95. *Ibid.*, p. 85.
96. Since the unconscious is a permanent and stable part of the mind, it could not be increased by volition. Therefore, "the greatest poet must be one who has had a full and fortunate life—and particularly a rich and favorable emotional development in childhood and youth" (*ibid.*, p. 100). Prescott's confusion on the nature of the unconscious—whether it contained the experiences of childhood or the "deeper truths of the race," or, if both, the nature of the relationship between these two—can be seen here and elsewhere.
97. *Ibid.*, p. 94.   98. *Ibid.*, p. 116.   99. *Ibid.*, p. 117.   100. *Ibid.*
101. *Ibid.* This explanation would seem to derive from Jung; actually the image is Emerson's. Aside from the reference to Jung's *Psychology*

The individual mind might share not only the mind of contemporaries but also that of its ancestors: "Man must have 'innate ideas' (in some sense) and sentiments which cannot be explained as arising from his individual experience."[102] The unconscious mind might also contain some premonition of future events; it could be considered prophetic in that it was capable of giving expression to wishes latent in the mind of the race which might then be fulfilled in actuality.[103] The unconscious mind basically, however, was the storehouse of the aspirations of the individual. Prescott admitted that these desires might also be the source of poetry: "A shallow or selfish desire may produce poetry—even an insane one may produce something analogous to it . . . . But to be valuable . . . poetry must be the product of high desire; to be communicable it must be the product, not of merely selfish but of shared desire. The greatest poetry is inspired by our highest and most nearly universal desires."[104]

The part played by the unconscious in the production of poems was much larger than was generally supposed. Although both "sudden inspiration" and "laborious composition" were necessary to produce a poem, not merely the content but in some cases also the form was presented to consciousness by the unconscious.[105] Prescott's statement on this matter is reminiscent of Coleridge's concept of organic unity: "If the feeling is right, if it is vivid and sincere, and especially if it is a deeper and more unconscious one . . . then the whole product will be right, will grow and organize itself, taking what is its own by true affinity . . . . It will have unity, as a tree or flower will have, because it is alive."[106]

That Prescott derived other elements of his critical theory from the critics of the nineteenth century is clear from his discussion of the imagination. Despite the fact that he explicitly rejected the Wordsworth-Coleridge distinction between Fancy and Imagination on the ground that it was "not really definite or intelligible,"[107] Prescott's own definition of the poetic imagination as that part of the mind which "accomplishes a fusion of images from without,

---

of the Unconscious, mentioned earlier, Prescott does not refer to Jung. It is difficult to believe, however, that the similarity between these two conceptions is mere coincidence.

102. *Ibid.,* p. 118.
104. *Ibid.,* p. 130.
106. *Ibid.,* p. 138.
103. *Ibid.,* pp. 120, 293.
105. *Ibid.,* p. 41.
107. *Ibid.,* p. 143.

and images and feelings, or images colored by feelings, already stored in the mind, from within"[108] is in accord with the definition of imagination given by major Romantic critics, at least insofar as it emphasized the *fusing* power of the imagination and the element played by *feeling* in retaining mental images. Furthermore, despite his disavowal of Coleridge's distinction between a mechanical Fancy and an organic Imagination, Prescott himself divided the imagination into two kinds: "the reproductive, which merely presents to the mind actual images, as they are remembered; and the productive, which makes over actual images, combining them with earlier experiences, to form new ones, ideal in nature."[109] It is the latter type of imagination which is at work in the production of dreams and poetry, wherein external sensory data are modified under the pressure of desire.[110]

But why are some sense data chosen to "become phantasmogenetic" and others rejected? Prescott answered that images utilized by the imagination in poetry may come either from recent or from older events, but that "there is no question of the paramount importance in poetry of impressions . . . [that] have been stored in the mind over a long period extending even as far back as childhood."[111] Although dreams seemed frequently to originate in trivial or indifferent material, it had been shown by Freud and others that this material was only seemingly indifferent—that actually it was a substitute or screen for an earlier experience which was highly charged emotionally. Such, Prescott argued, was also the situation in poetry. Furthermore, just as dreams rarely utilized profound emotional experiences of the present or recent past, so too "as a rule the imagination does not at once poetize important matters with which the emotions are deeply engaged."[112] In this sense, "Wordsworth was doubtless right in thinking that poetry 'takes its origin from emotion recollected in tranquillity.' "[113]

The accumulated images stored in the mind were retained largely because of their emotional significance. The imagination used these images, which were linked to each other by "associations, slight or strong, of contiguity or resemblance."[114] Many of the links, however, were unconscious. When a scene appeared

108. *Ibid.*, p. 154.   109. *Ibid.*, p. 145.   110. *Ibid.*, p. 146.
111. *Ibid.*, p. 155.   112. *Ibid.*, p. 156.   113. *Ibid.*, p. 157.
114. *Ibid.*, p. 162.

"poetical" to a poet, it was because something in the present situation had set up a train of unconscious associations with an experience of the past, whose emotional tone now colored the present experience. The utilization of this network of images in the imaginative production of a poem, Prescott concluded, was "a matter so complex and intricate that it is beyond the reach of critical analysis."[115] Some insight into the process, however, could be gained by examining the analogous process in dreams of fusing images from the past and images from immediate experience.

In discussing the similarities between these two processes, Prescott returned to the analogy he had used earlier in *Poetry and Dreams* between the "dream work" and the "poetic work." Essentially the same points were brought out, elaborated at greater length, and supported by numerous examples from literature. He discussed the concept of condensation in relation to punning and word play, and restated his earlier position that great works of the creative imagination were "over-determined," that is, had multiple meanings: "Some meanings are superficial, some are latent; the latter are most significant. Some can be comprehended, some can be felt only; the latter are most poetical. Some are conscious, others unconsciously produced; the latter are the richest products of the imagination. Some are readily expressible, others are under repression and must be veiled and hidden; the latter . . . are the truest subjects of poetry."[116]

The creation of literary characters and the creation of people in dreams had many parallels. The mechanism of displacement could be seen operating in fiction, where there was an autobiographical narrator who was essentially neutral, and a second character who was the vehicle of the artist's own emotions. As in the dream, fictional characters might be either an "identification" or a "composition." One of Freud's tenets was that in the dream the dreamer himself always appeared somewhere, if not in person then in disguised form as one of the dream characters. Prescott saw in this an analogy to fiction: "This suggests the possibility that every literary fiction will contain besides characters drawn from other persons, one character at least which bears the writer's ego—in the composition of which the person of the writer himself enters, perhaps in spite of appearances, as the largest ingredient."[117]

115. *Ibid.*, p. 166.   116. *Ibid.*, p. 183.   117. *Ibid.*, p. 192.

Autobiographical characters, however, were also partly idealized and modified in accordance with the author's desires.[118] Although "composite characters" could be formed by selecting and combining traits from several individuals, this was not done by a conscious process; they were rather fused into organized wholes in the unconscious. As in other forms of creativity, the intellectually constructed character would be inferior to the one created by the imagination, "first in naturalness and truth to life, and secondly in originality and depth of significance."[119]

Prescott next examined the nature of symbols and tropes in poetry. One of the characteristics of the imagination he found significant was its ability to perceive analogies. Although he objected to a hard and fast distinction between metaphor and simile, Prescott concluded that since in general the metaphor was the product of the "visionary imagination," it was superior to the more consciously contrived simile.[120] A complete "interpretation" of any poem, in the sense that one could make conscious all its intended meanings, was impossible, partly because there were many meanings of which the poet himself might be unconscious, and partly because the reader might legitimately have associations of his own to any particular image.[121] "Meaning" in poetry, then, was to a considerable extent subjective, both in reader and writer.

Prescott's earlier idea of poetry as the result of both "impulse" and "control" reappeared in *The Poetic Mind* in slightly changed form: the poetic impulse was here considered the inventive factor, furnishing the raw material; the control was the shaping force which gave form to this material, "not merely (1) to the structure, language, and verse of the finished poem, but even (2) . . . to the antecedent poetic vision itself."[122] Quoting Carlyle's statement that "in a symbol there is concealment and yet revelation," Prescott added that the concealment was a product of the control, the revelation a product of the impulse.[123] Poetry arose from the conflict between impulse and authority: ". . . when . . . the primary desire is met by the secondary one [the desire to conform to the social demand], when the impulse is controlled, the imagination affords not a direct image, but an equivalent associated one, which, however, is accompanied by the same feelings and supplies

118. *Ibid.*, p. 193.   119. *Ibid.*, p. 187.   120. *Ibid.*, p. 229.
121. *Ibid.*, p. 231.   122. *Ibid.*, p. 240.   123. *Ibid.*, p. 245.

a similar gratification."[124] In other words, an unconscious wish, perhaps representing some buried "complex" or desire from childhood, was forbidden to enter consciousness by the censor; there were then produced substitute images, more acceptable to consciousness. These "substitutes" appeared into consciousness without any apparent motivation, and brought with them feelings seemingly unrelated to the images themselves.[125] "The direct representation might seem more satisfying than the indirect, veiled, or symbolical one. It is not so; the veiled representation both liberates the individual and 'squares' him with society, and is thus doubly grateful."[126]

Turning to the question of the "poetic madness," Prescott reiterated that the question of the poet's sanity was not a profitable one, since the distinction between sanity and insanity was so blurred as to make it practically useless. Furthermore, there was the view that individual suffering might result in racial profit.[127] Prescott therefore tried to use the word "madness" in a neutral sense, defining it to mean little more than that the poet had access to more intense feelings than most and that there was less censorship on his part of feeling and image.[128]

Agreeing with Keble, Prescott saw the function of poetry as a "safety-valve," preserving the health of both reader and writer by allowing them to express desires through a fictional representation. Because they were controlled, the desires were given a "safe, regulated expression."[129] This concept had been expressed before in *Poetry and Dreams*; Prescott now added that frequently accompanying this catharsis of expression was a psychological "analysis" through which the poet came to an understanding of his conflict.[130] In *The Poetic Mind*, furthermore, the prevention of madness was considered merely the negative use of poetry; there was a more positive function which transcended its individual "use." Dreams

124. *Ibid.*, p. 247.   125. *Ibid.*, p. 249.
126. *Ibid.*, p. 250.   127. *Ibid.*, p. 261.
128. Even if he were to grant that the poet was more insane than sane, Prescott would still place a positive value on insanity. Irrationality, he argued, was "in large part a natural and healthful condition of the human mind" (*ibid.*, p. 268).
129. *Ibid.*, p. 274.
130. *Ibid.*, p. 276. This idea was derived, according to Prescott, from Stekel's "Poetry and Neurosis."

were in some sense prophetic, in that the wishes they embodied, when brought to consciousness (even in disguised form), enabled the individual to realize his desires and thus act upon them. In Prescott's view, poetry had a similar prophetic function. "The poet, through his high desire and vision, sees the future in the present."[131] He also "secures our spiritual inheritance," by putting us in contact with the racial aspirations of our progenitors.[132]

In the last chapter of *The Poetic Mind*, Prescott made it clear that he was essentially writing a defense of poetry: "I must insist more strongly than on anything else in this book," he wrote, "that poetry is not an activity 'useless as regards the preservation of the individual' or the race."[133] And further: "We must rise above an individual to a generalized conception of the poetic process—to the conception of man universal as poet and creator. Science, which generalizes tardily, must still look upon such a conception as speculative and transcendental; poetry, always first in the unifying and constructive work which constitutes human progress, not only suggests but enforces such a conception . . . . The poetic dream and creation are our nearest approach to 'the vision and faculty divine.' "[134]

From *Poetry and Dreams* to *The Poetic Mind* there was a progressive turning away from a "scientific" (or Freudian) view of the poet to one conceiving the poet as fulfilling a moral or "divine" function. It is odd that Prescott made no direct reference to the works of Carl Jung, whose conception of the mind as consisting of the conscious, the personal unconscious, and the racial or collective unconscious would have been a useful frame of reference for Prescott's own discussion and might have prevented a good deal of the confusion in his conception of the unconscious. It might also have mitigated somewhat his reaction to "science's" view of man; like Jung, Prescott apparently could not accept the Freudian view of the unconscious as being a repository solely for individual desires. His reasoning was somewhat as follows: poetry transcends the individual ego; its source is the unconscious; therefore, the unconscious must contain emotions and impulses which are supra-personal. His strong feeling that poetry possessed a value far greater than merely serving as a protection against mental im-

---

131. *The Poetic Mind*, p. 286.   132. *Ibid.*, p. 291.
133. *Ibid.*, p. 292.   134. *Ibid.*, p. 296.

balance in both creator and audience necessitated a postulate that the unconscious was the source of superior insights into the nature of reality. Like Jung, Prescott is open to the charge of "romanticism," or a tendency toward "mysticism"—the attitude which seeks to preserve mystery rather than to dispel it. Of the two books, *The Poetic Mind* was much more "guilty" of this, although at the same time it offered a more complete view of the process of poetic creation than did its predecessor.

The tendency to move from a "scientific" to a more romantic view of poetry was even more pronounced in Prescott's third book, *Poetry and Myth*, published in 1927, where the Freudian view of the poet was totally discarded. In the intervening five years between the publication of *The Poetic Mind* and *Poetry and Myth*, Prescott apparently either changed his mind about the truth of Freud's theories, or had come to feel that they were irrelevant to the question of the nature of poetry. *Poetry and Myth* was concerned with tracing the "mythopoeic" element in all "really great" poetry (a category which had been narrowed to include the works of relatively few poets other than Wordsworth and Shelley) with an end to demonstrating that poetry and religion were essentially the same, both embodying "divine truths" which were outside the scope of a materialistic-rationalistic approach to reality. If *The Poetic Mind* was in large part a defense of poetry, the later book was basically a defense of Christianity, which Prescott considered the greatest of all myth-poems. *Poetry and Myth* is an extremely disappointing and shallow study, and is of interest only insofar as it clarifies the general direction in which Prescott can be seen to have moved—from an eager acceptance of whatever contributions science or psychology might make toward an understanding of poetry in *Poetry and Dreams* to a more qualified acceptance of it in *The Poetic Mind* to a full-scale rejection of science in *Poetry and Myth*. Freud's tenets were not specifically rejected in *Poetry and Myth*, they were merely ignored; Freud's name does not appear in the index. By 1927, therefore, Prescott had ceased to be a critic using the concepts of depth psychology as a promising approach to literature.

The significance of Prescott's first two books as documents of the Freudian approach lies partly in the fact that in them one is able to see clearly that the use of depth psychology in criticism was an outgrowth of the romantic theories of the nineteenth century. Basically, what Prescott did was to graft the idea of the Freudian unconscious onto Wordsworth's and Coleridge's conceptions of the imagination. (In *The Poetic Mind*, particularly, the terms "unconscious" and "imagination" are almost interchangeable.) Coleridge's emphasis on the poetic process rather than on the finished poem, his use of the metaphors of the seed and the plant as analogies to poetic creation, his distinction between a mechanical Fancy and a spontaneous Imagination—all these paved the way for a consideration of the poetic process as largely an involuntary, unconscious activity.[135] Prescott defined the imagination as that part of the mind which fused "images from without, and images and feelings . . . from within," a definition similar to many given by the Romantics; what he added to this was the concept that the feelings occasioned by "images from without" were usually *repressed* feelings, emotions which could not enter consciousness either because they were too powerful or because they were of such a nature that, if admitted into the conscious mind, they would cause feelings of guilt or shame.

Prescott's view of the function of poetry as a "safety-valve" against madness also had its roots in romantic poetic theory, exemplified by Byron's well-known statement that poetry was "the lava of the imagination, whose eruption prevents an earthquake"; to this older view Prescott and other Freudians added the idea that poetry served as a catharsis for the audience as well as for the poet, and clarified the cathartic process itself with reference to the specifically Freudian tenets of repression and displacement. Prescott's denigration of the part played by the conscious will in the poetic process, and his insistence that "true" poetry only originated in unconscious sources—elements in the critical theory of most Freudians—was in large part an outgrowth of the nineteenth century preference for works of the "imagination" rather than the "fancy." Much of the twentieth-century opposition to

135. M. H. Abrams, in *The Mirror and the Lamp*, says, ". . . in some German critics, recourse to vegetable life as a model for the coming-into-being of a work of art had, in fact, engendered the fateful concept that artistic creation is primarily an unwilled and unconscious process of mind" (p. 173).

these tenets, therefore, was colored by a reaction against the romantic view of poetry as well as a reaction against the Freudian view of the mind.

The many reviews which *The Poetic Mind* occasioned were almost uniformly unfavorable, the main point of attack, oddly enough, being Prescott's "unscientific" approach. The *Times Literary Supplement* approved of some sections of the book, but concluded with the harsh statement that it "does little more than to put into diffuse academic language a theory which gives little that is new to any thinking student of poetry."[136] In an article in *The Journal of Abnormal Psychology*, Cary F. Jacob, a thorough-going rationalist, criticized it vigorously. Jacob primarily objected to Prescott's implication that the poetic mind was "divine" or that the visions of prophets and poets had more "truth" than the rational mind could apprehend: "To say that the minds of prophet and of poet function similarly and that, therefore, the product of the poetic mind is divine and above comprehension is only to avoid the issue and leave the entire subject unexplained . . . ."[137] *The Poetic Mind* was unsatisfactory in that it left unexplained also the question of how the poetic mind differed either from the creative mind or from the unconscious mind. In short, it had neglected to discuss the actual process of poetic composition.

Thomas Jewell Craven, reviewing the book in *The Dial*, accused Prescott of "loose thinking," which was a result of his "departure from the solid ground of perceptual experience."[138] Prescott's procedure was false from the start, since poets were "notoriously unreliable" as scientific witnesses. Like Jacob, Craven argued that Prescott had discussed the process of inspiration to the neglect of composition, with the result that his picture of the poetic

136. *Times Literary Supplement*, June 15, 1922, p. 398.
137. Cary F. Jacob, "The Psychology of Poetic Talent," *The Journal of Abnormal Psychology*, XVII (October-December, 1922), 237. Jacob's strong "scientific" orientation made him suspect any experience not directly connected with the senses or any conclusion not arrived at by reason: "Seriously, if one accepts visions at all, how is one to distinguish truth from error, revelation from sheer fraud? Why should what a man sees when his faculties are overpowered or benumbed be of greater value than what that same man sees when he is in full possession of them all!" (*ibid.*, p. 238).
138. Thomas Jewell Craven, "The Freudian Incubus," *The Dial*, LXXIII (July, 1922), 104.

process was almost wholly worthless: "The psychology of art has to do with form and composition . . . . The evolution of a work of art—the slow, constructive growth from the diversified materials of experience to the unity of the finished poem—escapes [Prescott] completely."[139]

Mark Van Doren's review of *The Poetic Mind* was less negative than this, on the whole, but ultimately he too was dissatisfied with it: "Mr. Prescott does not explain it [poetry] to me. With all the will in the world, I cannot find that he has made an intelligible connection between the poetic mind on one side of the field and the poetic product on the other . . . . I cannot admit that his elaborate Freudian structure stretched across empty space is better than a cobweb. I still do not know where poetry comes from."[140] Van Doren's position was that psychology would never be able to explain poetry until it granted that poetry was the product of the whole mind, both conscious and unconscious. As might be expected, he objected to Prescott's division of poetry into two kinds, a division which left out such poets as Pope; the only meaningful division of poetry to Van Doren was into good poetry and bad. The trouble with Prescott, he argued, was that "he must spell his poetry with a capital 'P.' He must search for a source instead of accepting an instinct. The source for a superstitious Greek was heaven . . . . The source for a superstitious psychologist is the hypostatized Unconscious Mind."[141]

What most annoyed Conrad Aiken, reviewing the book for *The New Republic*, was Prescott's attempt to hide his "mysticism" behind the pretense of being scientific. "If we can pardon him . . . for his religious attitude toward poetry, we cannot at all pardon him for conducting his investigation so persistently and prayerfully in a dim religious light. What we want is the dry light of science."[142] Aiken found the book "extraordinarily confused," and

139. *Ibid.*, p. 106. Craven further objected to Prescott's inexact psychology, his confusion of "images with stimuli and processes with meanings," and his subscribing to the "fetish of primitivism."

140. Mark Van Doren, "The Poetic Mind," *The Literary Review* (June 3, 1922), p. 700.

141. *Ibid.*

142. Conrad Aiken, "The Analysis of Poetry," *The New Republic*, XXXI (June 19, 1922), 222. Aiken's own approach to the use of psychology in literary criticism is discussed in Chapter 4.

eclectic in its use of psychology. When Prescott accepted the "Freudian lead," as in his discussion of symbolism, he was on solid ground, but when he departed from this to the point of equating the unconscious with the "soul," the book became absurd. Furthermore, Prescott's position that poetry which proceeds from the unconscious must be good was an error. "A poem is good," Aiken commented, "if the poet's sensibility is good; a bad poem is the result of a 'deficiency of sensibility.' " Not all products of the unconscious mind were "original," as Prescott had believed. They might be, and even were, as "dull as ditchwater."

The consistently negative reviews of *The Poetic Mind* are somewhat surprising, for in retrospect the book appears to have a good deal of intrinsic value. Curiously, the primary objection was not that Prescott used Freudian psychology as an approach to literature, but that he did not make *enough* use of it, that in a sense he had turned against the premises of the new science. Prescott's relatively cautious use of Freudian theory in his explanation of poetry compares very favorably, to say the least, with several extreme, dogmatic books of "literary criticism" then current, written by men who used psychoanalysis not to shed light on but to explain away the process of creativity.

Probably the worst offender among this group was Albert Mordell, whose book *The Erotic Motive in Literature* had appeared three years before *The Poetic Mind*, in 1919. The epitome of all that is bad in psychoanalytic criticism, the book was dogmatic, misinformed, badly written, and remarkably insensitive to any qualities of form and style in literature. Mordell believed explicitly in the infallibility of Freudian doctrine. "In every book," he wrote, "there is much of the author's unconscious which can be discovered by the critic and psychologist who applies a few and well tested and infallible principles."[143] His acceptance of a rigid psychological determinism led Mordell into absurdities like the following: "Thus with a man's literary work before us and with a few clues, we are able to reconstruct his emotional and intellectual life, and guess with reasonable certainty at many of the events in his career . . . . I do not think it would be difficult for us to deduce from the facts we have of Dante's life that he

143. Albert Mordell, *The Erotic Motive in Literature* (London: Kegan Paul, Trench, Trubner and Company, 1919), p. 1.

naturally would have given us a work of the nature of the Divine Comedy."[144]

Like most Freudian critics, Mordell's central tenet was that there existed a close analogy between the dream and the work of art. He also took the Freudian position that the writer had cured himself of his anxiety by giving vent to his feelings in his writing. One function of the critic was to observe how this had been accomplished and to point out the unconscious elements that the writer had brought forth. Despite the baldness of Mordell's manner of expressing it, this would have been fairly acceptable to most Freudians. For the most part, however, Mordell's application of Freudian principles (to ignore for the moment the manner of this application) was frequently wrong. Beginning with the erroneous premise that the "unconscious is largely identical with the mental love phantasies in their present and past life," he proceeded to explain Keats by means of Fanny Brawne, Shelley by Harriet Grove, and Poe by Mary Devereux.[145] Writers from Vergil to Swinburne were examined in order to demonstrate the presence of an erotic subcontent in all their works, with the implication that this was their "meaning." Flying, for example, was considered in Freudian dream theory a common symbol for the sexual experience. "To a Skylark," therefore, was nothing more than an expression of Shelley's unconscious sexual urge.[146]

It is difficult to believe that *The Erotic Motive in Literature* was accepted seriously at the time, but apparently it was.[147] One reviewer felt that the book was "not a little like peeking through

144. *Ibid.*, pp. 2-3.
145. *Ibid.*, pp. 6-7. Mordell's misconception of the unconscious can be further seen in his statement that "conscience, self-sacrifice, moral sense, love are unconscious sentiments" (p. 12). His misuse of psychology was severely criticized by Hanns Sachs, who reviewed the book in *The International Journal of Psychoanalysis*, I (1920), 477-78.
146. This approach to literature—the reduction of meaning to latent sexual desires—was also used by Frederick J. Farnell in an absurd article, "Erotism as Portrayed in Literature," *The International Journal of Psychoanalysis*, I (1920), 396-413. Here Shelley's "Ode to the West Wind" (the wind "in phallic worship is a fructifier and a creator") was boiled down to the same "meaning" as Mordell found in "To A Skylark." One wonders why these critics bothered to read such monotonous poems.
147. Freud himself actually approved of the book. See his letter to Mordell, May 21, 1920, reprinted in Ernest Jones, *The Life and Work of Sigmund Freud* (New York: Basic Books, 1955), II, 442.

the keyhole of a lady's bedroom," but added that "all agree that [Mordell] opens up wide avenues of suggestion."[148] The reviewer admitted that Mordell had gone a bit too far in his approach—particularly when he found such innocents as Renan, Wordsworth, and Longfellow "reeking in sexual symbolism," but concluded that on the whole the book "sheds some light on the nature of genius, and especially literary genius."[149]

The Erotic Motive in Literature was sufficiently well received to be chosen as the "book of the month" by *The North American Review*. Its review in April, 1919, was ironic in tone: "Mr. Mordell's book provides rare sport . . . . Emitting the glad cry of the pursuing Freudian following a scent, he sets forth hot-foot after such unsuspecting victims as Dickens and Wordsworth, Cowper and Keats, Tennyson, Longfellow, and Charles Lamb. The chase is delectable indeed."[150] The reviewer, Laurence Gilman, objected to the study as being "unduly naïve," and felt that in some respects it was detrimental to the more sophisticated attempts to investigate the problem of the relation of the unconscious to literature. His conclusion, however, praised Mordell for his "honesty, his inexhaustible curiosity, his gusto, his complete conviction," and judged the book to be "challenging and provocative."[151]

Mordell and Prescott were linked together as typical psychoanalytic critics in a lecture on "Psychoanalysis and Literary Criticism" delivered at Rice University in 1924 by Louis Cazamian, then professor of English literature at the University of Paris. Although agreeing that literary criticism could derive much of benefit from psychoanalysis, Cazamian felt that most of the attempts made up to that time to solve individual riddles of literature were unsatisfying. He accepted *The Poetic Mind* in general, particularly Prescott's use of the concepts of condensation and displacement, but rejected his attempt to "give diagrams of the subconscious activity of the poetic mind," since this reduced poetry

148. "Psychoanalyzing Great Poets and Novelists," *Current Opinion*, LXVII (July, 1919), 51.
149. *Ibid.*, p. 52.
150. Laurence Gilman, "Literature Unveiled," *The North American Review*, CCIX (April, 1919), 557.
151. *Ibid.*, p. 561. One wonders if the reviewer did not have his tongue in his cheek here and elsewhere.

to a false "mechanical precision."[152] For neither Mordell nor Ernest Jones, Cazamian's other representative of psychoanalytic criticism, did he have a kind word. He concluded that so far, psychoanalytic critics had been in error, and that the error was one of exclusion and emphasis: "Their fault is not that they introduce an awkward complexity into our notion of the mind, but that they narrow and simplify it overmuch. What is one element among many, most often of negligible value, hardly ever predominant, is thus magnified into the all-in-all of motive, theme, and expression."[153]

The influence of psychology on literary criticism was felt in England as well as in America. The British poet, Robert Graves, produced two strange books in 1922 and 1925 which described a theory of poetry obviously influenced by current psychoanalytic theories. Graves's psychology, however, was peculiarly individual, apparently deriving more from the British psychologist and anthropologist, W. H. R. Rivers, than from Freud.[154] To Graves, poetry was the result of an interior mental conflict between the poet's two selves or his "sub-personalities." The process of composition was therefore partly a "self-protective device" that "lets the pen solve the hitherto insoluble problem which has caused the disturbance."[155] Because of Graves's fanciful style,[156] it is difficult to comprehend the exact nature of these "sub-personalities." At one point he described them as follows: "The mind of the poet is like an international conference composed of delegates of both sexes and every shade of political thought, which is trying to decide on a series of problems of which the chairman has himself

152. Louis Cazamian, "Psychoanalysis and Literary Criticism," *The Rice Institute Pamphlet*, XI (April, 1924), 146.

153. *Ibid.*, p. 152.

154. Graves stated that he became interested in Freud in 1918 "as a possible corrective for my shell-shock," and that he wrote several poems at this time which consciously made use of Freudian material. Further on he added, "I would like to make it quite clear that I am no longer in sympathy with the sentiments or the psychological tenets embodied in this poem." See *Poetic Unreason and Other Studies* (London: Cecil Palmer, 1925), p. 108; see also pp. 126-32, 141.

155. Robert Graves, *On English Poetry* (New York: Alfred A. Knopf, 1922), p. 26.

156. As he himself said, "I am afraid that extravagance has broken down my determination to write soberly, on almost every page" (*ibid.*, p. 39).

little previous knowledge—yet this chairman, this central authority, will somehow contrive to sign a report embodying the specialized knowledge and reconciling the apparently hopeless disagreements of all factions concerned. These factions can be called, for convenience, the poet's sub-personalities."[157] In any event, the "subpersonalities" of the poet were conceived to be denizens of the conscious rather than the unconscious mind.[158] Aside from viewing poetry as a result of a mental conflict, Graves made use of the analogy between poetry and the dream and of the idea that poetry was a form of psycho-therapy: "Being the transformation into dream symbolism of some disturbing crisis in the poet's mind . . . poetry has the power of homeopathically healing other men's minds similarly troubled, by presenting them under the spell of hypnosis with an allegorical solution of the trouble. Once the allegory is recognized by the reader's unconscious mind as applicable the affective power of his own emotional crisis is diminished."[159]

Graves's application of his theory of poetry to specific literary works resulted in some highly ridiculous interpretations. His method was to take the poem and from it "reconstruct" a hypothetical situation in which the poet found himself; he would then examine the hypothetical mental conflict which presumably took place in the poet's mind.[160] On the whole, Graves's two books were not coherent pieces of criticism. They were written in a light, journalistic style which relied heavily on improbable metaphors to carry the burden of thought, and such psychology as was used was highly questionable. The books were sharply criticized by both F. L. Lucas and by Conrad Aiken. Lucas disagreed with every one of Graves's tenets: that poetry was "automatic writing";

157. *Ibid.*, p. 34.
158. Graves himself saw no need to explain his concept by any system of psychology: "It is hardly necessary to quote extreme cases of morbid psychology . . . to explain the subpersonalities of the poet's mind," since any observation of children's fantasies and play demonstrated that this was a perfectly natural phenomenon (ibid., p. 117). In *Poetic Unreason* the sub-personalities were spoken of in terms of "Jekyll and Hyde," terms which corresponded loosely to the intellectual and emotional sides of the poet.
159. Graves, *On English Poetry*, pp. 84-85.
160. See, for example, the analyses of *The Tempest* and of George Herbert's "The Bag," in *Poetic Unreason*.

that bad poetry was poetry which did not have reference to the reader's own complexes or conflicts. He particularly objected to the whole romantic tendency to see "associative thinking" as a process as "grown up and respectable" as logical thought.[161] Aiken's criticism was even more damning. "The plain facts are," he wrote, "that the book [*On English Poetry*] is thoroughly bad, and not merely bad in the sense of being mediocre, but offensively bad."[162] To Aiken, with his strong scientific orientation and his intense desire to give criticism a scientific basis, Graves's false psychology and careless method of approach were intolerable: "Mr. Graves has taken a few vague, psychoanalytic notions out of the air, added a few half-comprehended observations of his own behavior before, during and after poetic composition, and written a pompous, fatuous and gloriously inaccurate book. It has not the slightest scientific value."[163] In retrospect, Aiken's judgment seems perfectly sound.

The increasingly frequent appearance of psychoanalytic criticism, both theoretical and applied, was bound to arouse protest. One main line of attack came from critics of the "formalist" school, that is, from aestheticians who defined art as "expressive form." A representative article of this type was Leone Vivante's "The Misleading Comparison Between Art and Dreams," in *The Criterion* in 1926, the central thesis of which was that dreams were inferior to art, and that in the analogy between art and dreams there was "more error than truth."[164] The dream resembled art in being an indirect or symbolic expression; unlike art,

161. F. L. Lucas, "Critical Unreason," in *Authors Dead and Living* (New York: The Macmillan Company, 1935), p. 260. "It is rather fashionable at the moment," Lucas wrote, "to be tired of logical thought." He was also annoyed by Graves's fanciful discussion of *The Tempest*, and asked a question that must have echoed in the minds of many of those opposed to psychological criticism: "Who cares if Caliban represents the Man in the Moon or the Binomial Theorem?" (*ibid.*, p. 262).

162. Conrad Aiken, "Sludgery," *The New Republic*, XXXII (November 22, 1922), 340.

163. *Ibid.*, p. 341.

164. Leone Vivante, "The Misleading Comparison Between Art and Dreams," *The Criterion*, IV (1926), 436. It is not surprising that several critical articles antagonistic to the Freudian approach to literature should have appeared in this journal, whose editorial policy during this time reflected the strong influence of T. S. Eliot's "impersonal" theories of art.

however, the dream was not intimately modelled by an idea but was only an approximation of an idea. Dreams lacked "the unity of concept and expression" which was the hallmark of art[165]—in other words, they lacked the "controlling intelligence" of the artist. The concept that art expressed ideas not palatable to the consciousness of civilization, and that therefore these ideas were presented in disguised form, Vivante dismissed as absurd. Any subject matter was acceptable in art, provided only that it was well treated. "To read what Freud writes on the Oedipus Tyrannus, it would seem that the subject there unfolded ought to move an audience and have artistic value by whomsoever chosen and developed! The value of art is *in rendering the material intelligible* . . . ."[166] Vivante spoke favorably of the "moderate conception" of Prescott's *The Poetic Mind*, but still argued that the similarity between dream and art had been largely misused, that "the connection between the two must either be wholly avoided or considered as secondary and, relatively, irrelevant."[167] Dreams, in short, were inferior to art, a point which Vivante would consider hardly worth making were it not for the current tendency to pay homage to the "divinity of the unconscious."[168]

The most articulate spokesmen of the "formalist" school were the British aestheticians, Clive Bell and Roger Fry. The major criticism of both men was in the field of the visual arts, but the attacks they made on psychoanalysis were directed specifically against its encroachment on the field of literature. Bell attacked Freud in an irate article in *The Nation and the Athenaeum* for his presumption in speaking on matters on which he was not qualified. Quoting Freud's position in *The Introductory Lectures on Psychoanalysis* that the artist longed to attain "honor, power, riches, fame, and the love of women" but that, unable to attain this in the real world, he secured gratification for his desires in the life of fantasy,[169] Bell commented: "This is . . . a pretty good account

165. *Ibid.*, p. 439.
166. *Ibid.*, p. 440. Vivante further added, "Whatever is most obscure does not constitute poetry: the essence of poetry is intelligibility" (p. 441), which is a rather extreme position.
167. *Ibid.*, p. 451.   168. *Ibid.*, p. 453.
169. See Sigmund Freud, *A General Introduction to Psychoanalysis* (New York: Boni and Liveright, 1920), pp. 326-27; the passage is the same in both works.

of what housemaids take for art," since housemaids' novels *were* "wish fulfillment in a world of phantasy."[170] This, however, was not art. "The artist is not concerned with . . . the 'sublimation' of his normal lusts, because he is concerned with a problem which is quite outside normal experience. His object is to create a form which will match an aesthetic conception . . . ."[171] The artist's problem was wholly an aesthetic one; Shakespeare was concerned with a proper form for *Lear*, not with satisfying the wishes of the young lady on the third row, and for this reason made Cordelia die. Furthermore, art had nothing to do with dreams: "The artist is not one who dreams more vividly, but who is a good deal wider awake, than most people . . . . His grand and absorbing problem is to create a form that shall match a conception . . . . He is a creator, not a dreamer."[172]

Freud's problem, according to Bell, was that he assumed that his own reactions to a work of art were the reactions of everyone. This was not true, for Freud obviously lacked the aesthetic sense: "Of [the problem of creating artistic form] Dr. Freud, unluckily, knows nothing. He knows nothing about art, or about the feelings of people who can appreciate art . . . . There is no reason why he should know anything about either only, being ignorant, he should have held his tongue."[173] The aesthetic response to art involved not the fulfillment of our dreams of the desirable life, but something which life could never give—"that peculiar and quite disinterested state of mind which philosophers call aesthetic ecstasy."[174]

Many of Bell's pronouncements were overly harsh, and his interpretation of Freud seems deliberately to misconstrue his meaning. In the passage from Freud quoted by Bell, Freud was not necessarily speaking of the artist's *conscious* desire for wealth, fame, and so forth, which is what Bell took him to mean. Freud would have granted the artist's conscious preoccupation with form, although perhaps interpreting this preoccupation as itself a ra-

170. Clive Bell, "Dr. Freud on Art," *The Nation and the Athenaeum*, XXXV (September 6, 1924), 690. This article was reprinted in *The Dial*, LXXVIII (April, 1925), 280-284, and reprinted in digest form under the title "Psychoanalysis Fails to Account for the Artist," in *The Literary Digest*, LXXXIII (October 4, 1924), 32.

171. Bell, "Dr. Freud on Art," *The Nation and the Athenaeum*, p. 690.

172. *Ibid.*   173. *Ibid.*   174. *Ibid.*

tionalization for deeper, less conscious motivations. To Bell, who apparently denied the concept of unconscious motivation altogether, Freud's whole theory was merely absurd. Few Freudians, moreover, would have taken the position that wish-fulfillment appeared in an unalloyed form in literary works. Just as in a dream there were frequently certain resistances which blocked a complete fulfillment of the dreamer's wish, so too unconscious resistances in the artist could decree that the hero be killed at the end of a novel or play. Dimitri Karamazov cannot be allowed to go unpunished for the murder of his father—for psychological reasons as well as for reasons of "form."

Bell's main arguments were presented in a calmer and more convincing fashion by Roger Fry in a small book entitled *The Artist and Psychoanalysis*, published in 1924. Originally delivered as a lecture to an audience of psychologists, the essay opened with the statement that the artist would welcome the psychologist if he could help to shed light on the problem of creativity, but only on the condition that before the psychoanalysts told the artist what he was doing and why, they should first take the trouble to understand what the artist *thought* he was doing and why he was doing it. To Fry, there were at least two types of artist: "One of these groups . . . is mainly preoccupied with creating a fantasy-world in which the fulfillment of wishes is realized. The other is concerned with the contemplation of formal relations. I believe this latter activity to be as much detached from the instinctive life as any human activity that we know . . . . I consider this latter the distinctive aesthetic activity."[175] Fry admitted that the two aims might both appear in any given work of art, but insisted that fundamentally they were different, at least in their functions if not in their origins. If it were to be proved that art originated in the sexual feelings, Fry argued, this would be an interesting and important discovery, but it would still not explain the significance of art for human life. Almost every human activity had its original roots in the physical; science, for example, could be seen as an outgrowth of the instinct for self-preservation. At the present time, however, science had passed beyond these origins and now devoted itself to the pursuit of truth, rather than mere sur-

175. Roger Fry, *The Artist and Psychoanalysis* (London: Hogarth Press, 1924), p. 4.

vival. By the same token, art should be studied at its present stage, where it had evolved considerably since its origin.

The art that psychologists studied, and from which they drew their conclusions, was impure art, that is, it appealed to emotions other than the aesthetic emotion, which Fry defined as "an emotion about form."[176] Mankind's responses to a work of art, he suggested, were of two kinds—aesthetic and "associated." The "associated" response involved the viewer's experience of emotions which were stimulated by the resemblance of the particular art work to situations or objects which had in the past evoked the emotion. A landscape painting, for example, might remind the viewer of an actual scene (or even another landscape painting) viewed previously in his past which was associated with pleasant feelings; if so, he would judge the painting to be a "pleasant" one. Essentially this type of viewer was not reacting to the art work *qua* art work at all. The majority of people, according to Fry, lacked the aesthetic emotion; their reactions were largely of this "associated" kind. Popular art was art which had deliberately subordinated formal design to the excitation of emotions associated with objects.[177] Genuine works of art, in contrast, those which had outlived their immediate time period, satisfied the formal sense.

Like Bell, Fry quoted Freud's passage in the *General Introduction to Psychoanalysis* which treated the artist as a creator of fantasy. "The portrait of the artist here given," Fry argued, "is drawn on the lines of a widespread popular fallacy about the 'artistic temperament.' "[178] According to Fry, Freud had seen the artist as the stereotyped Bohemian, an image that was, in fact, an image of the impure artist. The pure or formal artist was in reality a "thoroughly bourgeoise person" who was "far too much interested in [his] job to spend [his] time kicking over the traces."[179] The wish-fulfillment of which Freud spoke applied to popular art, but not to, say, a great novel. The latter depended for its effect upon a *detachment* from the instinctive life: "Instead of manipulating reality so as to conform to the libido, [great artists] note the inexorable sequence in life of cause and effect, they mark the total indifference of fate to human desires, and they endeavor

176. *Ibid.*, p. 7.   177. *Ibid.*, p. 9.   178. *Ibid.*, p. 11.
179. *Ibid.*

to derive precisely from that inexorability of fate an altogether different kind of pleasure—the pleasure which consists in the recognition of *inevitable* sequences . . . a pleasure derived from the contemplation of the relations and correspondences of form."[180]

Certain psychologists, such as Oscar Pfister, had conducted experiments with neurotic patients in which they examined the latent contents of a patient's writings. "Art" of this kind, argued Fry, might be of value to the analyst, but it was worthless as an indication of the nature of genuine art. Nothing was more contrary to the essential aesthetic faculty than the dream; moreover, "in proportion as the artist was pure he was opposed to all symbolism."[181] The subject matter of a painting was nothing; it was the treatment of the subject that mattered.[182] If this were true, then great art must be considered as a product of the ego rather than the libido. It was concerned with reality; it was *"objective* and *dis-inter-ested."*[183]

Towards the end of his essay Fry partially qualified his extreme formalist position. It was true, he admitted, that the experience of beauty was not wholly formal; the experience was "suffused with an emotional tone" as if the work of art were "arousing some very deep, very vague, and immensely generalized reminiscences . . . as though art had got access to the substratum of all the emotional colours of life, to something that underlies all the particular and specialized emotions of actual life."[184] He concluded, apparently as a gracious gesture to his audience, that it was in this area that the artist would appreciate the psychologist's explanation.

Despite its brevity, *The Artist and Psychoanalysis* includes several good points of criticism of the Freudian theory of literature.[185] As the most succinct statement of the "formalist" school, it is a useful corrective, in some ways, to the position taken by F. C. Prescott and others who concentrated on the unconscious element

180. *Ibid.,* p. 12.   181. *Ibid.,* p. 16.
182. "Rembrandt expressed his profoundest feelings just as well when he painted a carcass hanging in a butcher's shop as when he painted the Crucifixion . . ." *(ibid.)*
183. *Ibid.,* p. 18.   184. *Ibid.,* p. 19.
185. For Ernest Jones's attempt to answer Fry's arguments, see his chapter on Freud's conception of the artist in Jones, *Life and Work,* III, 408-13.

in literature to the exclusion of the part played by the conscious mind of both the artist and his public. The quarrel between the "formalists" and the Freudians, however, did not constitute a genuine dialogue. The Freudians, by and large, viewed the appeal of art almost wholly in terms of its unconscious elements, while the "formalists" maintained that the artistic process was a completely conscious activity. Each side merely denied the basic premise of the other, with the result that no genuine argument, or even communication, was possible.

One reviewer of Fry's *The Artist and Psychoanalysis* was the British critic, Herbert Read, whose reaction was largely negative. Fry, he stated, "believes in the existence of a specific aesthetic emotion; he believes that this emotion is an emotion about form; and that it is this formal element which alone gives vitality to art."[186] To Read, this was the "obverse of sentimentality," since the criteria for judging art were reduced to instinctive physical reactions. Because Fry refused to distinguish between contents, his aesthetics lacked a scale of values. The psychoanalysts also suffered from this absence of any criteria for evaluating works of art: "To anyone who sees the immense importance and utility of Freud's general theory, nothing is so dismaying as the utter futility of *all* the psychoanalysts in the presence of art. They cannot understand that art is a triumph over neurosis, and that the symbolistic and mystical imaginings which they ask us to consider as art are the very denial of art, lacking order, form, and discipline."[187]

Read's own view of the uses of psychoanalysis in criticism was set forth in an excellent article he wrote for *The Criterion* in 1925.[188] Defining literary criticism as a science and as "the val-

186. Herbert Read, Review of *The Artist and Psychoanalysis, The Criterion,* III (April, 1925), 471. For a favorable review of the book, see W. C. Blum, "Improbable Purity," *The Dial,* LXXVIII (April, 1925), 318-23. The only objection Blum made was that Fry was inconsistent in admitting that unconscious urges might have something to do with pure art. If this were true, Blum argued, then "it does not appear improbable that the dream process is the prototype of the unconscious process not only of bad art, but of pure art too" (p. 322).

187. Read, Review of *Artist and Psychoanalysis,* p. 472.

188. Herbert Read, "Psychoanalysis and the Critic," in *The Criterion,* III (January, 1925), 214-30. The essay is reprinted in Herbert Read, *Reason and Romanticism* (London: Faber and Gwyer, 1926), pp. 83-106.

uation, by some standard, of the worth of literature,"[189] Read attempted to explore what light the science of psychoanalysis could shed on the problem of literary value. One fundamental distinction between the two "sciences" was that psychoanalysis was concerned with the processes of mental activity, whereas literary criticism was concerned with the product; to the analyst, art was no more significant than any other expression of mentality. Because of this, it was doubtful if the analytic approach of psychology could help much in the problem of literary valuation: "Analysis involves the reduction of the symbol to its origins, and once the symbol is in this way dissolved, it is of no aesthetic significance: art is art as symbol, not as sign."[190] The attempt to translate works of art in terms of personal, individual fantasy—the approach to art then commonly made by psychologists—was therefore unprofitable.

But psychology could possibly be useful to the literary critic in other ways. Read posed three questions which the critic might profitably explore: (1) What general function did psychoanalysis assign to literature? (2) How did psychoanalysis explain the process of inspiration in poetic creation? (3) Did psychoanalysis cause us to extend in any way the functions of criticism? Familiar with the theories of Freud, Jung, and Adler, Read drew more heavily on those of the latter two, contending that only Jung had gone beyond the individual aspect of art and had worked out a theory of the function of literature in any detail.[191] One conclusion he found latent in Jung's theory of fantasy was that "the poetic function is nothing else but this active phantasy [of the normal man] in its more-than-individual aspect. The poet, in fact, is one who is capable of creating phantasies . . . of universal appeal."[192] Read here stated in a slightly different form the theory of art as therapy for both the artist and his audience: "Thus art has for psychoanalysis the general function of resolving into one

189. Read, *Reason and Romanticism*, p. 84.
190. *Ibid.*, p. 86.
191. Read's source here was Jung's remarks in *Psychological Types* where romantic and classic art were considered in terms of introversion and extroversion. Although he does not mention it, Read may also have been familiar with Jung's "On the Relation of Analytical Psychology to Poetic Art," published in 1923.
192. *Reason and Romanticism*, p. 91.

uniform flow of life all that springs from the inner well of primordial images and instinctive feelings, and all that springs from the outer mechanism of actuality—doing this, not only for the artist himself, from whose own need the phantasy is born, but also, by suggestion and by symbol, for all who come to participate in his
imaginative work."[193] Jung, discussing the difference between abnormal and artistic fantasies, had concluded that the difference
lay in the "social validity of the symbol," in the degree to which
the artistic symbol possessed a common social value or whether
its value was restricted to the individual creator. Read found this
idea striking, and suggested that if psychoanalysis could aid the
critic in testing the "social validity of the symbol," it could make
a significant contribution to literary criticism.

Read further relied on Jung in describing the process of inspiration. In the artist's mind (as in the minds of all men), there were
two general tendencies—one which directed the attention outward
to the world of forms, and one which directed the attention inward
to the world of subjective images, the "fresh elemental imagery"
of the unconscious. Perfect art was achieved when both tendencies
or forces were present in equilibrium, when there was a harmony
between the "romantic" and the "classic" impulses. In the process
of inspiration, an unconscious image or memory was fortuitously
brought into active consciousness, where it was scrutinized and
either selected or rejected, developed or transformed, in order
to serve the artist's prevailing affectivity at the moment. This
process of inspiration was common to both the artist and the
average man; the difference between the two, according to Read,
was the difference in "the nature of the ideal or affective tendency
to which [the artist's] whole creative life is subservient."[194]

The psychoanalysts' attempts to define the nature of this abnormal mentality of the artist had not been too successful. Rejecting Ernest Jones's theory that the aesthetic sense arose out of
the child's rebellion against his "original excremental interests,"
Read preferred instead Adler's explanation of the artist's unique
interest in beauty and ideal forms in terms of the "goal of godlikeness" which arose as a compensation for the child's feeling of inferiority because of his position in the family circle. The artist

193. *Ibid.*   194. *Ibid.*, p. 96.

"takes this goal of godlikeness seriously, and is compelled to flee from real life and compromise to seek a life within life; and he is an artist in virtue of the form and ideal perfections which he can give to this inner life."[195] Unlike the neurotic, whose fantasy world remained unstructured and unformed, the artist was able to give his fantasies concrete expression, and thus eventually achieved the "honor, riches, fame, and the love of woman" that Freud saw as being ultimately the artist's conscious or unconscious goal. If the artist succeeded in making his fantasies communicable and socially valuable, he was able to escape his neurosis and find his way back to reality. Psychoanalysis could thus be of aid to the critic in being able to discriminate between the "real" and the "neurotic" in any given artistic expression: "Psychoanalysis finds in art a system of symbols, representing a hidden reality, and by analysis it can testify to the purposive genuineness of the symbols; it can also testify to the faithfulness, the richness, and the range of the mind behind the symbol."[196]

On the third question, whether or not psychoanalysis caused the critic to extend the functions of criticism, Read was less specific. After analyzing briefly Jones's study of Hamlet, he concluded that "whether Dr. Jones' explanation is tenable or not, it does provide what is at present the only way out of a critical impasse, and for that reason alone it merits consideration."[197] The new approach used by Jones and other psychoanalytic critics might supply a "corrective to the narrowness of criticism."[198] Further, psychoanalysis might possibly be of aid in solving the age-old conflict between romanticism and classicism, for in the light of Jung's classification of introversion and extroversion the two could be seen as the "natural expression of a biological opposition in human nature";[199] neither standpoint should be considered as an intellectual fallacy, but a matter of natural neces-

195. *Ibid.*, p. 97.
196. *Ibid.*, p. 99. Exactly how psychoanalysis could do this, and what its criterion of value would be in making this judgment, Read did not say. He admitted that the critic himself could determine the borderline between the real and the neurotic "by general critical principles," but suggested that psychoanalysis might offer a shorter path to the goal. This claim that psychoanalysis could help explain the universal significance of artistic symbols was also made by Alfred Booth Kuttner. See above, p. 47.
197. *Ibid.*, p. 102.   198. *Ibid.*, p. 103.   199. *Ibid.*, p. 104.

sity for the individual, depending upon his psychological type. The critic, therefore, "must resort to some criterion above the individual," and "take up a position above the conflict."

In conclusion Read suggested yet another possible way for psychology to aid criticism. Relying again on Jung, he discussed the hypothesis that myth and religion originated in the unconscious, and suggested that the psychologist could help us learn the nature of the "vague desires that exist in the collective mind" which occasioned the primordial images that appeared recurrently in literature. Read's point here—and this is in general true of the whole essay—was suggestive rather than definitive. The article was a tentative exploration of how criticism might avail itself of the concepts of the new psychology in order to achieve its central function, the evaluation of the work of art. Read's suggestions were general rather than specific. Despite its lack of precision, his essay was one of the more sophisticated attempts to derive something of benefit from psychoanalysis over and above the usual approach as an aid to biographical understanding, and was one of the rare attempts to relate it to criticism as evaluation rather than comprehension.[200]

It was primarily the theories of Jung rather than Freud that Herbert Read found most useful for the literary critic. Other aspects of Jung's psychology were applied to the problem of creativity by John M. Thorburn and by Maud Bodkin. Thorburn's views of the artist were set forth in 1921 in an article entitled "Art and the Unconscious" and in a book of the same name published four years later. Like Bell and Fry, Thorburn was primarily an aesthetician concerned with the visual arts rather than a literary critic, but his theories embraced literature as well as painting, sculpture, and music. He tried to resolve in his article the problem of why religious art still maintained its meaning and beauty to those who no longer shared a belief in the intellectual content

200. In his critical practice, Read made relatively little use of psychology. The exception to this is his essay on the Brontes, discussed in Chapter 3. For Read's later views on psychoanalysis and the critic, see his excellent article, "Psychoanalysis and the Problem of Aesthetic Value," *The International Journal of Psychoanalysis*, XXXII, Part 2 (1951), 73-82. In this much more sophisticated essay, Read discarded his earlier reliance on Adler, and attempted a synthesis of the troublesome form-content problem by way of Jung, Susanne Langer, and the Gestalt theorists.

of its symbols, or in other words, how art was able to communicate with peoples possessing different cultural values. To solve this problem Thorburn used the dream-art analogy: I "believe," he wrote, "that this analogy is very far-reaching, and that its elaboration and application with all due criticism and care will be one of the most powerful methods of aesthetic in the near future."[201] When awakening from a dream, our emotions are intensified in the instant of revelation when the meaning of the dream symbol becomes conscious. By analogy, the religious artist worked with symbols whose meaning was to him unconscious;[202] in contrast, succeeding generations possessed a conscious awareness of the symbol's significance. Later ages were thus able to interpret the "dreams" of the past, and had an added dimension of response. The greatest artists used symbols originating in the unconscious while at the same time possessing a conscious awareness of their meaning: "One of the great contributions that art makes to human life is in its interpretation of the marvelous symbols our unconsciousness whether individual or social is continually bringing up to us."[203]

In *Art and the Unconscious*, Thorburn made a more extensive attempt to apply depth psychology, especially the theories of Carl Jung, to aesthetics. He began by stating that through the discoveries of the new psychology, science for the first time possessed a meaningful approach to art:

We need the new psychological method in its application to an artists's work, not primarily to explain the aberrations of his temperament; but because it is worthwhile more deeply to understand the nature of art itself, and to see its value in true perspective with the other values of life. If our reading of art in terms of "the unconscious" is to have

201. John M. Thorburn, "Art and the Unconscious," *The Monist*, XXXI (October, 1921), 589.
202. Thorburn's use of the word "unconscious" is somewhat ambiguous. He apparently meant here that the religious artist was not aware of his symbol *as symbol*; the intercession of the Virgin, for example, he took as literal truth. Thorburn's conception of the unconscious was derived from Jung, who maintained that primordial images were of their very nature untranslatable.
203. Thorburn, "Art and the Unconscious," p. 594. At the other extreme from the great artist was one who attempted consciously to manipulate unconscious symbols. Thorburn found several twentieth century artists, Picasso among them, to be guilty of this.

significance, it cannot be by regarding art only as a phenomenon that a new psychological method can analyse and explain—perhaps explain away—as a mere by-product. The application to art of a psychology of the unconscious can have significance only in relation to a problem of value . . . .[204]

The central idea contributed by modern psychology to aesthetics was the parallel between art and the dream. If some art conveyed an irresistible impression of being like a dream, Thorburn argued, all art might in the last analysis demand interpretation through the same analogy.[205] The parallel between art and the dream, however, was not to be regarded as final, for the dream experience was one that more or less ruled out conscious direction and control. "Dreams come unwilled and are natural phenomena rather than products of individuality. The analogy, therefore, however significant we may find it, is bound to leave us with some of the essentials of art unaccounted for, in the last resort."[206]

Thorburn defined the dream as a "counterpart of an attitude,"[207] by which he meant that the dream was an unresolved or unexpressed idea which found expression in sleep. This definition is unusual primarily because the dream is conceived of in terms of repressed *ideas* rather than repressed emotions or *desires*. The two characteristics of the dream which Thorburn stressed were also rather unusual: the "reality" of the people appearing in one's dreams,[208] and the fact that the dream possessed a "unity— a dramatic unity—a real unity of action."[209] Dreaming differed

204. John M. Thorburn, *Art and the Unconscious* (London: Kegan Paul, Trench, Trubner and Company, 1925), p. 5. My discussion of this book is confined to Part I; in Part II, Thorburn applied his theories to art of different eras (i.e., the architecture of the Byzantine and Gothic periods), and deals with non-literary material.

205. *Ibid.*, p. 7.   206. *Ibid.*, p. 8.   207. *Ibid.*, p. 9.

208. "The denizens of the dream are 'real' people . . . . By real, I mean that they are not inventions, or in any sense artificial . . . . They are centers of vitality whose self-motion is not to be controlled by the dreamer . . . . That is to say, the denizens of the dream are at the extreme opposite of anything like a logical fabrication. The best of novelists or playwrights occasionally lapses into a logical fabrication, or is guilty of a logically consistent heroine. The dream, never. All in that realm are themselves, exactly as the Almighty created them, and they show no trace of the artificially devising touch of man" (*ibid.*, pp. 12-13).

209. *Ibid.*, p. 13. Thorburn granted that this unity was sometimes apparent only through close scrutiny, but insisted that no dream was ultimately chaotic.

from daytime thought in that it could not be translated into action: "The advent of sleep deprives the idea conceived in conscious life of all possibility of carrying itself into effect in practice. But instead of being applied to practical life, it seems somehow to give unity to the activity of the people of the dream. It is in the dying of the idea as a practical possibility that these little people live their lives and experience their individualities."[210] This "dying of the idea into a dream" is a concept central to Thorburn's theory of the creative process in art.

In his brief examination of the nature of poetry, Thorburn postulated that in great poems there was a balance between "spontaneity" and "control." Shaw exemplified the artist who suffered from too much control, with too little spontaneity, and *Prometheus Unbound* the imbalance of the opposite type, where the idea (the conscious meaning of the poet) was too completely absorbed by the "denizens of the dream" (i.e., the unconscious flow of images).

Returning to the differences between the dream and art, Thorburn made one of his most important points. The main distinction between the dream and art was that art was a symbolic expression in a particular medium:

Dreaming is that kind of art which has no medium; or, if it be preferred . . . art is that kind of dream which expresses itself in some material medium. For how is it that the artist can go about literally awake . . . and yet dream the dreams of art? My answer must be that it is because of his medium—for the poet, sonorous words; for the sculptor, marble; or for the builder, stone. It is the artist's medium that keeps him unconscious. The sculptor, if it were not because he is continually mesmerized by clay . . . would wake up and become the mere vulgar deviser of commonplace shapes. The presence of marble and a chisel keeps him asleep.[211]

Medium functioned to keep the artist unconscious, to induce in him a sort of hypnotic trance which enabled him to make contact with his unconscious creative powers; at the same time, because of its inherent interest, it kept him from descending into actual sleep, where the creative fantasy was dissipated and not given permanent form. The artist was thus one who "dreamed awake."

Another significant distinction between art and the dream was that the dream had meaning only for the individual dreamer,

210. *Ibid.*, p. 16.   211. *Ibid.*, p. 37.

whereas art had a "higher value," communicating a wider social meaning. The problem of articulating this "higher value" prompted Thorburn to a discussion of the various theories of Freud and Jung. Though he appreciated the "tremendous" contribution of Freud, he criticized his school strongly. According to Thorburn, the Freudians refused to regard religion or art as a thing of value, treating them as merely pathological phenomena.[212] They considered art to be a symptom of a failure in adaptation: "The dream, if it be a veiled wish, is also an ungratified wish—a wish that never can be gratified. It is thus essentially a symptom of failure."[213] Viewed in this light, art not only had no biological value, it was actually a product or result of biological failure. This concept Thorburn could not accept, since the "negative attitude towards the imagination" inherent in the theories of Freud and his school was contrary to human experience, which rightly valued it highly. He further objected to Freud's tendency, in explaining the art work in terms of the fundamental psychological relation of the child to the mother, to explain away the work itself.[214]

It was Jung's *Psychology of the Unconscious* that to Thorburn satisfactorily explained the social value of art. According to the Freudians, the inevitable transformation of the original infantile libidinal desires was necessary in order for primitive races to progress toward a more complex culture. But Jung had discovered in religious symbolism other possible functions, less negative than the mere absorption or transformation of a dangerous energy: "The embodiment of individual phantasy and racial myth in works of art and in ceremonies and monuments of religion has given us things of 'imperishable beauty.' Now that is a value, a positive value, and not a mere safeguard, not just a sublimation of destructive force."[215] Jung's view suggested that religious fantasies marked the transition from a lower to a higher stage of culture and that it was through these fantasies, and by their aid, that the higher stage was reached.[216] Thus, Jung had restored the

212. *Ibid.*, p. 54. Thorburn cited in this connection Freud's study of Leonardo in which, he stated, "the reader would have no inkling that the art of Leonardo might be a thing of beauty," since Freud showed only its pathology.
213. *Ibid.*   214. *Ibid.*, p. 57.   215. *Ibid.*, p. 59.   216. *Ibid.*, p. 60.

"higher value" of art. The unconscious was not merely the repository of repressed infantile desires, but the storehouse of racial memory and a source of unconscious knowledge, a sort of "intuitive wisdom" which could teach the conscious mind. The deeper the artist delved into this unconscious, the greater would be his art. The artist's problem, as Thorburn saw it, was to reconcile this archaic past with his own individual history. "So far as the archaic can be recognized and made integral with individual and social experience it necessarily gives an enlargement and enrichment of these experiences."[217]

Thorburn accepted Jung's definition of the archetypal image as "an expression for that of which no rational account can be given at the time when the symbol possesses its highest value,"[218] adding: "The symbol is regarded as something placed over against the conscious standpoint. Or rather, the image or the phantasy, in all the fullness of its emotional resonance and with all the apparent thought-content through which it may have been elaborated, becomes a symbol through the adoption by consciousness of a definite attitude towards it."[219] What Thorburn borrowed from Jung was essentially the idea that Freudian symbols were themselves symbols of something else—i.e., what Freud interpreted as a wish to return to the womb represented for Jung and his followers a symbol for the desire to be reborn, or more expansively, for the desire for a new life. That is, the Jungians tended to see in Freud's interpretation of individual experience in terms of the child a symbol of the universal desires of man's psyche. Archetypal or mythical images involving the primal Oedipal situation were thus interpreted in terms of man's longing to unite with the sources of his being, and images involving the conflict with the father viewed in terms of man's universal need to escape from tyranny and to free himself from repression. (Freud, of course, would see this very longing to escape from tyranny as merely a sublimated form of the original, primal desire to escape from the restrictions imposed on the child by the father.) Jung's system was much easier than Freud's to reconcile with the premise of a "higher value" of art, a premise which was for Thorburn, as for Prescott, necessary to any coherent aesthetic.

217. *Ibid.*, p. 72.   218. *Ibid.*, p. 74.   219. *Ibid.*, p. 75.

Returning to the concept of the dream, Thorburn discussed the tendency of the dream to "dream through objects,"[220] that is, to dramatize emotions and ideas by projecting them upon a concrete object. When the artist handled his medium, he also "dreamed through an object." The artistic "dream," however, was a slower and more complex process than ordinary dreaming, since the artist projected his emotion onto his creation and at the same time distanced himself from it, making it more regular, more "formal." In romantic art, the first process—the projection of the emotion— was more prominent; in classic art, the "distancing" played the larger role.

Thorburn's use of the dream-art analogy while maintaining at the same time that the difference between the two lay in the artist's conscious manipulation of a medium in order to achieve a specific form was an interesting attempt to mediate between the psychological view that the fundamental characteristic of art was its appeal to the unconscious and the insistence of formalists like Clive Bell and Roger Fry that art was primarily form. *Art and the Unconscious* is a provocative but not wholly successful work; the vagueness of much of Thorburn's writing unfortunately leaves unexplained many questions concerning the specific relation between the conscious and the unconscious elements in the creative process.

Some of this vagueness was clarified by Maud Bodkin in an article discussing both Prescott and Thorburn entitled "Literary Criticism and the Study of the Unconscious," an article which is a helpful addendum to Thorburn's book. Like Thorburn and Read, Miss Bodkin was concerned with the problem of how and to what extent psychoanalysis could aid the literary critic.[221] Like Thorburn also, she found the works of Carl Jung much more suggestive than those of Freud.[222] Agreeing with Thorburn that the

220. *Ibid.*, p. 104.

221. In an earlier article, "The Relevance of Psychoanalysis to Art Criticism," *The British Journal of Psychology*, XV (October, 1924), Part II, Miss Bodkin had discussed the relevance of psychoanalysis to criticism of the pictorial arts in connection with Roger Fry's lecture. Her conclusion here was that "the bearing of psychoanalytic investigations upon art criticism must be mainly indirect, operating by way of suggestion upon the mind of the critic pursuing his own problems in his own way" (p. 182).

222. In "Literary Criticism and the Study of the Unconscious," *The Monist*, XXXVII (July, 1927), she says, "Dr. Jung has urged that wherever creative phantasy is freely manifested, we find the primoridial image or

attitude toward archaic psychic material marked the differences between the various schools of psychology, she added:

If, with Jung, we believe that the archaic images appear in dream and phantasy with a prospective significance, undergoing transformation in accordance with the urgencies of the inner life of the moment, then there is opportunity for conscious purpose to ally itself with all there may be of promise in these unconscious productions. Whether they be used for the ends of art or of practical life, they are means of access to a reservoir of power. To those holding this view, the interaction of conscious and unconscious throughout the sphere of art becomes a problem of great significance and gives a clue with which to approach it.[223]

The unconscious, according to Miss Bodkin, played a larger part in human activity than was generally recognized. Not only creative thought, but much reflective thought as well had its roots in the unconscious mind. Her criticism of Prescott rested on this premise. By making a strict dichotomy between the type of undirected associative thinking akin to dreams and "ordinary thought," Prescott had presented a misleading picture of the mind. He had contrasted associative thought only to "the mechanical kind of thinking with familiar verbal counters,"[224] and had thus left unexplained the part consciousness played in the creative process. To Miss Bodkin, Thorburn was closer to the truth in distinguishing the poet from other dreamers and thinkers who were not artists because of the poet's command of a particular medium in which his thoughts and dreams could find expression. She also found Thorburn's application of the analogy between art and the dream more useful to criticism than Prescott's. Thorburn had seen in dreams a unity between the various scenes. "On the other side of the analogy," said Miss Bodkin, "he expresses the relation between the unity of the poem and the conscious idea with which the poet may begin his work, by saying that the idea must, as

---

archetype, a mythological figure or situation characterized by peculiar emotional intensity, corresponding to some inherited 'resultant of countless typical experiences of our ancestors,' " (p. 456). Her reference to Jung's concept of the archetypal image is from his important essay, "On the Relation of Analytical Psychology to Poetic Art," a brief discussion of which can be found in Appendix B.

223. Bodkin, *"Literary Criticism and the Study of the Unconscious,"* p. 457.

224. *Ibid.,* p. 462.

idea, perish, but its nature will remain recognizable 'even after its absorption into the action and by the characters which it brings to birth.' "[225] The poet's idea was absorbed into his characters or images in the same way that the dreamer's emotional life was unconsciously absorbed into the dream images. If these images could be interpreted, they would reveal something of the underground currents of the dreamer's (or artist's) being. To Miss Bodkin, this explanation helped clarify the part played by the conscious mind in the production of a poem. Conscious intelligence furnished an idea or theme, which could then be absorbed by the unconscious and rendered in terms of images. Consciousness played a further part in judging and selecting the images welling up from the unconscious: "The poet is in some measure necessarily the critic of his own work. The vital idea that passes, in almost dream-like fashion, into expression through the poet's rapport with his medium, must be at least partially discerned and understood by him, that he may perfect its expression."[226]

The great artist was one who was able to experience the primordial images of the unconscious and to shape these into a form fitted to the needs of his time, so that the images could stir man afresh. By means of psychoanalytic theory, the literary critic was better able to understand the nature and function of art:

Our initial question was as to whether the study of the unconscious with the help of the new methods could contribute anything of value to the literary critic. I have tried to show how, in the work of art, we find meanings lifted from the welter of unconscious experience, displayed in terms of a sensuous medium, as objects for social contemplation. The task of the philosophic critic involves a further detachment of meaning, from the particular medium, and from the conventions that govern at any particular period the expression in that medium. It is by the abstraction and consolidation of such meanings . . . [that] a higher degree of understanding can be established between one appreciative mind and another, and between art-consciousness of different ages.[227]

Through her frequent use of examples to explain her points—interpretations of her own dreams, a comparison of the Faust theme in Marlowe and Goethe, an analysis of Ibsen's *An Enemy of the People*—Miss Bodkin made concrete several of Thorburn's more

225. *Ibid.*, p. 450.   226. *Ibid.*, p. 466.   227. *Ibid.*, p. 468.

difficult points. "Literary Criticism and the Study of the Unconscious" is a valuable article for this reason, and because of the light it throws on Miss Bodkin's later important work on archetypal images in literature.

Herbert Read, John M. Thorburn, and Maud Bodkin all departed from a strict Freudian interpretation in their attempts to come to grips with the problem of creativity. The difficulty with the Freudian position, as Clive Bell and Roger Fry had argued, was that it left out of account the element of form, which was the primary difference between art and the dream. One other important critic to speculate on the use of the new psychology in the study of literature was Kenneth Burke in a now well-known article, "Psychology and Form," which first appeared in *The Dial* in 1925. Burke's use of the new psychology was highly individual in character and reflects a general absorption of ideas current at the time rather than the adoption of any particular psychological theory. On the whole, Burke felt that psychoanalysis had been detrimental to literature. The vigorous rise of science, he argued, had been such that men had not had time to make a "spiritual readjustment" to it, and the application of psychology to art had resulted in a "derangement of taste": "Psychology has become a body of information . . . . And similarly, in art, we tend to look for psychology as the purveying of information. Thus, a contemporary writer objected to Joyce's *Ulysses* on the ground that there are more psychoanalytic data available in Freud."[228] This approach to art was false, according to Burke, since the real value of a work of art lay in what he called the psychology of form. The new source of knowledge about human behavior had unfortunately also led the artist to place emphasis on the giving of information, with the result that art had substituted "the psychology of the hero" (the subject) for "the psychology of the audience" (form).[229]

Like almost all critics who attempted to apply psychology in an effort to understand the literary process, Burke made reference in this article to the dream-art analogy, but he used it with a striking difference: ". . . Folk tales are just such waking dreams. Thus

228. Kenneth Burke, "Psychology and Form," *The Dial*, LXXIX (July, 1925), 36.
229. *Ibid.*, p. 37.

it is right that art should be called a 'waking dream.' The only difficulty with this definition . . . is that today we understand it to mean art as a waking dream for the artist. Modern criticism, and psychoanalysis in particular, is too prone to define the essence of art in terms of the artist's weaknesses. It is, rather, the audience which dreams, while the artist oversees the conditions which determine this dream. He is the manipulator of blood, brains, heart, and bowels which, while we sleep, dictate the mould of our desires."[230] The artist's "manipulation of the audience's dream" is *form*, the "creation of an appetite in the mind of the auditor, and the adequate satisfying of the appetite."[231] The end of art was what Burke called "eloquence," defined as "the result of that desire in the artist to make a work perfect by adapting it in every minute detail to the racial appetites." In adopting this position, Burke stood somewhere in between critics like Prescott, who viewed art in terms of the dream, and the aestheticians, Bell and Fry, who saw it in terms of "significant form." Burke's position cannot be said to reconcile these two opposing views, but it does offer another approach to the problem by defining both art and form in terms of the audience rather than the artist.

The central issue of concern to literary critics interested in the potential use of psychoanalytic theory was the nature of the relationship between art and the dream, an issue which involved the question of the respective parts played in creativity by the "conscious" and the "unconscious" elements in the artist's personality, and whether the art work was to be viewed as the result of personal or supra-personal forces. The literary qualities of certain dreams, and the dream-like qualities of some works of art, had been noticed long before Freud and his followers provided a key to the mystery of dream symbolism. The dream-art analogy seemed a natural and logical one: if "science" could explain the dream, it might also help the critic understand the mysterious origin and function of art. Freud's dream theories, however, appeared to place only a negative value on the dream, which functioned as a "safety-valve" to preserve the psychic equilibrium of the dreamer by allowing him to give disguised expression to unacceptable wishes and impulses. An extension of this view to the work of art was

230. *Ibid.*, p. 40.   231 *Ibid.*, p. 35.

unpalatable to the majority of the early literary theorists—particularly those like Prescott, Thorburn, and Fry who were not psychologists. Great art had its roots in the unconscious—most critics agreed on this—but its value to mankind could not be merely to discharge unacceptable desires, a theory which would turn art lovers (and critics) into little more than sophisticated and self-deluding, albeit unconscious, erotomaniacs. The means of avoiding this implication was in one way or another to deny Freud's premise, either by maintaining that the significance of art lay in its form, or by modifying the concept of the unconscious along the lines of Jungian theory, which allowed greater scope for "meaning" in art than the repressed desires of artist and audience. Either alternative was preferable, and the literary theorists availed themselves of both.

The extensiveness of the debate over the applicability of the new science to literary theory indicates a widespread feeling on the part of critics that the new psychology did have an important bearing on problems of literary criticism, although there was considerable confusion as to the extent and the precise method in which the new knowledge of the mind could be used.

The problem of art and the dream seems to have usurped the secondary question of whether or not art was the product of neurosis. Unlike the practitioners of psychoanalytic criticism, the theorists for the most part seem to have agreed that although the artist himself might be neurotic, the impulse to create art was a healthy one. Few of these critics discussed the use of psychology as an aid to interpreting biography, as a tool which could be used to explain the relationship between the personal character of the poet and the art product he created, or as a system of thought which could aid the critic in his role as interpreter of individual works. The use of psychology in the critical process of making value judgments was in general limited to a common faith that products of the "unconscious" mind were somehow superior to those of the conscious, and to the expression of the hope that psychoanalysis would at some time in the future be able to discover some method for separating meaningful or "socially valid" unconscious expressions from morbid or unhealthy ones. The concern of the early theorists was primarily with the nature of art itself; practical problems of literary criticism were largely left to the many contributors to psychology journals who, accepting implicitly the premises of Freud, proceeded to trace with great earnestness the tell-tale signs of the Oedipus complex in English and American literature.

3. *Freudian Criticism: The Practitioners*

The majority of the literary theorists intrigued by the possibilities of a new scientific approach to creativity were fairly sophisticated and articulate men. With one or two exceptions, their discussions of the use of Freudian theory in literary criticism are still useful and stimulating. The same, unfortunately, cannot be said about the earliest writers who applied the theory to individual works of literature. The general run of such criticism is offensively dogmatic, over-simplified, and woefully lacking in appreciation of aesthetic expression. For the most part, the initial attempts at practical psychoanalytic criticism represent the worst kind of formula-writing. Proceeding from an *a priori* assumption about the "meaning" of literature, the literary psychologists persisted in translating symbols and themes in terms of unconscious erotic drives and "proving" the validity of their explications by referring to Freudian authority. This kind of circular argument, self-enclosed as it is, is difficult, if not impossible, to refute. As Mario Praz has recently pointed out, once its initial premise is accepted, psychoanalytic criticism can hardly fail to be "successful": "Symbolic figuration, condensation, scission, and in desperate cases, when an important link in a dream is missing (or in the waking dream: a work of art) then the intervention of a 'censor' put forward to account for the suppression of the link . . . . It must be plain to all that with these trumps in his hand the psychoanalyst is bound to win every game. He can turn the smallest card into a trump, or even, for lack of legitimate cards, produce surreptitious ones out of his sleeves, his pockets, or even his nose."[1]

The findings of the psychoanalytic literary analysts were singularly monotonous; to defend themselves against this charge, they would have no doubt replied that they were not responsible for the fact that unconscious material reduces itself to only a few simple "universal" themes. But whether the monotony resides in the unconscious itself or in the eye of the critic examining it, the major fault of most psychoanalytic criticism, particularly of this early period, is its dullness. Despite its frequent failure to provide convincing interpretations of literary works, however, this early criticism does provide insights into the manner and method of critics exploring a new technique for analyzing the life and works of the world's literary artists. An examination of such criticism can expose its limitations, evaluate the validity of its approach, and perhaps suggest the conditions under which a psychoanalytic investigation of literature can be profitably pursued.

The most frequent application of psychoanalytic theory in criticism was in the field of biography. This is in no way surprising, since the study of an author's life for the purpose of shedding light on his works and, conversely, a study of the works as an aid to an understanding of his character, was a common approach in literary criticism during the last part of the nineteenth century. Psychoanalysis was a tool that could extend one's knowledge of a writer's "inner life," an interest inherited from nineteenth century biographical studies. Pre-Freudian psychology had frequently been invoked to explain the temperament of various artists suffering from what are now called neurotic disturbances. Furthermore, there had been several studies of the nature of genius, such as those of Lombroso, in which attempts were made to relate it to degeneracy, insanity, or some other type of biological or psychological malfunction. All of these factors therefore prepared the way for the application of psychoanalytic concepts to literary biography.

Behind Freud's view that the writer's creation was in some sense a sublimated form of a neurosis lay the earlier idea that genius was a product of insanity. This idea was the subject of

1. Mario Praz, "Poe and Psychoanalysis," *Sewanee Review*, LXVIII (Summer, 1960), 385-86.

dispute in an essay in the *Scientific American Supplement* in 1913 which clarifies the background of the problem of the artist's relation to disease. Arthur Jacobsen's "Literary Genius and Manic-Depressive Insanity, with Special Reference to the Alleged Case of Dean Swift" was written in reply to an earlier article by Eva C. Reid, "Manifestations of Manic-Depressive Insanity in Literary Genius." Miss Reid had maintained that literary geniuses suffered from a manic-depressive type of insanity and that their literature was an outlet for their "abnormal feelings and passions." Jacobsen objected strongly to this implication that geniuses were geniuses *because* they were insane. The literary genius, he argued, was in the special position of having left a record of his emotions, but this did not mean that he was any more disturbed than any other type of genius, or indeed, than any non-genius. If insanity and genius were equated, it would follow that the productions of the schizophrenic and the artist were not different in kind: "It seems an odd thing to this writer that a great literature is not emanating from the asylums of the land, if it be true that the relation of genius and insanity is so close. The answer is that the great genius must be eminently sane. He must possess in the highest degree the critical faculty directed toward his own literary productions. No great literary work can possibly be produced if this endowment is lacking."[2]

Turning to the specific case of Swift, which Miss Reid had cited as evidence for her thesis, Jacobsen granted that in many respects Swift's character presented a clinical picture of neurasthenia, but he denied emphatically that the "neurasthenia" was the cause of his genius. Swift was not a lunatic of any kind or degree, said Jacobsen, but one of the greatest men of his time. And, he added, although genius might be conducive to insanity, in the sense that the two very frequently appeared together, the insane temperament was not conducive to genius. His conclusion, apparently reached without any knowledge of Freud, expressed succinctly the position taken later by many Freudian critics: "The genius is usually, if not always, of insane temperament, but his best creative work reflects the man at his best, that is to say, his sanest. To the de-

2. Arthur C. Jacobsen, "Literary Genius and Manic-Depressive Insanity: With Special Reference to the Alleged Case of Dean Swift," *Scientific American Supplement*, LXXV (January 4, 1913), 2.

gree that clinical insanity enters in, to that degree is his work vitiated. Insanity is the Nemesis of the delicately balanced genius, never his good angel . . . . Certain psychopathological states undoubtedly at times excite and color the creative labors of true geniuses, but they are not geniuses because of . . . psychopathology . . . . The thesis of Dr. Reid [is] utterly fallacious. Genius is not a disease."[3]

Few Freudians would have disagreed with Jacobsen's position on insanity and genius. The question of the extent to which art was a product of *neurosis*, however, or whether it was an achievement accomplished in spite of neurosis, was, of course, an open one. Many authors of biographical studies of literary artists ignored the theoretical problem altogether, and limited themselves to studying the artist's personality without attempting to relate his neurotic character traits causally to the works he produced.[4] John H. Cassity followed this procedure in his analysis of Lord Byron in *The Psychoanalytic Review* in 1925.[5] Superficial in treatment, the essay examined Byron's character with particular emphasis on his narcism, his sadism, and his "Don Juan" complex, all of which were traced back to his relationship with an over-protective mother. Byron's incestuous attachment to Augusta Leigh was analyzed in terms of the Freudian formula whereby the sister was a typical displacement for the mother in the Oedipal situation.

Writers of the Romantic era were generally the best targets for psychoanalytic analysis. The more neurotic the writer, the more plausible was the use of the psychoanalytic formula to explain his eccentricities. For this reason, Edgar Allan Poe was an excellent subject.[6] Poe's turbulent life and diseased fantasies were a

3. *Ibid.*

4. There was an implicit assumption in these studies, however, that the neurosis and the art work were related causally in some way, else there would be little justification for demonstrating at length that Byron and Shelley were any more neurotic than their anonymous contemporaries.

5. John H. Cassity, "Psychopathological Glimpses of Lord Byron," *The Psychoanalytic Review*, XII (October, 1925), 397-413. More psychoanalytic criticism appeared in this journal than in any other; on the whole, the essays printed here were guilty of the worst sins of the psychoanalytic critic—dogmatism, superficiality, and an insensitivity to literary values.

6. Poe had been a favorite subject for psychological analysis long before Freud. Several phrenological discussions of his character suggested that

gold mine for would-be psychoanalysts. He could be (and was) approached from the standpoint of his alcoholism, his drug addiction, his status as an orphan, poor heredity, and, of course, the Oedipus complex.[7] In an article in *The American Journal of Psychology* in 1920, studies by not only Freud, Jung, and Adler, but Lombroso, studies of the behavior of the only child, and physiological psychology were used to explain his disturbances. The conclusion reached by way of all this was that Poe in his later life suffered from the effects of congenital syphilis and that the majority of his neurotic character traits could be explained on the basis of Adler's concept of the Will Power.

The author of the article, Lorine Pruette, found in Poe's family a "decided organic inferiority." This inferiority, which Poe inherited, demanded compensation, a compensation the young Poe found in drawing and in writing stories and poems. This alone was not a satisfactory outlet in Poe's case, however: "His 'will to power' . . . would brook no superior, nor even equal, in either physical or mental pursuits, and it was this intolerance . . . which brought upon him in later life the enmity of much of the literary world."[8] Despite his literary successes, Poe's "masculine protest" remained unsatisfied, necessitating his denigration of other literary figures, such as Longfellow. Miss Pruette stressed the effect on Poe of having been raised by the Allans as an only child; since, in her view, Poe's mother died too young for him to have developed any Oedipal attachment,[9] his recurrent poetic and fictional theme of the death of a loved woman was explained in terms of the women who died during Poe's later life. She ignored the ques-

---

a "split" or Jekyll-Hyde personality was indicated by the dissimilar halves of his face. Other early psychologists attributed Poe's difficulties to bad heredity, to alcohol, or to "psychic epilepsy." See Phillip Young, "The Earlier Psychologists and Poe," *American Literature*, XXII (January, 1951), 442-54.

7. The two most important full-length psychoanalytic studies of Poe were Marie Bonaparte's *Edgar Poe, Étude Psychoanalytique* (Paris: Denoël et Steele, 1933), which bore the imprimatur of Freud himself; and Joseph Wood Krutch's *Edgar Allan Poe* (New York: Alfred A. Knopf, 1926). The latter is discussed in detail in chapter 4.

8. Lorine Pruette, "A Psychoanalytical Study of Edgar Allan Poe," *The American Journal of Psychology*, XXXI (1920), 375.

9. The Oedipus situation as the cause of Poe's neurosis and the consequent necrophilia in his works is the thesis of Marie Bonaparte in the work cited in n. 7 above.

tion of homosexuality or impotence, and suggested that Poe's sadistic impulses were derived from the practice of flogging boys in school. "All through his life," she wrote, "the two things are found together: the will to power thwarted, demanding sadistic revenge, his sadism gratifying and enforcing his will to power."[10] Although she quoted frequently from Poe's works to demonstrate his neurotic character, Miss Pruette made little attempt to examine them as works of art. She concluded that the poems revealed "a very considerable degree of introversion (in the sense in which Jung uses the term) and a flight from reality."[11] A highly eclectic and comparatively shallow study of a complex neurotic personality, Miss Pruette's treatment is interesting primarily as an example of the rare application of Adler's psychology to a literary artist.

Another poet of the Romantic era, Percy Bysshe Shelley, was the frequent target of psychoanalytic criticism. Shelley's poems were the subject of several analyses, and an attempt at psychoanalytic biography was made by Edward Carpenter and George Barnefield in 1925.[12] Their book, *The Psychology of the Poet Shelley*, consisted of two brief essays. The first, by Carpenter, merely gave a stamp of approval to Barnefield's thesis that Shelley was bisexual or at least a latent homosexual. The burden of Carpenter's essay was the suggestion that bisexuality or hermaphroditism (which Carpenter maintained Shelley proposed as a future ideal for man in "The Witch of Atlas") might be a form of life superior to heterosexuality. Carpenter, the author of several anthropological studies, among them one entitled *The Intermediate Sex*, cited the existence of hermaphrodites in primitive tribes and "bisexual" geniuses such as Leonardo and Michelangelo to substantiate his point.

Carpenter's essay itself contributed little, functioning only as a somewhat awkward apologia to Barnefield's analysis of Shelley's character in terms of strong repressed homosexual impulses. The actual evidence cited in proof of this was slight: Shelley's general feminine appearance, his early boyhood friendships and later ones

10. Pruette, "A Psychoanalytical Study," p. 391.
11. *Ibid.*, p. 380.
12. Edward Carpenter and George Barnefield, *The Psychology of the Poet Shelley* (London: George Allen and Unwin, 1925).

such as those with Hogg and Trelawney, his idealization of women, his paranoia (according to psychoanalytic theory, frequently a defense against homosexuality), the bisexual nature of some of Shelley's literary characters, his attraction to Greek statuary and to the *Symposium*. None of this is, to say the least, conclusive, even psychoanalytically. Shelley's relation to his father was mentioned in one paragraph, and his other family relationships were ignored. Barnefield apparently wrote on the assumption that homosexuality was simply a physiological fact; his use of Freudian psychology extended only to his argument that Shelley's repression of his homosexual tendencies was the causative factor in his life-long melancholia and in his pursuit of a love ideal which could never be satisfied precisely because its real object was unknown to the poet's consciousness. Barnefield did not attempt any literary evaluation, nor did he relate his thesis to the poems themselves. What virtue his essay has lies in the tentativeness of its postulate and the fact that the postulate itself—that Shelley was effeminate in nature—is hardly so astounding that it would not be accepted as a matter of course by most readers of Shelley's poems.[13]

If homosexuality was the clue to Shelley's character, an overly strong attachment to a highly sensual mother was found to be the causative factor in the neurosis of Shelley's contemporary, John Keats. Rejecting the standard interpretations of Keats in a long review of Amy Lowell's biography, Conrad Aiken resorted to this psychoanalytic interpretation in order to explain what was to him "the most completely and consciously sensuous poetry ever written."[14] In Aiken's view, Keats's outstanding personal characteristic was his emotional instability. His habit of "passionate and conscious abandonment to sensation" Aiken attributed partly to his mother's "unusually vivid sexual nature,"[15] and to Keats's strong emotional attachment to her, which was not abandoned even at her death. It was her influence, more than Hunt's, which "led to the excesses of *Endymion*," and it was Keats's inability

13. A far cruder and more dogmatic analysis of an artist in terms of homosexuality was Clement Wood's *Amy Lowell* (New York: Harold Vinal, 1926), in which Freudian psychology was used to mask a personal spite. The study is wholly worthless from any standpoint.
14. Conrad Aiken, "John Keats," *The Dial*, XXVII (June, 1925), 483.
15. *Ibid.*, p. 478.

to find an adequate substitute for her in Fanny Brawne that caused the "abject implorings and yearnings of the love-letters."[16]

Aiken construed Keats's embarrassment at his father's menial occupation (he was an ostler) as being something more than a self-consciousness over low social status; it was rather a sign of the child's deeper resentment towards the father as an obstacle in the path of possession of the mother. Aiken noted the presence of the Oedipal theme in Keats's two epics, one dealing with the love of a goddess for a mortal, the other with the dethronement of the "father," Saturn. The sensuousness of the poems and the sensuality of his life[17] were both the result of Keats's "feverish search for luxury as a replacement of his mother."[18] His melancholy and emotional instability, in this view, could not be accounted for simply by biographical facts: "The situation is analogous to that of Hamlet; we see him peculiarly unbalanced, unbalanced to the point of insanity, but we do not see on the surface any wholly adequate cause."[19] It was only by reference to unconscious factors that Keats's personality was explicable.

Aiken's examination of the poems centered on the ambivalence toward death found in the Odes. In these poems, according to Aiken, the affective burden—the melancholy—dominated and tended to negate the surface logic of the narratives, in which Keats pretended to find peace. The "curious obsession with death" revealed in Keats's poetry was traceable, Aiken suggested, to his obsession with his mother; death, to Keats, had a "profoundly erotic significance."[20] Excerpted in this way, Aiken's interpretation of Keats's life and poems may sound more strained than it is in the essay itself, which is, on the whole, one of the more convincing of the Freudian analyses of the Romantic poets.

The life of Charlotte Brontë was interpreted with the aid of the new psychology by both Herbert Read and Lucile Dooley. Miss Dooley's study, the more strictly Freudian interpretation, is relatively successful, owing partly to her temperate approach to her subject, and partly to the ease with which the material lent itself to a psychoanalytic analysis. Charlotte Brontë's life was compara-

16. *Ibid.*, p. 479.
17. Aiken believed that Keats sought to escape dependence on his mother through sexual promiscuity which led eventually to his contracting syphilis.
18. *Ibid.*, p. 485.   19. *Ibid.*, p. 483.   20. *Ibid.*, p. 488.

tively simple in outline; her biographies were well documented; and she left behind her a considerable number of works, many written during the period of adolescence, which were partly or wholly autobiographical. The substance of Miss Dooley's thesis was that Charlotte, whose mother died when she was five years old, suffered from a strong repressed father-fixation. Accepting the Freudian theory of the artist, Miss Dooley attributed the literary power of Charlotte Brontë's fiction to her neurosis: "She could not possess this power [in her writing] unless the primordial unconscious soul of her remained unchanged and accessible as it does in the abnormally developed personality—the neurotic or the genius . . . . The secret of this tremendous power of passion in her fiction is emotional conflict in her own soul. This conflict involves a partial repression of its exciting cause into the lower strata of subconsciousness, but the emotional energy attached thereto finds its way out through the channel of novel writing with force unabated."[21]

The key to Charlotte's personality was the dominant role played by her father in her emotional life. The normal childhood attraction of a young girl to the father was heightened in Miss Brontë's case by her mother's death and by the completely closed-in nature of the Brontë household.[22] Devoting much attention to Charlotte's adolescence, Miss Dooley pointed out many neurotic symptoms during this period—her insomnia, superstitions, nervous terrors, strong feelings of inferiority, frequent headaches and depressions. These symptoms, Miss Dooley speculated, were the result of Charlotte's being forced into the role of mother to the family at the death of her elder sisters when she was nine years old, and the awakening of the desire to have a child during the adolescent period, with the consequent ambivalent feelings this occasioned.

Charlotte's love for her teacher in Brussells, Monsieur Heger, was in part determined, according to this interpretation, by his inaccessibility, making him thereby a pattern for her father. The

21. Lucile Dooley, "Psychoanalysis of Charlotte Bronte as a Type of the Woman of Genius," *The American Journal of Psychology*, XXI (July, 1920), 222-23. Miss Dooley was a pupil of the psychologist, G. Stanley Hall, under whose direction this study was written.

22. The "family complex" was further complicated in Charlotte Bronte's case "because it continued so long paramount" (*ibid.*, p. 226).

two men had many traits in common; as in the case of her love for her father, Charlotte was forced to renounce her love for the professor. After this renunciation, she produced her best novels. Miss Dooley objected strongly to the common suggestion that the power of *Jane Eyre* and the other novels was a result of the failure of her love affair with Heger: "Too much has been made of the attachment to Heger . . . . It was not this passion only she poured out in her romantic fiction, it was not this store of repressed feelings alone that forced her to write."[23] The passion for Heger was merely the "precipitating agent," reawakening as it did her earlier forbidden love for her father.[24] Had Charlotte not at that time found an outlet for her emotions in her writings, Miss Dooley suggested, she might possibly have become insane.

The conflict which demanded expression was unconsciously portrayed in many of her works, but particularly in *Jane Eyre*, a novel which Miss Dooley examined at some length and with considerable skill.[25] To her, the novel was a veiled expression of the child's wish to marry the father, a wish that was blocked in the novel by the discovery that the desired object was already married. Rochester's blindness at the end of *Jane Eyre* satisfied the "resistance" to the fulfillment of the wish: "The story did not demand that Rochester be made blind, but conflicting forces of the author's unconsciousness required it . . . . [It] was introduced to satisfy a demand of the unconscious complex of the writer, out of which complex the story grew."[26] The death of Paul at the end of *Villette* served the same function, according to Miss Dooley. This novel she considered Charlotte's masterpiece; its greater power arose from the fact that she was treating her personal complexes more directly here, although the father theme appeared also in her

23. *Ibid.*, p. 251.

24. "Out of her original Father Complex her need for emotional expression would have grown without the aid of any new love experience" (*ibid.*, p. 253).

25. The "conflict" in Charlotte Bronte was, of course, an unconscious one; "It is because a large part of her conflict remained subconscious that it could find a perfect and uncensored expression in creative, imaginative, writing" (*ibid.*, p. 252).

26. *Ibid.*, p. 226. Miss Dooley also suggested that on the unconscious symbolic level Rochester's blindness functioned to prevent his seeing who it was he was marrying, and noted that Miss Bronte's father was going blind at the time of the composition of *Jane Eyre*.

other books.[27] The consistency of her findings in both the life and work of Charlotte Brontë makes Miss Dooley's interpretation rather convincing, once the original Freudian premises are granted. Her treatment of sexuality was moderate while at the same time consistent in its broad outlines with psychoanalytic tenets. She avoided a rigidly dogmatic stand and treated her subject with respect and good taste.

Herbert Read was apparently unaware of this study, for he made no mention of it in his own psychological interpretation of the life and art of the Brontës. A discursive essay which touches on many points, Read's "Charlotte and Emily Brontë" centered on the problem of the relation in the Brontë sisters between genius and neurosis. He discussed first their physical heredity and added: "A neurosis, however, is never of a direct physical origin; the psychical complement, too, must be sought, and perhaps the mother provided this also by her early death in 1821, when Charlotte was but five and Emily three years old. The strong instinctive link between mother and child is never thus abruptly broken without unseen compensations and reverberations. I tread on delicate ground here—ground I would willingly leave to the expert psychologist."[28]

In Charlotte's juvenile writings there were frequent evocations of the figure of the Duke of Wellington. Miss Dooley had interpreted these in terms of the fantasy of the ideal father. Read hesitated to make any such definite statement, commenting: "Interpretations of such a phantasy as this might differ: Adler would see in it an unconscious attempt on the part of the neurotic weakling to free herself from a feeling of inferiority by the creation of a compensating ideal of superiority; whereas Jung would find the unconscious origin of such a hero phantasy quite specifically in a longing for the lost mother."[29] In any event, a sense of inferiority or incompleteness, an essential character of neurosis, was evident in Charlotte's case.

In the case of Emily the same causes, Read suggested, produced

27. Charlotte's later life was also examined by Miss Dooley in the light of her relation to her father. It was even suggested that Charlotte's death during pregnancy was possibly complicated by psychogenetic features.

28. Herbert Read, "Charlotte and Emily Bronte," *Reason and Romanticism* (London: Faber and Gwyer, 1926), p. 161.

29. *Ibid.*, p. 162.

a "masculine protest" of a more complex kind, involving "the typical features of what I think we must, with the psychoanalyst, call psychical hermaphroditism."[30] Anne and Branwell also manifested neurotic characteristics. Although all four children presented diverse symptoms, these were all traceable to the one cause, which Read delineated as "the early rupture of the maternal bond of affection and protection, the counteraction of a stern, impassive father, the formation of inferiority complexes in the children, and the consequent compensations by phantasy."[31] Read was not content to rest with this as an explanation for the art of the Brontës, however. What must be emphasized in their case, he said, was that art was a triumph over neurosis; that although it may have originated in a neurotic tendency, it represented a "coming-out-against" this tendency; and that in the case of the three sisters the sublimation was achieved: "Their art is not neurotic in kind; no art is. It is only when we search for causes and origins (as we have a perfect right to do) that we discover the neurosis; in the effect, according to the measure of its success, all is health and harmony."[32]

The experiences of the Brontë sisters did not *cause* their artistic development, Read continued. In order for an artist to be produced, experience must be united with a previous disposition to create an imaginary world, a disposition which probably had its origins in psychological factors present during infancy and adolescence. In the case of the Brontës, "when bleak disillusionment was added to [their] already sufficiently bleak existence . . . when expression became a more serious necessity as an escape from emotional agitations too strong to be repressed with impunity, then the mere mechanism of literary expression was ready at their command."[33] In other words, an early artistic tendency, accentuated and perhaps even caused by factors in the family situation, was intensified by later experience; but both the tendency (loosely, the impulse to the particular craft of literary expression) and the experience must combine to produce an artist.

Read concluded his essay by comparing Charlotte Brontë to Jane Austen, the former typifying the romantic temperament, the latter the classical temperament. In attempting to judge between

30. *Ibid.*
31. *Ibid.*, p. 163.
32. *Ibid.*, p. 164.
33. *Ibid.*, p. 172.

these two modes of expression, Read again used the concept of introversion-extroversion he apparently found so attractive in Jung. His conclusion here was identical to that expressed in his article on psychoanalysis and the literary critic: "The psychologist does not venture to take sides in such an opposition [between romantic and classic] but resorts to his theory of types, and sees here the dry bones of his structure take on perfect flesh. It would be difficult to discover a more exact illustration of the main distinction he draws between faculties directed inwards, to the observation of feeling, and faculties directed outwards, to the observation of external things. The psychologist must halt at this distinction . . . . But the critic must pursue the matter to a judgment."[34]

Read's use of Jung and Adler resulted in a more general analysis of the Brontës than Miss Dooley's detailed study of Charlotte along Freudian lines. He was less concerned with a strictly biographical treatment than with the relation between art and neurosis, using the Brontës as specific examples. Relying on Adler and Jung, Read viewed the Brontës' art in terms of a compensation through fantasy for some feeling of inferiority, without relating any specific motif in their lives to their works. Although not without interest, the essay is of less value as a study of the Brontës than Miss Dooley's more thorough work.

A provocative though brief analysis of the life of the poet Francis Thompson was made in 1925 by Ella Freeman Sharpe, whose essential thesis was that Thompson's life and poetry were an expression of an "original psychical fixation of libido at the oral level."[35] These offensively technical terms make the point sound absurd, but in Miss Sharpe's presentation, the thesis makes progressively more sense. Frequent reference was made to Thompson's poems, and the cumulative effect of the images lent probability to the theory that some form of psychic infantilism was present in Thompson's mental makeup. Instead of "reducing" the poems to a Freudian formula, their religious symbolism was enriched by Miss Sharpe's explication of the more primary psy-

34. *Ibid.*, pp. 183-84. Read's own judgment was ultimately for romanticism, because it attempted more. "It is, finally, a question of courage—of throwing into the attempt for truth not only intelligence, spirit, faith, but also feeling, emotion, self" (p. 185).

35. Ella Freeman Sharpe, "Francis Thompson: A Psychoanalytic Study," *The British Journal of Medical Psychology*, V (1925), 341.

chological situations which may have been their ultimate cause. Her tone throughout the essay was respectful, and she avoided the frequently irritating naïveté and dogmatism that marred much criticism of this type.

A collection of brief psychoanalytic studies of a series of American writers appeared in 1920. Written by Harvey O'Higgins and Dr. Edward H. Reade, *The American Mind in Action* attempted to define the American character with the aid of the concepts of the new psychology. The book reflects the somewhat childish animosity towards "Puritanism" present among certain American intellectuals in the years following the first World War; viewing the American character in terms of the heritage of repression passed down to their descendants by the Puritan fathers, the authors put forward the thesis that the "condition of blind repression and worried insecurity seems still to be the subconscious state of the typical American." This tendency to repress the instinctual life explained in large part "why the typical American is so idealistic, so practical, so inventive, so unphilosophical, so unartistical, so worried, restless, anxious, and ambitious, so apparently self-confident and yet so sensitive to criticism, so successful in achieving his aims and so unhappy in their achievement."[36]   To illustrate this rather inclusive thesis, the authors examined the lives of a variety of specimens of the American character: Twain, Lincoln, Carnegie, Anthony Comstock, Emerson, Franklin, Longfellow, Whitman, Mark Hanna, P. T. Barnum, Julia Ward Howe, Anna Howard Shaw, and Margaret Fuller. These analyses varied considerably in their degree of success, and the book as a whole can hardly be said to have demonstrated conclusively the authors' thesis, but as psychoanalytic portraits they had the virtue of being relatively free from Freudian dogmatism (rigid Freudian theory is several times attacked in the book) and were generally stimulating. Not all of the personalities examined were considered to be neurotics: Franklin and Longfellow represented successful psychological adaptations to their external environments and to their internal needs and goals. For the most part, however, the men discussed were viewed as having failed to use to the full their po-

36. Harvey O'Higgins and Edward H. Reede, M.D., *The American Mind in Action* (New York: Harper and Brothers, 1924), pp. 24-25. Originally appearing in 1920, the book was reprinted in 1923 and again in 1924.

tential as human beings and as creative artists. Frequently the authors showed some insight into the nature of these failures— as in their view that Emerson's outstanding weakness as a writer was his inability to confront the existence of evil, a psychological evasion of reality through the mechanism of denial—and in at least two cases, in the studies of Mark Twain and of Margaret Fuller, these brief analyses represent in some respects more rounded portraits of their subjects than the full-length Freudian biographies of them written at the same time.

Katherine Anthony's study of Margaret Fuller appeared in 1921. The book does not pretend to be purely objective. A warm admirer of Margaret Fuller, Miss Anthony frankly stated in her Preface that Margaret Fuller's story "needed to be told by someone who could sympathize with her struggles and affirm her ideals. Therefore, while striving for realism and impartiality, the following study does not pretend to avoid the warmth of the advocate."[37] The biography opens with a discussion of Margaret Fuller's childhood. She was raised almost entirely by her father; the mother, a very passive woman, apparently had little influence on the child's upbringing. Like Charlotte Brontë's, Margaret Fuller's father was a dominant presence in her life, according to this interpretation, and because of the mother's passivity, he played the roles of both mother and father to the young child.[38] As both her father and her teacher, he exercised a profound influence over her, and her identification with him led her to develop strong masculine traits.[39]

Margaret Fuller left a fragment of an autobiography, part of which discussed her childhood with some candor. In it were cited several early dreams, at least one of which is an almost classic example of the Freudian concept of wish-fulfillment. Miss Anthony used these dreams to support her thesis that much of Miss Fuller's "hysteria" was the result of a strong repressed sexual wish for the father. "The tie between father and daughter is never

37. Katherine Anthony, *Margaret Fuller: A Psychological Biography* (New York: Harcourt, Brace & Co., 1921), p. v.
38. The authors of *The American Mind in Action* strongly disagreed with this view, arguing that Mrs. Fuller was a strong personality who exercised a considerable influence on Margaret Fuller's personality development (O'Higgins and Reede, *American Mind*, pp. 305-7).
39. Anthony, *Margaret Fuller*, p. 6.

without some tinge of sex-attraction, and in the over-stressing of that tie lies the possibility of much neurotic suffering. In Margaret's case, without doubt, this early and natural affection was forced by the circumstances of her home-life into a premature strength and intensity. It became an *amour* which the sensitive consciousness was forced to drive down into the deepest and most secret recesses of its abandoned memories . . . . Her childish love was the mainspring of her whole career."[40]

Several other dreams involved the imagined deaths of her sister and her mother. These were also interpreted in terms of wish-fulfillment: "In this good child's heart, there were evil wishes which she had to keep secret even from herself. She had a primeval and murderous wish to attend the funeral of her beloved mother."[41] As a child, Margaret Fuller suffered from attacks of anxiety and frequent nightmares. Miss Anthony concluded from an examination of a recurrent childhood anxiety dream that these dreams indicated that the child underwent considerable suffering as a result of "the terrible burden of her precocious sexuality and painful repressions."[42]

Katherine Anthony's thesis was not based on the evidence of the dreams alone. As in the case of Charlotte Brontë, an examination of the events of Margaret Fuller's life, particularly if made by one who accepted Freud's theories of neurosis, led naturally to the view that here was a classic case of an unresolved Oedipal problem. To Miss Anthony, at any rate, Freud's theory of hysteria was a "perfect fit":

As one of the Freudians has said, "it may be more comfortable to believe that hysteria is due to a toxic process than to psycho-sexual conflicts," but we shall have to make ourselves uncomfortable for the moment in the interests of the truth about Margaret Fuller's childhood. But how can an innocent child be the victim of a psycho-sexual conflict, someone protests. "The passions are not unfrequently felt in their full shock, if not in their intensity, at eight or nine years old." This is not a statement of those profoundly irritating Freudians but of Margaret Fuller herself, who wrote it in a book review in 1846. She frequently wrote the most surprising statements about the love-impulse which showed that she had more than an inkling of the truth about its nature and its history.[43]

40. *Ibid.*, p. 25.   41. *Ibid.*, p. 17.   42. *Ibid.*, p. 19.
43. *Ibid.*, pp. 23-24. Miss Anthony frequently emphasized Margaret Ful-

The repressed father fixation was seen as the source of Margaret Fuller's failure to form any satisfactory love relation with a man until very late in life, her emotions until the age of thirty-seven being more typically directed toward women. Quoting T. W. Higginson, Miss Anthony argued that "she was one of those maidens . . . who form passionate attachments to older women."[44] While not directly discussing Margaret Fuller's psychosexual constitution in terms of homosexuality, the author did remark that "the feminism of women, like the corresponding form of sex-solidarity among men, is based on a social impulse which is in turn, rooted in an erotic impulse towards others of one's own sex."[45] The repressed libidinal attachment to the father was sublimated in another form in Margaret's early interest in mystical spiritism, and in her invention of a "demon" to explain her creative powers.[46]

Miss Anthony confined her psychological analysis largely to the early chapters of her study; she did not attempt to explain the reason for Margaret Fuller's marriage to Count d'Ossoli (an event which puzzled most of Margaret's friends) in psychoanalytic terms, or in connection with the original father complex which presumably was the "mainspring" of Margaret's life. Her only suggestion was the following: "[Ossoli] filled up the place left vacant in her life by her favorite brother Eugene and she restored in him the long-cherished maternal image."[47] Nor did she offer an explanation for Margaret's strange passivity in the face of death and her refusal to attempt to save herself when her boat was shipwrecked only fifty yards from shore except by the comment that "These things were manifestations of hysteria, and Margaret had long been known to have a neurotic constitution."[48]

Basically, Miss Anthony's analysis is typical of the popularized

---

ler's precocious intuitive grasp of Freudian principles. The tone of the passage quoted is typical of Miss Anthony's style throughout the book.
44. *Ibid.*, p. 35.
45. *Ibid.*, p. 57. In general, the handling of sexual matters in these early Freudian studies, particularly in those done by women, was much more delicate than in later works.
46. "Thus she tried to analyze the power of the unconscious, that unknown and inexplicable force—repressed yet irrepressible, forgotten but indestructible—by which she felt herself enthralled but which was at the same time the source of all her energy" (*ibid.*, p. 53).
47. *Ibid.*, p. 161.   48. *Ibid.*, p. 210.

Freudian biography; the limited success it achieves is due to the circumstance that the biographical facts of Margaret Fuller's life did not have to be stretched too far in order to portray her as a classic Freudian case of neurosis resulting from an unresolved Oedipal conflict. Miss Anthony was relatively moderate in her interpretations and made no attempt to analyze where no data were available. On the other hand, she frequently omitted details of Margaret Fuller's life and character which did not fit the Freudian scheme—although this may have been a consequence of ignorance rather than conscious intention. Her obvious affection for her subject resulted at times in manifestly unfair treatment of her material, as in her attempts to discredit Hawthorne's unflattering remarks on Margaret Fuller by charging that they were only reflections of his own neurosis. Stylistically, the book left a great deal to be desired, but despite its naïveté it had the virtue of readability; and as far as the psychologizing went (which, as has been pointed out, was not really very far), although it was superficial and one-sided it conformed, essentially, to Freudian principles as they were understood at that time.

A more impressive full-length Freudian biography was Axel Uppvall's dissertation on August Strindberg done under the direction of G. Stanley Hall at Clark University and published in 1920. Despite its early date,[49] the book is a good interpretative analysis of a complex figure. In his preface, Uppvall wrote that the study had been worked out "mainly along Freudian lines," although he personally agreed with Hall that Freud, in emphasizing sexuality exclusively, had given a "one-sided" view of man's psychic life.[50] He apologized for not using the theories of Jung, which any complete analysis, he felt, would have taken into account, and explained his use of Freud by saying that it "applied beautifully to Strindberg," and that furthermore its simplicity "naturally appealed strongly to the inexperienced analyst."[51] Strindberg was an excellent subject for a psychoanalytic treatment because of his

49. It is a curious fact of early psychoanalytic criticism that there was no progressive improvement in the works written between 1912 and 1926. Well-informed and sound interpretations appeared both early and late, as did interpretations that lacked value either as criticism or as psychology.

50. Axel John Uppvall, *August Strindberg: A Psychoanalytic Study* (Boston: The Gorham Press, 1920), p. 5.

51. *Ibid.*, p. 6.

marked neurotic behavior, the autobiographical nature of much of his writing, and his own rather remarkable insights into the nature of his conflicts, which frequently anticipated Freudian theory.[52]

Subtitled "A Psychoanalytic Study with Special Reference to the Oedipus Complex," the book outlined briefly the major events in Strindberg's life; Uppvall relied here mainly on Strindberg's own autobiographical writings. Disagreeing with Adler's analysis of the playwright in terms of an over-compensation to organ inferiority and the will to power,[53] he found the origin of Strindberg's neurotic disturbance in his extraordinary sensitiveness as a child coupled with the existence of an extremely harsh, tyrannical father who resembled in many respects the stereotype of the authoritarian Victorian father figure. "The significance of the influence," Uppvall wrote, "conscious and unconscious, of the father upon Strindberg's life can hardly be overestimated . . . ."[54] In Strindberg's case the basic Oedipal conflict was complicated by a severe ambivalence toward his mother, an ambivalence reflected in his adult relationships with women.[55] The cause of his reputed misogyny, however, was never adequately explained in this book, although Uppvall offered several possible interpretations: the ambivalence toward and fear of the mother, and a strong latent homosexuality.[56] Strindberg's fear and dislike of women were exaggerated by his disastrous first marriage, from which he was unable to free himself for fourteen years. His later religious mysticism, after his complete breakdown, was viewed by Uppvall not as a solution to his problems but as an escape from them: "Strindberg's conver-

52. For example, referring to his passionate ambivalence toward his wife, to whom he related as a son to his mother, Strindberg wrote: "Is that an unnatural impulse? Am I the product of the caprice of nature? Are my feelings those of a degenerate, since I am in possession of my mother? Is this unconscious incest of the heart?" (*ibid.*, p. 56).

53. This interpretation is to be found in Poul Bjerre, *The History and Practice of Psychoanalysis*, trans. Elizabeth N. Barrow (Boston: Richard C. Badger, 1916). For a brief discussion of this book, see Appendix B.

54. Uppvall, *August Strindberg*, p. 37.

55. Strindberg's marriages were unusually stormy; he was three times divorced.

56. This latter interpretation is unsatisfactory since the homosexuality would have been the product of the ambivalence toward the mother, rather than a cause of it. According to the standard analytic interpretation of homosexuality, it is a defense against the Oedipal conflict.

sion was . . . a strategic retreat, a compromise . . . . Hence
his flight into alchemy, magic, mysticism and occultism and then
to the Cross, the everlasting symbol . . . of the inability on the
part of the individual to cope with and master the problems of
earthly life."[57]

The fascination of Uppvall's study lies probably in the subject
himself, who was one of the most intensely neurotic geniuses of
the last century and whose plays, with their strange symbolism and
dream-like situations, reflect a marked use of unconscious material. Uppvall's application of psychoanalytic analysis was informed and judicious, and he made no attempt to explain away
Strindberg's genius on the basis of his neurosis. There was little
literary criticism in this study, which was primarily biographical,
although *The Father* and one or two other plays were discussed
in relation to certain themes which reflected recurrent personality
conflicts in the author's life. This absence of literary analysis is
to be regretted, as is the book's brevity, for the subject is an unusually fruitful one for psychoanalytic investigation.

A survey of these early Freudian biographical studies of literary artists reveals, on the whole, a rather monotonous series of
Oedipal complexes. Generally speaking, Freudian theory was not
used to explain the artistic process itself but was limited to clarifying certain characteristics of the artist's personality. The more
successful writers exercised tact in their use of psychoanalytic material and avoided a rigid insistence that their hypotheses were the
only interpretations possible. Apparently several factors are necessary for a sound analytic biography, besides the indispensable
prerequisite of an intelligent biographer: the subject must have a
markedly neurotic temperament; the record of his life, particularly
the early years, should be fairly thorough; and there should be a
considerable body of autobiographical writing, preferably including several of the subject's dreams. Of the many early attempts
at psychoanalytic literary biography, these elements were present
only in the cases of Strindberg and Charlotte Brontë, with the result that these studies alone have much real value at the present
time.

Psychoanalytic criticism of the drama in the post-War decade

57. Uppvall, *August Strindberg*, p. 88.

was quite extensive. The precedent for applying the concepts of psychoanalysis to dramatic works had been set, of course, by Freud himself, who in *The Interpretation of Dreams* had analyzed Sophocles' Oedipus to explain his idea of the Oedipus complex and had made some suggestive remarks on *Hamlet* which Ernest Jones later developed into a full-length study.[58] Furthermore, the psychoanalytic process itself involved what Freud, using Aristotle's troublesome term from the *Poetics*, called the "cathartic method."

The similarity between the psychoanalytic patient's "purging" of his emotions and the "catharsis" achieved by the witness to a tragedy was noted early by readers of Freud. Albert Chandler's prize essay at Harvard in 1911, mentioned earlier, was among the first to use Freud's ideas to explain an audience's reaction to serious drama. The problem Chandler set himself to solve via *The Interpretation of Dreams* was this: in real life, man tended to avoid unpleasant or tragic situations; why then did he seek them in art? In his analysis of *Oedipus Rex*, Chandler stated, Freud had explained why we were horrified, but he had not explained why we were fascinated. The answer, according to Chandler, was that "tragedy attracts us because it depicts situations which our suppressed complexes demand."[59] The audience's identification with the tragic protagonist allowed them to express temporarily their repressed unconscious feelings of hostility, power drives, or sexual desire. At the same time, in the structure of tragic drama, the hero, with whom the audience had identified, was ultimately punished; this satisfied the audience's "resistances" to their unconscious wish and thus placated their civilized consciences. "The structure of tragedy," Chandler pointed out, "is like the structure of a dream, since its fundamental motives are derived from the lower stratum, and these motives are forced to express themselves in a guise acceptable to the upper stratum."[60] The relief afforded by a "safe" expression of unconscious desires constituted the "catharsis."

The tragic catharsis, however, afforded not merely relief; it had

58. Jones's essay on *Hamlet* is examined in detail in Chapter 5.

59. Albert R. Chandler, "Tragic Effect in Sophocles Analyzed According to the Freudian Method," *The Monist*, XXIII (January, 1913), 77.

60. *Ibid.*, p. 86.

a "higher," curative aspect, that of sublimation: "Tragedy does not merely release the energy of the suppressed complexes, but turns it into profitable channels."[61] This was the moral function of tragedy: the energy bound up in the "lower" complexes was freed to strengthen the higher, ethical complexes. The mere release of energy without sublimation would be dangerous; the unconscious complexes might even be strengthened, as a muscle is strengthened through exercise. "It would be very difficult," Chandler wrote, "to say just how often a person should visit a tragedy to give his complexes relief without increasing their future demands."[62] Because of the danger that there would be an incomplete sublimation, he concluded, tragedy was a mixed good, although he added that art should not be justified on the basis of its moral "good" but on its "intrinsic value as a form of art."

The naïveté of Chandler's mechanical system of "energy" being transposed from "lower" complexes to "higher" ones would not be accepted today, of course, but much of this is a reflection of the author's youth and the fact that Freud's ideas were at that time extremely new. His fundamental concept of catharsis was similar to that later (and better) expressed by Prescott and others, and his assumption that drama appealed to something in the unconscious of the audience was basic for any psychoanalytic critic of the drama. As a theoretical exposition, Chandler's effort initiated the examination of a problem which is still an intriguing one.

Applications of psychoanalytic theory to drama were varied. Apart from Freudian analyses of individual plays and individual characters, there were examinations of mythical motifs and sexual symbolism in various plays,[63] and more specific applications of Freudian tenets. Samuel A. Tannenbaum demonstrated examples of Freudian slips of the tongue and other "symbolic actions" in Shakespeare,[64] analyzing in Freudian terms Caesar's epileptic fit

61. *Ibid.*, p. 87.   62. *Ibid.*, p. 89.
63. For example, W. J. Lawrence, "The Phallus on the Early English Stage," *Psyche and Eros*, II (May-June, 1921), 161, which traced the use of the phallus as part of the devil's costume in pre-Renaissance drama in an effort to suggest "how far-reaching in its implications [is] the Freudian metaphysic."
64. Samuel A. Tannenbaum, "Shakespeare and the New Psychology," *The Dial*, LIX (December 23, 1915), 601-3; "Slips of the Tongue in Shakespeare," *The Dial*, LXI (August 15, 1916), 89-91; and "Psych-

and Othello's "trance," an instance of rationalization in Brutus' soliloquy (II.1), and Desdemona's repression of a painful incident (III.2). His purpose in these essays was to illustrate from Shakespeare the "simpler Freudian mechanisms," his thesis being that Shakespeare intuitively understood such mechanisms as slips of the tongue and introduced them into his plays as a means of portrying character.[65] Tannenbaum's most extensive examination of a Freudian "error" was that of Coriolanus' inability to remember the name of a Volscian man who had once helped him and whom he wished to reward (I.9.79-92). Applying Freud's concept that such lapses of memory were not accidental, Tannenbaum suggested that Shakespeare introduced this incident to point up Coriolanus' dislike of being indebted to a member of the lower classes.[66] In general, Tannenbaum's use of Freud was very circumspect, and the instances he cited were frequently convincing.

As both a psychotherapist and a noted Shakespearean scholar, Tannenbaum was in the odd position of having become interested in psychology via his studies of literature.[67] As co-editor of both *Psyche and Eros* and *The Journal of Sexology and Psychanalysis*, he was responsible for the publication of several comparatively good pieces of psychoanalytic criticism. By the early 1920's, however, he had decided that psychology was not a sufficiently scientific discipline for literary scholarship and turned sharply against Freud.[68] This reversal can be seen in his article, "The Heart of Hamlet's Mystery," in 1923, a lengthy sarcastic protest against current Freudian productions of the play.[69] To reduce the com-

---

analytic Gleanings from Shakespeare," *Psyche and Eros*, I (July, 1920), 29-39.

65. Tannenbaum, "Slips of the Tongue," p. 89.

66. Tannenbaum, "Shakespeare and the New Psychology," p. 602.

67. He had read in 1910 a psychological interpretation of *Othello* which interested him in psychoanalysis; two years later he went to Europe to study under Freud. See John J. McAleer, "The Gladiatorial Dr. Tannenbaum," *The Bulletin of the New York Public Library*, LXVI (November, 1962), 557.

68. Tannenbaum's rejection of all of Freud's major tenets can be seen in his editorial, "A New Journal of Psychanalysis—Why?" *The Journal of Sexology and Psychanalysis*, I (January, 1923), 4-5, wherein he accused Freud of "mysticism," among other things.

69. Arthur Hopkins produced *Hamlet* in 1922 in New York with John Barrymore in the title role. The production followed Ernest Jones's interpretation, and was apparently rather overdone. For another strong pro-

plexity of Hamlet to a lust for his mother was to travesty Shake-speare's art, Tannenbaum argued. "It will be difficult to find a complex that cannot be nailed on [Hamlet] and made a key to the play." Such, he added ironically, "was the greatness of Shake-speare's polymorph-perverse genius."[70]

Dr. Tannenbaum's combination of literary and psychoanalytic training was unfortunately rare. More representative than his work are the articles on contemporary drama written by Louise Brink and Smith Ely Jelliffe, two practicing analysts of the time, which were published in book form under the title *Psychoanalysis and the Drama* in 1922. These essays are excellent examples of a type of criticism the premise of which was that literature was therapy and that the literary artist could be of great "use" to the therapist. Brink and Jelliffe analyzed dramas not in terms of their artistic value but as an adjunct to psychotherapy. "Psycho-analysis," they announced in their preface, "seeks to enlarge the extent of intellectual knowledge and control of the unconscious mental life. It therefore welcomes the drama as an important means toward this end."[71]

Written primarily for doctors, the book contained an examin-ation of individual plays showing how they illustrated "universal themes of the unconscious"; in effect, each drama was treated as an object lesson in the basic tenets of psychoanalysis. Brink and Jelliffe had a Jungian, rather than a Freudian, predisposition, and their use of Jung's ideas too frequently resulted merely in senti-mental enthusiasm over the wondrous workings of man's libido and the marvels of sublimation. There was also a good deal of what can be only called psychoanalytic moralizing, of which the following, selected at random, is typical: "The sordid and the gay, earthly love and heavenly joy, merry making and religious festival, and even the gentle kindness of ministration and the darker things of envy and greed, all these lie closer to the unconscious than we are accustomed to think. Conscious thought rudely separates them

test against it, see G. K. Chesterton, "Hamlet and the Psychoanalyst," in *Fancies vs. Fads* (London: Methuen and Company, 1923), pp. 20-34.

70. Samuel A. Tannenbaum, "The Hearts [sic] of Hamlet's Mystery," *The Journal of Sexology and Psychanalysis*, I (May, 1923), 323.

71. Louise Brink and Smith Ely Jelliffe, *Psychoanalysis and the Drama* (New York and Washington: The Nervous and Mental Disease Publishing Company, 1922), p. iii.

from one another—this is the imperfect attempt to dissolve the mystery of the evershifting confluence of the varying elements of life . . . ."[72]

However, despite irritating passages of this sort, which are as much a fault of style as of method, *Psychoanalysis and the Drama* did include a few suggestive analyses of plays in terms of the artist's treatment of universal emotional conflicts originating in the mental life of the child. It is a curious coincidence, however, that the most successful analyses, such as that of J. M. Barrie's *Dear Brutus*, were of plays which utilized in their plots dreams and motifs publicized by psychoanalytic theory. Brink and Jelliffe did not suggest that the authors of these dramas were consciously using psychoanalytic material, but one suspects that much of the "universality" of the dramatic situations was a product of the playwright's knowledge of Freud.[73]

The chief objection to Brink and Jelliffe's approach is their implicit assumption that the artist's function was to present psychoanalytic object lessons. Drama, in their view, was a species of therapy:

The spectator need not be consciously aware of the close relation to himself of the problems presented in the drama. His intense interest in their progress, and the solution or the disaster that follows . . . lies chiefly in the unconscious where his own problems largely lie hidden. The mission of the drama is to apply healing, sometimes through a solution objectively presented or perhaps only through the laying of these open to a certain amount of psychic ventilation. This may occur through a tragic exposure of the problems and their results. The existence of the problems may even be unguessed, the need of healing may be the least acknowledged reason for seeking pleasure in an evening's performance.[74]

Whatever truth there may be in this theory, it can easily lead to bad literary criticism. It led Brink and Jelliffe to interpret drama as a psychoanalytic parable of the unconscious and to inflate common moral platitudes with psychoanalytic language.[75]

---

72. *Ibid.*, p. 77.

73. The plays selected for discussion were all performed between 1919 and 1922. A further objection to this book is that since these works are by now largely unknown, the sketchiness with which the plots were outlined leaves much to be desired.

74. Brink and Jelliffe, *Psychoanalysis and the Drama*, p. 12.

75. Brink and Jelliffe's earlier interpretation of *The Wild Duck* (*Psycho-*

If poor Jungian critics tended to be guilty of sentimental ef-
fusions over the wondrous manifestations of the unconscious, poor
Freudians were guilty of reducing art works to a single meaning.
Strindberg's *The Father*, for example, was analyzed by Leo Kaplan merely to point out how an unsatisfactory sexual relationship
between the parents could lead them to substitute the child as a
love object. The disturbance of the protagonist was traced back
to an Oedipal conflict, which in turn was said to reflect Strindberg's own neurosis.[76] The writings of Isador H. Coriat, an American psychoanalyst, also exemplify this reductive approach. One
of his articles, "The Sadism in Oscar Wilde's *Salome*," did little
more than illustrate the overt sadism in the play (according to
Coriat "one of the finest examples of the portrayal of the sadistic
impulse in literature"), and state that such expression could be
accomplished only by a man with "well-marked sadistic feelings."[77] The point of another essay, "Anal-Erotic Character Traits
in Shylock," was that Shylock "was not of a particular racial type
[but] that such character traits can be found in all individuals . . . ."[78] The "anal-erotic" character traits which Coriat
found in Shylock included orderliness, parsimony, obstinacy, the
love of children, disobedience, procrastination, and sadism. It
goes without saying that merely to give Shylock a psychoanalytic
label does little to clarify either his character or the play.

Psychoanalytic critics found the plays of Shakespeare good
hunting ground. Freud himself had been intrigued not only by
Hamlet but by *Macbeth*.[79] Following Freud's cue, Coriat produced a most absurd Freudian study in a small book, *The Hysteria*

---

analytic Review, VI (October, 1919), 357-78) was also marred by sentimentality and psychoanalytic moralizing, although their analysis of Gre-
gers Werle in terms of his unconscious hatred for his father was fairly
successful.

76. Leo Kaplan, "Strindberg's *The Father* Analyzed," *Psyche and Eros*,
II (July-August, 1921), 215-21. Like much criticism of this kind, one of
the main purposes of the essay was to point out how Strindberg intuited
much of Freudian theory.

77. Isador H. Coriat, "The Sadism in Oscar Wilde's *Salome*," *The Psychoanalytic Review*, I (July, 1914), 259.

78. Isador H. Coriat, "Anal-Erotic Character Traits in Shylock," *The
International Journal of Psychoanalysis*, II (September, 1921), 360.

79. See "Some Character Types Met With in Psychoanalytical Work,"
a brief discussion of which can be found in Appendix B.

of Lady Macbeth, considered by some psychoanalytical writers to be a "classic." Coriat's reductive approach can be seen from his general statements about art in his introduction. Previous literary critics, he wrote, had failed to perceive that "every literary creation was the product of the author's unconscious and could not be separated from it."[80] It was only in the light of modern psychoanalysis that an insight into the true meaning of works of literature could be achieved, since these works were "merely the projections into artistic form of the unconscious mental life of the author."[81] Coriat's analysis of Lady Macbeth's "neurosis" assumed her existence as a human being apart from her dramatic role. She was diagnosed as a typical hysteric suffering from dissociation because of two repressed "complexes"—her ambition to be queen, which was itself a substitute for her thwarted desire to have a child, and her guilt feelings over the murder of Duncan. Coriat's analysis was both pedestrian and pompous, and merely translated into psychoanalytic jargon standard critical interpretations of Lady Macbeth's character.[82] Other Shakespearean "studies" included an essay on *Coriolanus* by J. E. Towne, who found in that play a variant of the Oedipus tragedy;[83] Hanns Sachs's analysis of *The Tempest* and the other late romances in terms of Shakespeare's own sexual love for his daughter and his guilt over the death of his son Hamnet;[84] and an interesting examination of the scene between York and Aumerle in *Richard II* in terms of York's unconscious

80. Isador H. Coriat, *The Hysteria of Lady Macbeth* (Boston: The Four Seas Company, 1922), p. x. The first edition of this book appeared in 1912.

81. Coriat quoted from Taine to substantiate his position that only psychoanalysis could enable the critic to grasp the full meaning of literature. Of Shakespeare Taine had written: "As the complicated revolutions of the heavenly bodies become intelligible only by the use of a superior calculus . . . so the great works of art can be interpreted only by the most advanced psychological systems" (*ibid.*, p. 2).

82. For an equally silly analysis of Lady Macbeth in terms of her "pathological" sleep-walking, see Dr. I. Sadger, *Sleep Walking and Moon Walking: A Medico-Literary Study* (New York and Washington: Nervous and Mental Disease Publishing Company, 1920). Sadger found the cause of Lady Macbeth's neurosis in her Oedipal problems with her father.

83. Jackson E. Towne, "A Psychoanalytic Study of Shakespeare's *Coriolanus*," *The Psychoanalytic Review*, VIII (January, 1921), 84-91.

84. Hanns Sachs, "The Tempest," *The International Journal of Psychoanalysis*, IV (January, 1923), 43-88. This article is one of the better Freudian analyses.

identification of Aumerle as the personification of his own guilt in betraying the king.[85]

Although, with the exception of Coriat's treatment of Macbeth, the studies of Shakespeare had some merit, taken as a group, early Freudian studies of the drama were bad. When the psychoanalytic critics departed from dramatic theory to actual analyses of individual plays, they tended to confine themselves to pointing out how a particular character reflected particular neurotic traits (which could be traced back to an Oedipus complex), or saw in the plays a psychoanalytic moral. Even the Shakespearean studies, if we exclude Jones's excellent work on *Hamlet*, cannot be said to constitute a significant contribution to an understanding of Shakespeare in particular or of drama in general. Possibly because of Freud's own interest in the drama, there was a greater volume of psychoanalytic studies of dramatic literature than of any other genre, but their quantity was not matched by quality.

There were several early analyses of non-dramatic literature by those intrigued by the new psychology. In numerous articles, writers pointed out how a certain piece of literature exemplified a certain pathological symptom, or demonstrated that a particular author was a "literary forerunner" of Freud.[86] Critics elucidated common literary themes in Freudian terms,[87] suggested programs for analyzing experimentally an author's work,[88] discussed the poetic process by means of atrocious poems written by mental

85. M. P. Taylor, "A Father Pleads for the Death of His Son," *The International Journal of Psychoanalysis*, VIII (January, 1927), 53-55.

86. For the first type, see Sylvia Stragnell, "A Study in Sublimations," *The Psychoanalytic Review*, X (April, 1923), 209-13, and Francis T. Russell, "A Poet's Portrayal of Emotion," *The Psychological Review*, XXVIII (May, 1921), 222-38; for the latter, see Helen W. Brown, "A Literary Forerunner of Freud," *The Psychoanalytic Review*, IV (January, 1917), 64-69 (on Matthew Arnold), and L. C. Martin, "A Note on Hazlitt," *The International Journal of Psychoanalysis*, I (1920), 414-19.

87. See, for example, John T. MacCurdy, "The Omnipotence of Thought and the Phantasy of the Mother's Body in the Hephaestus Myth and a Novel by Bulwer Lytton," abstracted by Louise Brink in *The Psychoanalytic Review*, VII (July, 1920), 295-300, and Leo Kaplan, "The Psychology of Literary Invention," *Psyche and Eros*, II (March-April, 1921), 65-80 (on the Don Juan theme in literature).

88. See J. E. Downey, "A Program for a Psychology of Literature," *The Journal of Applied Psychology*, II (1918), 366-77, and R. A. Tsanoff, "On the Psychology of Poetic Construction," *The American Journal of Psychology*, XXV (October, 1914), 528-37.

patients,[89] and analyzed the psychological function of technical aspects of poetry, such as rhyme and refrain.[90] More typical, however, were Freudian dissections of individual works. Poetry, on the whole, was more frequently attacked (the word is consciously chosen) than the novel. J. W. Preger's outlandish analysis of two of Blake's lyrics is an excellent demonstration of the extreme length to which some Freudians went in their interpretations. Beginning with the premise that "The Garden of Love" could have little meaning "for any but the psychoanalytically informed,"[91] Preger quoted the poem in full and analyzed it in terms of Blake's unconscious conflicts. The last line of the first quatrain ("where I used to play on the green") symbolized his mother's lap; the "Chapel" symbolized the mother's matrix. The second stanza of the lyric "developed the incest-prohibition," which forced the poet to seek a mother-substitute in the "sweet flowers." The last stanza, according to Preger, expressed the realization of the child's incestuous desire, for, through death, he was enabled to return to the mother's womb: ". . . the 'graves' and the 'tombstones' can here stand for but one thing, the consummation of his desire, and symbolize, by virtue of their form and relation the female and male sex-organs respectively . . . . Through death, he returns whence he came to his mother's matrix; whilst through the priests and the briars he identifies himself with Christ who was crowned with thorns and crucified by the priests that here stand for Blake's father, whose existence meant the Crucifixion of his son's 'joys and desires.' "[92] His analysis of the second lyric, "The Defiled Sanctuary," in terms of onanism, was, if possible, even more extreme. To Preger this poem was obviously inspired by Blake's reminiscence of his parents' cohabitation; like those of the first poem, its images "fail to convey, except to those ac-

89. For example, J. C. Hill, "Poetry and the Unconscious," *The British Journal of Medical Psychology*, IV (1924), 125-33.

90. K. Weiss, "Rhyme and Refrain, A Contribution to the Psychogenesis of the Poetic Means of Expression," abstracted by Louise Brink in *The Psychoanalytic Review*, VI (January, 1919), 101-4. This article traced rhyme back to the infantile pleasure in repetition, originally an autoerotic activity based ultimately on suckling.

91. J. W. Preger, "A Note on William Blake's Lyrics," *The International Journal of Psychoanalysis*, I (1920), 196.

92. *Ibid.*, p. 197.

quainted with psychoanalysis, any idea bearing on human experience."[93]

A different kind of absurdity to which Freudian critics of poetry were liable is exemplified by Margaret K. Strong's "A New Reading of Tennyson's 'The Lotos Eaters.'" This "new reading" saw the poem as a portrait of a patient undergoing analysis. Miss Strong found in "The Lotos Eaters" a "description of a psychoanalytic process which could be possible only in relation to our most modern mental clinics," although freely admitting that this was an anachronism.[94] Still, to those who read it so, the poem could be seen as a "true presentation of the conflict of a dissociated personality . . . presenting the emotional experience of the neurotic carrying you with him from trough to crest of the 'mounting wave' and back again."[95] Although it may be true that "The Lotos Eaters" portrays a conflict, and that this conflict can be seen as analogous to other conflicts, even those of a neurotic patient, to make an interpretation of this sort, admitting at the outset that it has nothing whatever to do with the poet's intended expression, is to deny poetry any real meaning at all.

The two examples just discussed illustrate the depths to which Freudian criticism could sink. The picture would not be complete, however, without including a sample of the Jungian approach, the worst feature of which was its sentimentality. An example is Thomas V. Moore's interpretation of "The Hound of Heaven" as a parallel of the Jungian *libido*, in which the flight that is the subject matter of the poem was seen in terms of the wanderings of the libido in its attempt to escape conscience (the "Hound of Heaven").[96] This adds little to one's understanding of the poem, merely translating as it does the traditional interpretation into Jungian terminology. To Moore, however, "The Hound of Heaven" took on marvellous new meaning when read in these terms:

93. *Ibid.*, p. 198.
94. Margaret K. Strong, "A New Reading of Tennyson's 'The Lotos Eaters,'" *The Psychoanalytic Review*, VIII (April, 1921), 184.
95. *Ibid.*
96. Thomas V. Moore, "The Hound of Heaven," *The Psychoanalytical Review*, V (October, 1918), 346. After a fuzzy discussion of Freud's concept of the pleasure principle and the reality principle, Moore suggested that a third should be added—the "conscience" principle. The conflict between this and the libido Moore saw as the real subject of the poem.

"How luminous this poem appears when we read it from the psychoanalytical point of view as the autobiography of the author! It is the story of the strivings of the *libido*. At first, it is described as unchecked, uncompensated, and without any sublimation. Then we see the efforts of a poetic genius to direct the *libido*, first in one channel and then in another, and finally we witness the triumph of the individual over the *libido* in a religious sublimation."[97]

Not all psychological criticism during this time, of course, was quite this bad. Walter S. Swisher, in a psychoanalytic interpretation of Browning's "Pauline," avoided the extremes of both the Freudians and the Jungians at their worst. He saw the poem not as the dramatized fragment of a lover's confession but as an unconscious revelation of the psychic life of a young man who had just passed through adolescence and was emerging into manhood.[98] Swisher summarized the poem and its meanings as follows: "The poet confesses that he has been guilty of secret faults which are the result of introversion . . . being bound up in the dim orb of self. He relates two dreams to substantiate this, which deal with an infantile fixation upon his parents . . . . He imagines landscapes with swans and other birds, towers and snakes, fiends and witches, which disturb him . . . . He confesses a slavish worship for . . . Shelley, who is the surrogate for the father. Finally, he breaks down his resistances, breaks up the complex, abreacts, remolds the complex through religion, and feels himself a normal man."[99]

Odd as it may seem, this interpretation of the poem, although extreme in its language, is progressively convincing. In Swisher's view, the poem had a cathartic, therapeutic effect on Browning, and was written at a stage in the poet's life when he was unconsciously attempting to move beyond the autoeroticism of the child into mature adult life. According to Swisher, he succeeded; Browning as an adult was not a neurotic. Relying heavily on both Jung and Adler, Swisher analyzed the poem's images in terms of archetypes rather than as purely personal symbols. Such conflict as these images evinced reflected the conflict of the ego in its at-

97. *Ibid.*
98. Walter S. Swisher, "A Psychoanalysis of Browning's *Pauline*," *The Psychoanalytic Review*, VII (April, 1920), 115.
99. *Ibid.*, p. 133.

tempts to free itself from the "terrible mother" imago postulated by Jung.[100] Although such a reading of the poem would appeal only to one who accepted Jungian psychology, it remains one of the more convincing poetic analyses, although it is marred by a too-frequent use of scientific terminology.

An interesting study of a group of poems in terms of a single theme appeared in *The Psychoanalytic Review* in 1918, an exploration of the phenomenon, frequent in early poems such as *Beowulf*, the *Chansons de Geste*, and the legend of Cuchulain, of the relationship between the nephew and the maternal uncle. The hero of these stories (Roland, Cuchulain, Beowulf, Percival) frequently had as a father-figure his maternal uncle, who was represented as kind and genial and with whom a warm bond was maintained, while the actual father either was presented as a harsh figure or was reduced to dramatic insignificance in the plot of the narrative. This phenomenon had previously been explained on the basis of the theory of a matriarchal society existing in the early Indo-European family, traces of which had found their way into the later legends. Rejecting this theory as false on philological grounds, Albert Weinberg attempted an explanation in psychoanalytic terms, suggesting that the original father imago had been split into two people—the "good" uncle and the "bad" father. The reason for this splitting was dual: "We may posit for the kindness and affection attributed to the maternal uncle a two-fold significance. On the one hand it would by implication contrast with the severity of the father, a severity which may or may not be objective but which in either event has its reality in the subjective apperception of the son. On the other hand . . . it would establish an ideal father, a conception which has its prerequisite in the deficiency of the actual parent."[101] The choice of an uncle on the mother's rather than on the father's side was probably determined by the stronger associations of the father with the paternal uncle,[102] and by the fact that some of the maternal uncle's

100. It was refreshing to discover than Browning apparently did not suffer from an Oedipus complex. His relations with his father, according to Swisher, were entirely healthy.

101. Albert K. Weinberg, "Nephew and Maternal Uncle: A Motive of Early Literature in the Light of the Freudian Psychology," *The Psychoanalytic Review*, V (October, 1918), 394.

102. Weinberg pointed out that the paternal uncle, as in *Hamlet, Nich-*

fondness for his sister would be unconsciously transferred to her son. In his concluding speculations, Weinberg suggested that it was not mere coincidence that the hero should be presented as a nephew; it was possible that heroism itself was viewed by the unconscious in its primal form, the original act of heroism being the revolt against the father's domination. If this were so, these primitive figures were not heroes *and* nephews but in a sense heroes *because* nephews: "They have dared to replace the wonted relation of son and father with that of nephew and maternal uncle."[103]

Although some of his suggestions were tenuous, Weinberg's article was provocative and largely convincing. In general, Freudian analyses of older literature, particularly of those works closely connected with myth, tended to have more plausibility than those dealing with modern literature, and the closer modern literature approached myth, the greater likelihood there was that the work could profit from a psychoanalytic examination. The mythical elements in Ibsen's *Peer Gynt* lent themselves readily to this sort of treatment and received much attention, although unfortunately these early analyses were of comparatively little worth. Wilhelm Stekel examined the poem on the basis of its "dream work,"[104] and Leo Kanner analyzed Peer himself as a classic schizophrenic type,[105] concluding that the poem's success was due to Ibsen's ability to portray the precarious borderline between genius and insanity. A more lengthy analysis was made by Harold Jeffreys, who opened his study with a discussion of the feasibility of applying psychoanalysis to literature. If the art work were primarily an expression of the author's personality, he reasoned, it was susceptible to the same interpretation given to dreams. In literature,

---

olas Nickleby, Kidnapped, and other works both ancient and modern, was generally a figure of cruelty and oppression, probably because of his close association with the father (*ibid.,* p. 396).

103. *Ibid.,* p. 397.

104. Wilhelm Stekel, "Analytical Comments on Ibsen's 'Peer Gynt,' " *Psyche and Eros,* I (November-December, 1920), 152-56.

105. Leo Kanner, "A Psychiatric Study of Ibsen's *Peer Gynt," The Journal of Abnormal Psychology,* XIX (January, 1925), 381. Peer was found to be a "pathological liar, a day-dreamer, victim of illusions and delusions, with visual, auditory, and somatic hallucinations, self-satisfied, egotistical, emotionally indifferent, immoral, with no inhibitions, no insight, and no judgment." These characteristics "justified the psychiatric diagnosis of dementia praecox."

however, the analyst had no access to the author's free associations, which were necessary for any satisfactory dream interpretation. Moreover, a complete analysis could never be made on the basis of a single fantasy. The critic, however, could resolve this difficulty by using the principle of analogy, for "if the same group of associations occur in different poems, it is a legitimate scientific procedure to infer a similar origin in each person."[106] The results obtained by this method would have only a "moderate probability" if they were based on analogy alone, but if they led to a coherent psychoanalytical account of the work, they would "constitute a verification . . . and the whole will possess a probability amounting to practical certainty."[107] On the other hand, since no one work expressed the total personality of its author, biographical inferences should be avoided.

This caution in theory contrasted remarkably with the extravagance of Jeffrey's interpretation of *Peer Gynt* itself. In a detailed analysis extending for some thirty pages, he examined the conflict between Peer and Ase, which involved, according to him, not only the Oedipal conflict, but castration complexes and anal fixations as well. There was scarcely a line or an image in the poem which Jeffreys did not succeed in tracing back to its ultimate source in the digestive tract, the vagina, or the womb. This proliferation of Freudian symbols and themes was finally merely ludicrous, almost as if the author were writing a parody of the Freudian approach to literature. Whatever value the essay might have for the psychoanalyst, as literary criticism it is only an object of wonder.

Jeffreys' Freudian analysis of *Peer Gynt* stands in contrast to a detailed Jungian study of Shelley's poems by Eugene C. Taylor. Like Jeffreys, Taylor began with some remarks on the usefulness of psychoanalysis in criticism, referring favorably to Prescott's *Poetry and Dreams*, and describing in particular Jung's *Psychology of the Unconscious*. "Those who are familiar with this remarkable work, and with Shelley's poetry as well," he commented, "cannot but be struck with the almost literal exactness with which the poet's psychic growth followed the evolution of the human mind

106. Harold Jeffreys, "Ibsen's *Peer Gynt*," *The Psychoanalytic Review*, XI (October, 1924), 363.
107. *Ibid.*

in general, as it is outlined by Dr. Jung."[108] Taylor's purpose was to examine the various stages in Shelley's poetic growth as they paralleled the stages of the psychic evolution of the *libido*, or life energy. He discussed briefly Shelley's early life, emphasizing the poet's attempts to deal with the practical world, such as his interest in social reforms. *Alastor*, Shelley's first significant poem, appeared at a time when these attempts had failed. To Taylor, this was a critical moment in Shelley's career, for there was a danger that the libido, thwarted in its everyday existence, would cut itself off from reality and turn back upon itself in a futile introversion. Fortunately, Shelley found in his art a satisfactory form of expression, and was thus saved from a neurosis.[109]

The bulk of Taylor's essay was devoted to an analysis of Shelley's poems, which he divided into two types: those evidencing the "quest motif" and those which he called "dramas of emancipation." The first type was best exemplified by *Alastor*, which was given lengthy consideration. In the course of examining the poem's images, Taylor offered an interesting statement of one principle of psychological interpretation. Poets, he wrote, used both universal and purely personal symbols; the latter resulted "from a repressed wish or former disquieting experience struggling to relieve itself by expression. The symbols are discovered by their recurrence; if there is any constancy in the scenes with which Shelley surrounds his lovers . . . or if there is any set form in describing a woman herself, it is from these similarities that we may derive the erotic symbols themselves. Then, when they are repeated in a poem that is not overtly erotic we shall be able to recognize more exactly the poet's emotion as he composed the passage in question."[110]

Taylor found several of these erotic symbols in Shelley's poems, particularly in *Alastor*: the cave setting near a running stream, the boat propelled by the wind, and the image of the meteor. The ambiguity in *Alastor*—the discrepancy between what is stated in the Preface and what actually happens in the poem itself—

108. Eugene C. Taylor, "Shelley as Myth-Maker," *The Journal of Abnormal Psychology*, XIV (April-June, 1919), 64.

109. Taylor's view was that Shelley "by no means became a neurotic or a recluse. His life was healthy and normal . . ." (*ibid.*, p. 66).

110. *Ibid.*, pp. 68-69.

Taylor explained as the result of two conflicting tendencies in Shelley's mind, the "regressive" tendency to seek the absolute, and the "progressive" tendency of the libido to turn outward into the real world.[111] From his examination of two fragmentary poems composed shortly after *Alastor*, he concluded: ". . . the true purpose of the quest motif should be almost self-evident; the retrogressive libido was leading back to the golden age of childhood and to the mother, but . . . it was blocked by the incest prohibition. The Oedipus complex results."[112] He supported this thesis with biographical evidence, and cited six instances of the incest motif in Shelley's poems (particularly in the first version of "The Revolt of Islam," *Prometheus Unbound*, and "The Cenci.") The Oedipus complex here was not interpreted to mean the desire for the mother in the Freudian sense, however. It itself had symbolic significance; by using Jung's concept that the longing for the mother was "the unquenchable longing for all the deepest sources of our being, for the body of the mother, and through it for communion with infantile life in the countless forms of existence,"[113] Taylor was able to interpret the quest motif in psychoanalytic terms without doing any great violence to the surface meaning of the poems. According to Taylor, *Alastor* and other poems of this type were unsuccessful since they found their solution in death but in his later poems, particularly in *Prometheus Unbound*, Shelley achieved a higher synthesis.

In the remainder of the essay Taylor analyzed *Prometheus Unbound* in detail. Up to this point, his use of psychology had been fairly temperate. His interpretation of the images in "Episychidion" and "The Revolt of Islam" in terms of Jungian archetypes, however, became increasingly vague and generalized. One may discern elements of this vaporish quality in Shelley's poetry, but Taylor's interpretations were at times so expansive as to be barely meaningful. If the Jungian, rather than the Freudian, approach to Shelley's poems is more successful, it is primarily because the high level of abstract allegory in the poems lends itself to this type of treatment. This is particularly true of *Prometheus Unbound*; Taylor's interpretation of this poem is interesting, and hardly less believable than the attempts made by other critics to resolve the allegory into a rational scheme.

111. *Ibid.*, p. 72.   112. *Ibid.*, p. 73.   113. *Ibid.*, p. 74.

In summary, Taylor's analysis suggested that Jupiter represents the incest barrier, "the sum of all obstacles that block the libido in its circuitous course, first away from and then back to the mother and eternal happiness."[114] Asia is the mother surrogate with whom Prometheus is eventually united. The death of hatred in Prometheus' mind is the beginning of Jupiter's downfall: "Through self-sacrifice, the hero has successfully sublimated his desires; the incest barrier is no longer a terror; and hence is no longer hated. Disregarded it must necessarily cease to exist."[115] Demogorgon, residing in the underworld of the unconscious, represents the "repressed portion of the libido."[116] Asia, the "forward-striving libido of Prometheus," must establish communication with the "pent-up, incestuous, and retrogressive libido" of the unconscious;[117] this is accomplished in her descent into Demogorgon's cave. She is apotheosized and ascends triumphant. The result is Jupiter's fall, "for when the subconscious has been revealed and the retrogressive libido given progressive expression, the incest barrier must necessarily cease to exist." Demogorgon disappears with Jupiter since "there is no repressed libido in the perfect state which has been achieved in the universe."[118]

Taylor's interpretation of *Prometheus Unbound* in terms of an unconscious symbolic expression of a universal conflict in the mind of man is intriguing. Its acceptance, even provisionally, depends, of course, on an acceptance of the Jungian postulates of the nature of myth on which it is based. Like Jung's own writing, Taylor's suffers from an over-generalization and a tendency to expand into the "circumambient gas"; but perhaps for this reason the Jungian approach would seem to be a relatively successful method with which to examine Shelley's poetry. However the essay may be judged by students of Shelley, it remains one of the finest early Jungian studies of poetry.

There was less psychoanalytic criticism of the novel during this time than of poetry or of the drama. Two general essays approached fiction from the standpoint of the audience rather than the author with interesting results. Nelson A. Crawford's "Lit-

114. *Ibid.*, p. 81.   115. *Ibid.*   116. *Ibid.*, p. 86.   117. *Ibid.*, p. 87.
118. *Ibid.*, p. 88. It should be kept in mind that the skeleton of the interpretation, without including the evidence Taylor offered, tends to make it much less plausible than it is in the essay itself; see pp. 81-89.

erature and the Psychopathic" compared popular fiction with primitive legends. Both forms of literature, Crawford found, fulfilled the needs of the members of a particular culture, although modern fiction lacked the dignity of the primitive tale.[119] Both embodied a belief in magic, which appeared in popular fiction as sentimentality, the "mistaking of ideal connections for real ones."[120] Both forms of literature retained intact the cultural taboos of the society which produced them. To Crawford, the modern popular novel was unhealthy, its popularity being due to the neurotic character of its readers: "The public that seeks popular literature because it emphasizes the importance of the common taboos and because it makes use of magic shows one of the dominant traits of the typical psychopathic patient."[121] Like the neurotic, the reader of popular novels did not really want to rid himself of his neurosis. The cultural taboos embodied in this fiction were for him necessary; his objection to a realistic portrayal of sexuality in fiction was made "principally on the basis of an actual desire to keep sexual psychopathies intact, or to keep the general scheme of repression, which inevitably involves psychopathic conditions, intact . . . ."

Genuine art, in contrast, was a healthy form of sublimation, a "more conscious seeking for the same understanding that the common man instinctively seeks."[122] True art, Crawford maintained, represented the reality principle, whereas popular art was merely an escape fantasy. The former should be recommended to a patient as part of his cure; the latter should be abolished.

Floyd Dell, in an essay on the use of psychoanalytic material in contemporary fiction, focused on modern society's rejection of the artist. In his analysis, Dell used both the psychoanalytic and the Marxist approaches to literature, a combination which was relatively rare. Analyzing the "decadent" works of the late nineteenth century, which he considered "raw . . . fairly unassimilable fantasy creations,"[123] Dell saw their production as being a consequence of the advent of modern commercialism, a stage in

119. Nelson A. Crawford, "Literature and the Psychopathic," *The Psychoanalytic Review*, X (October, 1923), 441.

120. *Ibid.*, p. 443.   121. *Ibid.*, p. 445.   122. *Ibid.*

123. Floyd Dell, "Psychoanalysis and Recent Fiction," *Psyche and Eros*, I (July, 1920), 39.

the evolution of capitalism in which the artist loses his traditional function. Defining that function, he wrote: "Now art is not free dreaming, but a compromise effected between the individual need of fantasy-production and the social gratification of finding these fantasy-productions understood and shared by others. When the artist loses his popular audience he loses at the same time one of the factors of artistic creativity."[124]

With the loss of his audience, the artist's works tended to become more "raw"—that is, more childish and full of the " 'polymorph-perverse' tendencies of infancy." The public, reacting with shock to these fantasies, recoiled further from the artist, thereby increasing his alienation. In the present age, however, Dell suggested hopefully, because capitalism was beginning to solve some of its problems, society was becoming more tolerant of criticism; consequently, the artist's social function was being restored. Because the novel was the best potential vehicle for social criticism, he argued, it was the most significant art form of modern times.

One new aspect of human experience treated by contemporary novelists was the unconscious. Examining the writings of D. H. Lawrence, Sherwood Anderson, and other lesser writers, Dell concluded that their attempts to explore this area had not yet been successful, partly because these writers had tended to "forsake the role of analyst for that of patient."[125] In the future, he predicted, a knowledge of psychology would be as much a part of the writer's training as the study of anatomy was to the painter. In any event, the artist was once more beginning to fulfill his social function, which consisted in "elucidating and justifying the discontent of the common man" with a society which stifled his creative instincts. "The artist," Dell concluded, "is the psychoanalyst of human society. [It is] his task to liberate the very impulses which society so much fears from their age-old repressions . . . ."[126]

The application of the new psychology to specific works of fiction was scant, although Freud himself had set an excellent precedent in his study of Wilhelm Jensen's *Gradiva*, an analysis which is still a model example of psychoanalytic criticism.[127] Leo Kaplan produced a shallow examination of *The Picture of Dorian*

124. *Ibid.*, p. 42.   125. *Ibid.*, p. 44.   126. *Ibid.*, p. 49.
127. For a brief summary of *Delusion and Dream in Jensen's "Gradiva,"* see Appendix B.

Gray in terms of Wilde's narcism,[128] and Jackson Towne wrote a predictable analysis of Turgenev's *Fathers and Sons* in terms of the Oedipus complex of the central character, Bazaroff.[129] The use of the dream in fiction was noted by Albert K. Weinberg, who gave an interesting Freudian exegesis of a dream in *Jean Christophe*, but unfortunately did not relate his findings to the novel as a whole.[130] Gregory Stragnell analyzed at greater length the use of dreams in Russian fiction, examining various dreams in the novels of Dostoevsky, Gogol, and Turgenev as evidence that Russian authors intuitively understood more about the workings of the dream than other writers. To explain this, Stragnell postulated that the greater political censorship in Russia had accustomed these novelists to working in symbolic language in order to avoid political reprisals. As a result, "their constant conscious use of symbolic writing familiarized them with the symbol when they encountered it in their own unconscious dream material."[131] The interest of Stragnell's article lies mainly in his citations of dreams and his reproduction of the author's own interpretations, for in several instances, particularly in the case of Dostoevsky, these Russian writers clearly anticipated some of Freud's hypotheses.

The only really successful psychoanalytic analysis of fiction during this period was Alfred Booth Kuttner's study of Lawrence's *Sons and Lovers*. "It sometimes happens," Kuttner wrote, "that a piece of literature acquires an added significance by virtue of the support it gives to the scientific study of human motives."[132] Such works were of particular value to the psychologist, "for a new truth about ourselves, which may seem altogether grotesque and impossible when presented as an arid theory, often gains unexpected confirmation when presented to us in a beautiful work

128. Leo Kaplan, "Analysis of *The Picture of Dorian Gray*," *Psyche and Eros*, III (January, 1922), 8-21.

129. Jackson E. Towne, "Skepticism as a Freudian 'Defense-Reaction': A Psychoanalysis of Bazaroff, the Hero of Turgenev's *Fathers and Sons*," *The Psychoanalytic Review*, VII (April, 1920), 159-62.

130. Albert K. Weinberg, "The Dream in *Jean Christophe*," *The Journal of Abnormal Psychology*, XIII (April, 1918), 12-16.

131. Gregory Stragnell, "The Dream in Russian Literature," *The Psychoanalytic Review*, VIII (July, 1921), 247.

132. Alfred Booth Kuttner, "*Sons and Lovers*: A Freudian Interpretation," *The Psychoanalytic Review*, III (July, 1916), 295.

of literature as an authentic piece of life."[133] In approaching the novel in this way as a confirmation of psychoanalytic theory, Kuttner was following Freud's lead in his study of *Gradiva*. His essay was therefore directed primarily to the psychologist, although his sensitivity to literature as art prevented him from reducing the work to a mere psychological object lesson.

To Kuttner, Lawrence's study of the love life of Paul, the hero of *Sons and Lovers*, put into high relief a constant relationship between parent and child and gave it added significance. "The [readers'] instinctive recognition of their kinship with the hero of the book would go a great way towards explaining the potency of *Sons and Lovers*."[134] The fundamental theme of the novel was, of course, the Oedipal conflict, which Paul was unable to resolve because of two factors: his inability to identify with a father he could not admire, and his mother's excessive love for him as a replacement for her husband. Unable to move beyond childhood emotionally, Paul was ultimately drained of his will to live, and at the novel's end, was doomed to a continual restless wandering.[135] Relating this Oedipal theme to Lawrence's other works, where it also occurs, Kuttner concluded that Lawrence himself, unlike Paul, had through his art achieved a way out of the tragic impasse: "Out of the dark struggles of his own soul he has emerged as a triumphant artist. In every epoch the soul of the artist is sick with the problems of his generation. He cures himself by expression in his art. And by producing a catharsis in the spectator through the enjoyment of his art, he also heals his fellow beings. His artistic stature is measured by the universality of the problem which his art has transfigured."[136]

Like the biographical studies of Charlotte Brontë and August Strindberg, the success of Kuttner's essay seems largely due to the ease with which the subject matter lends itself to such an approach. D. H. Lawrence himself denied that he had any knowledge of Freud at the time of writing *Sons and Lovers*; if this is true, the novel is remarkable for the "confirmation" it gave to Freud's central hypothesis. Since its publication, *Sons and Lovers* has be-

133. *Ibid.*, pp. 295-96.   134. *Ibid.*, p. 307.
135. Kuttner's interpretation of the book's conclusion as wholly tragic is debatable.
136. Kuttner, "Sons and Lovers," p. 317.

come the classic instance in modern literature of the exploration of the Oedipal theme; Kuttner's analysis is therefore one of the few instances where the critical application of psychoanalytic concepts did not violate the surface meaning of the narrative.

With one or two exceptions, the early efforts at practical psychoanalytic criticism left much to be desired. The major fault of the Freudian studies was their reductiveness, their tendency to equate "meaning" or significance in literature with two or three unconscious themes. Too little respect was paid to the formal characteristics of the work or to the artist's conscious intention, insofar as that can be determined within the work itself. The monotony of the findings of the psychological analysts make their validity suspect; at the very least, it creates a thirst for a critical approach which treats the differences between literary works as well as their "universal" similarities. The Jungian critiques also manifested this reductiveness, although the primary symbols and themes uncovered by their approach were more metaphysical than physiological. In their enthusiasm and their relatively unqualified conviction that the new science could at last reveal the "truth" of literary art, early psychological critics suffered from the syndrome of most converts: a proselytizing zeal, a tendency towards dogmatism, a lack of objectivity, and a habit of taking themselves much too seriously.

All of these characteristics appeared in this early criticism at its worst; at its best, when the critic possessed the two prerequisites of critical intelligence and artistic sensitivity, and undertook to analyze either a literary work or figure having marked neurotic qualities or one who was more or less consciously exploring unconscious material, the resulting study produced illuminating glimpses into the artist's personality and added another dimension of appreciation to the art work itself. Although much early psychoanalytic criticism lacks permanent value, its widespread use reflects the eagerness with which the new psychology was adopted, partly in an attempt to put the discipline of criticism on a more scientific basis, and partly, perhaps, to borrow some of the glamour which surrounded the practice of psychoanalysis. The literary studies appearing in the professional psychology journals, with some exceptions, exhibited too little awareness of literature as art for their conclusions to be acceptable. Although many psychologists speculated about various authors and their works, the best psychoanalytic literary criticism in this period was done not by the psychoanalysts but by men of letters who had familiarized themselves, in varying degrees, with psychoanalytic theory and who could bring to criticism not only aesthetic sensitivity and respect for form but the added dimension of a new insight into content.

4. The Criticism of Conrad Aiken

Conrad Aiken's *Skepticisms*, a collection of essays that had previously appeared in such journals as *The Dial, The New Republic*, and *The North American Review*, was published in 1919.[1] As a poet, short story writer, novelist, and critic, Aiken's writings were strongly influenced by Freud's thought; although his critical approach was too eclectic to classify him technically as a "psychoanalytic critic," his application of depth psychology to criticism was a major pioneer effort to incorporate into literary theory the concepts of the new science.

Aiken was first introduced to Freud's ideas while at Harvard, from which he graduated in 1911. Because he lacked a knowledge of German, he was unable to read Freud in the original, but he read *The Interpretation of Dreams* in Brill's translation in 1915. According to one biographer, Jay Martin, "it is impossible to measure his indebtedness to Freud accurately. He read not only Freud, but also Adler, Pfister, Ferenczi, Rank and Wittels. And while he recognized Freud as the greatest of these, he soaked himself in his 'co-workers and rivals and followers,' who, he believed, 'were making the most important contribution of the century to

1. Conrad Aiken, *Skepticisms* (New York: Alfred A. Knopf, 1919). The essays were largely extended book reviews, which accounts for their brevity and for their emphasis on critical evaluation. Although my discussion of Aiken involves this work primarily, several of his later essays— those written between 1919 and 1926—are also included. These are reprinted in *A Reviewer's ABC* (New York: Meridian Books, 1958).

the understanding of man and his consciousness.' "[2] Throughout his life he maintained close friendships with several psychoanalysts; as Frederick J. Hoffman has commented, Aiken "grew up with and even *in* the psychoanalytic movement."[3] He was not, however, a doctrinaire Freudian, for he maintained a degree of skepticism towards certain aspects of Freudian thought as early as 1920. Henry A. Murray, a psychoanalyst and friend of Aiken's, has suggested that Aiken "allowed the Freudian dragon to swallow him, and then, after a sufficient sojourn in its maw, cut his way out to a new freedom. When he emerged he was stocked with the lore of psychoanalysis, but neither subjugated nor impeded by it . . . ."[4]

Aiken's application of Freudian concepts to literary criticism differs in several respects from that of most of his contemporaries. Believing that the central task of the literary critic was evaluation, he was intensely concerned with finding objective criteria for judgment to replace the subjective assessments which he felt had always been the curse of literary criticism. Science, he argued repeatedly, and particularly a science of the mind, was the only discipline which could provide such objective criteria, and it was primarily for this reason that Aiken was attracted to the new psychological theory of the creative process. Unlike many of the early psychoanalytic critics, Aiken never argued for a specifically psychoanalytic approach to literature, but borrowed from Freud's system of psychology only such ideas as seemed to him relevant to the critic's basic function—that of evaluation. Although he applied his knowledge of psychology primarily in the area of literary theory, on occasion he also used various Freudian concepts in his critical practice; here, too, however, they were utilized as a tool for evaluation rather than as a device for unravelling the unconscious meaning of a specific work or as a biographical technique.

Paradoxically, the very problem Aiken sought to solve by means of the science of psychology was made more acute by his awareness of Freud's theories. Temperamentally, Aiken seems to have

2. Jay Martin, *Conrad Aiken: A Life of His Art* (Princeton: Princeton University Press, 1962), p. 26.
3. *Freudianism and the Literary Mind* (Baton Rouge: Louisiana State University Press, 1957), p. 275.
4. Quoted by Frederick J. Hoffman in *Conrad Aiken* (New York: Twayne Publishers, Inc., 1962), p. 26.

been a skeptic and a materialist. Throughout his critical writings he opposed two of the tendencies he found in literary criticism: the tendency toward "impressionism," or the passing of aesthetic value judgments based only on the critic's own personal taste; and the tendency to define value in art in terms of an aesthetic or metaphysical absolute which was not scientifically demonstrable. Aiken turned to psychology—and particularly to Freudian psychology—as a corrective to both of these tendencies, in the hope that it could furnish the critic with an unimpeachable base for making critical evaluations. Unfortunately, the Freudian view of man as a being largely determined by unconscious needs and desires tended only to strengthen his original conviction of the inevitability of critical relativism: if art was merely a day-dream which satisfied the unconscious wishes of both artist and audience, the critic could not trust his own critical pronouncements to be anything more than an elaborately rationalized defense of his own unconscious needs. Each critic's opinions, therefore, would seem to possess as much (or as little) validity as any other's. Aiken's confrontation of this dilemma and the manner in which he confronted it are of great interest, for they present in its most acute form the problem faced by early literary theorists who felt it necessary to absorb and utilize the insights of the new psychology. Aiken's wide knowledge of psychology and his application of its principles in both his critical theory and critical practice make him almost unique among literary critics of his time. His critical writings can bear rereading today both for themselves and for the light they throw on the phenomenon of the absorption into literary criticism of the ideas of an alien discipline.

Aiken's title, "Skepticisms," reflects one of his central critical concerns—the inevitability of critical relativism. This belief is clearly stated in the prefatory essay, "Apologia Pro Specie Sua," the dominant theme of which is that personal bias is unavoidable, particularly in the case of a poet-critic. A critic of poetry who was at the same time a writer of poetry, Aiken argued, tended to favor either poems similar to his own or poems so different that they would not be perceived as competing with his own. If the imagist critic, for example, should approve of narrative or philosophic poetry, it would undermine his own theory of what poetry should be, and, by consequence, force him into the position of rejecting his own poems. A poet's criticism, therefore, even when written with the best of conscious intentions to be objective, of necessity involved a self-portrait. Eventually, Aiken suggested, this impasse might be resolved by science. Since the only true test of greatness in literature was the "test of time," the tastes of succeeding generations might reflect some permanent quality in the mind of man which psychology could some day define with precision: "If in the long run humanity prefers this or that sort of art, it should be possible to find the reasons for this, to say eventually just what chords of human vanity are thereby exquisitely and cajolingly played upon."[5] For the time being, however, the critic could do little more than warn his readers of the inescapable subjective element in his criticism.

Aiken's strong feeling that criticism could be rescued from its lack of objective standards only by science is reflected in his choice of the article, "The Mechanism of Poetic Inspiration," to begin his book. This essay, which originally appeared in *The North American Review* in 1917, was a review of Nicholas Kostyleff's *Le Mécanisme Cérébrale de la Pensée*, a work which had a notable influence on Aiken's thought. Aiken's initial remarks expressed his discouragement with the state of contemporary American literary criticism, which was still a "rather primitive parade of likes and dislikes . . . [with] little inquiry into psychological causes."[6] Although most critics, he wrote, were familiar with Freud's theory that poetry, like the dream, was a "release of complexes," this theory was not entirely satisfactory. Kostyleff, who felt that Freud's concept of the poetic process was insufficient to explain the phenomenon of poetic inspiration because it applied primarily to only one kind of poetry, "romantic" poetry, had concluded that in the last analysis poetry was a "purely cerebral affair and that it was not the result of a discharge or excess of emotion in the poet so much as a cerebral reaction to internal stimuli."[7] In his view, the poetic process involved the release of a series of verbal discharges which proceeded in associated chains which, stored in the unconscious and apparently forgotten, were self-generating once they had been set in motion by a stimulus. This

5. *Skepticisms*, p. 20.   6. *Ibid.*, p. 33.   7. *Ibid.*, p. 35.

theory seemed to account for the fact that the emotional content of the poetic product usually exceeded the stimulus from which the poem originated.

According to Kostyleff, poetic inspiration had two sources: the poet's sensibility and the "preformed mechanisms of verbal reactions,"[8] i.e., the individual's stored impressions and his unique verbal responses. Poor poets were those who lacked a "personal mechanism of verbal reactions," which was formed during childhood. Though he largely accepted this explanation, Aiken thought this concept of a "personal quality" was too vague. Imitative poets, he argued, had as large a fund of "associated chains" of verbal responses as did great poets; the difference therefore must lie in their different sensibilities, in the fact that the great poet possessed an individual, peculiar sensibility which enabled him to "extend the field of our consciousness in a new direction."[9]

Aiken also believed Kostyleff's system was biased toward a verbal, cerebral type of poetry and tended to ignore narrative or philosophic poetry in which the ideational content played a large role. Moreover, although he admitted that Kostyleff's theory might aid our comprehension of one mechanical aspect of poetic creation, he pointed out that it had not been reconciled with Freud's conception of the part the unconscious played in creativity. "We are shown parts of the machine," Aiken complained, "but not the machine in motion. What, after all, is the compelling power at the bottom of poetic creation?"[10] His answer was that the poet's reaction to stimuli was a selective process, determined by some affective principle of vital concern to the poet. This "selective principle" had a specific origin, seemed universally present in all poets, and arose in accordance with some definite need: "This . . . brings us back to the theory of Freud. It is to some deep hunger, whether erotic or not . . . that we must look for the source of the power that sets in motion the delicate mechanism . . . which Mr. Kostyleff has begun to illuminate for us. It is clear that this is not merely a sexual hunger . . . . Is it merely in general the hunger of the frustrate (which we all are) for richer experience?"[11]

Aiken found Kostyleff's theories useful as a supplement to the

8. *Ibid.*, p. 39.   9. *Ibid.*, p. 44.
10. *Ibid.*, p. 45.   11. *Ibid.*, pp. 46-47.

insights of Freudian psychology, and he applied these ideas on several occasions in his practical criticism. In "Confectionary and Caviar," in which he reviewed the work of several contemporary poets, Aiken used Kostyleff's theory to define imitativeness in poetry. The difference between the secondary and the original poet was that "in [the] former instance [the] verbo-motor mechanism is not deeply related to the poet's specific sensibility; in the latter it is."[12] In other words, the imitative poet responded to a poetic stimulus with a chain of merely literary associations or "stock responses" which were not a product of his immediate experience, whereas the responses of the genuine poet arose from personal experiences which had been absorbed into his unconscious.

Aiken used Kostyleff's ideas most extensively in his study of John Gould Fletcher. Kostyleff had theorized that part of the poet's peculiar sensibility was his "wealth of verbal reflexes"; the greater this wealth, the greater the poet. When actually applied to individual poets, Aiken wrote, some aspects of this theory were more illuminating than others; in some poets one factor was more important, in others, another. In Fletcher's case, "the striking feature has always been his habit of surrendering himself, almost completely to the power of these automatically, unravelling verbal reflexes."[13] A poem written by someone like Fletcher would be most successful when the stimulus was "of a nature to leave him greatest freedom," that is, when it was most generalized and not consciously restricted, since "any sort of conceptual framework prepared in advance with regard either to subject or form would be perpetually bringing him back to a more severely conscious plane of effort . . . ."[14] Early in Fletcher's career, when "impressions [came] up shining from their long burial in the subconscious," he was at his best, but when later he learned the trick of "not merely allowing, but precisely inviting, his subconscious to take possession of him,"[15] his poems were weakened. Throughout *Skepticisms*, Aiken maintained that great poetry emanates ultimately from the subconscious, but that a conscious exploitation of this subconscious material defeats the poetic process.[16]

12. *Ibid.*, p. 181.   13. *Ibid.*, p. 108.   14. *Ibid.*, p. 109.
15. *Ibid.*, p. 110.
16. The idea is first introduced to explain why Fletcher was more suc-

The idea that the power of poetry results from its unconscious derivation finds its fullest expression in the essay, "Magic or Legerdemain?" The term "magic" is one Aiken had used in an earlier article on D. H. Lawrence, in which he had tried to explain the function of melody and rhythm in poetry. The test of poetry, he had stated, was whether or not a poem possessed a "magic" quality, which was somehow related to a "conspicuous increase in the persuasiveness of rhythm."[17] He cited several poems possessing this characteristic which served as touchstones, but could explain them only by suggesting that they were "precious fragments cherished by the jackdaw of the unconscious."[18] In "Magic or Legerdemain?" Aiken developed the concept that "when the subconscious speaks, the subconscious answers,"[19] and attempted to settle the vexed question of the roles played by the conscious and by the unconscious in poetic creation.

Although the unconscious was responsible for a large part of the poetic process, it was only the finished product that the critic could submit to analysis.[20] The process itself, therefore, could be analyzed only after the fact. Speaking largely from his own creative experience, Aiken pointed out that "it is usually during a poet's best moments that his medium is least consciously under his control."[21] Poets who denied the "efficacy of the subconscious" were generally those who lacked "magic." Moments of poetic inspiration were not merely moments of a heightening of ordinary consciousness, but moments of a sort of "dual consciousness," during which there was greater freedom of communication between the conscious and unconscious portions of the mind. "During this state of dual consciousness," Aiken wrote, "there is a sense in which it is true that the poet has his subconscious under control."[22] This sense, however, was "peculiar," in that the poet was "aware of more than he precisely sees." His decisions concerning which words to choose, for example, were

---

cessful in short poems rather than in long ones. Although he admired the "Symphonies," Aiken could not ultimately consider Fletcher's poetry great, since it lacked both thought and deep feeling. It was vague word-music, successful when allowed to proceed in an unconscious flow, unsuccessful when repeated or forced, as it was in Fletcher's later and more ambitious productions.

17. *Skepticisms*, p. 95.   18. *Ibid.*, p. 97.   19. *Ibid.*
20. *Ibid.*, p. 273.   21. *Ibid.*, p. 274.   22. *Ibid.*, p. 275.

conscious, but the logical train by which he arrived at such a decision was largely unconscious: "The poet . . . no matter how much he may call upon the subconscious and deliver himself over to it, is at all times pretty much aware of what he is doing, and why . . . . It is with this fact in mind that some poets belittle the value of the subconscious . . . . The things in the poem which have greatest magic and beauty are usually not the product of skill, merely, but the skillful use of a wealth for the most part subterranean . . . a wealth in the deposit of which they have played as little conscious part as the surface of the earth plays in the crystallization of diamonds."[23]

Not all men, of course, could become great poets merely by "letting themselves go" to their unconscious. The genuine poet not only had a rich sensibility, but possessed the gift of craftsmanship, the "skill with which the poet turns his subconscious treasure to account." Poetry that was pure craft, lacking an unconscious source, aroused merely cool admiration, not the "full emotional surrender, the uncontrolled surrender of one's own aroused subconscious. When craftsmanship induces that surrender it proves itself to be more than craftsmanship."[24]

Several major critical tenets of Aiken's are articulated here. One is a variation on Henry James's dictum that the quality of a work of art always reflects the quality of the mind of its creator— the "subconscious mind," Aiken might add. Another is his belief that both craft and content, technique and idea, operated together to produce a successful poem. The reader's "uncontrolled surrender of his aroused subconscious" was apparently the criterion for judging whether or not a poem possessed "magic," a term left undefined and loosely equated with the heightened emotional responses of the reader of the poem. It should be noted, however, that despite this emphasis on emotional response, Aiken was highly critical of poetry lacking in ideas; his criticism at times seemed to be groping towards the criterion later enunciated by T. S. Eliot in his discussion of metaphysical poetry—that of "felt thought" or the emotional experience of an idea. Aiken was also quite capable of rejecting poetry for weaknesses of form. In his essay on Edgar Lee Masters, he concluded that Masters' poems

23. *Ibid.*, p. 279.   24. *Ibid.*, pp. 279-80.

ultimately lacked "art," and for this reason did not bear rereading: ". . . one derives pleasure in rereading a poem in proportion to its perfection—and perhaps even more important, its elaborateness—as a work of art," the "perfection" or "elaborateness" being the result of a combination of "fecundity and freshness of ideas and sensations" and "beauty, ease, and intricacy of form."[25]

Aiken criticized in his reviews excesses of both form and content, the former in his essay on Ezra Pound, and the latter in "Disintegration in Modern Poetry," a criticism of the poems of D. H. Lawrence. In this essay, Aiken utilized another concept of Freudian psychology to establish a further criterion for good poetry, the criterion of a balance between the "pleasure principle" and the "reality principle." Discussing Alan Seeger, he wrote: "If Freud's theory of the artist is correct—that the artist is one in whom the pleasure principle of childhood never gives way to the reality principle of maturity—then we have a particularly typical artist, in this sense, in Alan Seeger."[26] Poor poetry, particularly sentimental poetry, was the result of the pleasure principle unmodified by the reality principle and represented merely a childish wish-fulfillment. In contrast, artists such as Shakespeare, Euripides, and Turgenev "developed the pleasure principle and the reality principle side by side, achieving the perfect balance which we call greatness."[27] Although Aiken did not stress this concept or develop it at any length, it is an important one. By defining "good" poetry as poetry in which the pleasure principle was modified by the "reality principle," Aiken has suggested one answer to the criticism of the psychological approach to literature made by such people as Clive Bell when they complained that art which was "pure wish-fulfillment" was not genuine art.[28]

These criteria for judging poetry—of "magic" or "the balance between the reality and pleasure principles" (both of which were basically psychological criteria)—were not completely satisfactory to Aiken himself. His continual preoccupation with the problem of placing critical evaluation on a scientific basis, and his irritation at criticism which failed to do this, can be seen in several of his essays. Already noted is his review of *The Poetic Mind*, in which

25. *ABC*, p. 300.
26. *Skepticisms*, p. 133.
27. *Ibid.*, p. 134.
28. See above, pp. 78-79.

he took issue with Prescott for masking a romantic or mystical approach in scientific terms; on the same ground he criticized Benedetto Croce for claiming that his "metaphysical" view of poetry and art was a scientific one.[29] He also attacked the anthologist, William Stanley Braithwaite, for dissolving into an "O altitudo!" in the presence of any poem he liked: "Shall we never learn that there is nothing mysterious or supernatural about poetry; that it is a natural, organic product, with discoverable functions, clearly open to analysis? It would be a pity if our critics and poets were to leave this to the scientists instead of doing it themselves."[30]

Aiken's ambivalent response to I. A. Richards' *The Principles of Literary Criticism*, a book in which an attempt was made to ground criticism in science, is representative of this impatience with contemporary critics. He was basically in agreement with Richards' effort, at least until Richards betrayed his premises by "surreptitiously" readmitting the absolute into his concept of value. According to Aiken, Richards had retreated from his "social-psychological view of art" to avoid the implication that value was simply an equation between artist and audience. It was an unwarranted assumption of Richards', Aiken argued, that some art works were inherently superior to others, and that people who responded to "great" art did so because they had a more "finely organized mind." All that the critic could do, in Aiken's view, was to admit that there were different kinds of art which appealed to different audiences, study them according to the laws of their genre, and classify them "in terms of the simple-to-complex." To Richards' suggestion that the artist's mind was "better organized" than the average, Aiken replied that the opposite might be true. It was possible that the artist was one "whose mind was *less* efficiently organized for a life of 'action' than the average, and that his art was the process, analogous to the daydream, by which he seeks to maintain his balance. To those whose psychosis corresponds closely to his own, his work will be 'good'—it becomes their successful daydream."[31]

It seems apparent here that Aiken's adoption of the Freudian view of art as a "daydream" which fulfilled the unconscious desires of the audience tended to strengthen his belief in critical rela-

29. *ABC*, pp. 71-75.   30. *Skepticisms*, p. 132.

tivism. That Aiken was willing to carry this position to its extreme can be seen in his essay, "A Basis for Criticism," which appeared in *The New Republic* in 1923. This is Aiken's longest single critical essay and contains the heart of his critical beliefs. Essentially the article was an attack on current "aesthetic" criticism: "We can not . . . look very long or very hard at criticism," he began, "without noting that its most striking characteristic is its vagueness."[32] Aesthetic criticism, although it had some merits, had been largely an exercise in the "intense inane."[33] The problem was that the aestheticians refused to define beauty in any meaningful sense, shrinking from an attempt at a psychological definition. To them, the only admissible type of analysis of a work of art was the analysis of the document itself, "not of the mind and body which produced the document in response to pressure."[34] Moreover, the aestheticians insisted that beauty had nothing to do with the content of the art work but was a result of the "arrangement of the stimuli"—that is, of form. The implication of this position, Aiken maintained, was that the emotional appeal of the content was a "spurious sort of thing which interferes equally with the aesthetic operations of creator and critic" and should be, ideally, purged from the critical process.

Opposing this, Aiken argued that the value of art lay in the fact that the aesthetic stimuli were "keys to associations," and that the feeling or response which is called "beauty" resulted when the art work successfully played on the audience's associations. This explanation, however, was still unsatisfactory, for why this "absurd serious tickling of the soul" was felt to be so important to human beings was still left in question. Art must have a larger function than this; if this were true, the central question to which the critic should address himself was: "What, in the life of civilized man, is the function of art—social, biological, psychological?" It was essential that he arrive at an answer to this question, for

31. *ABC*, p. 77. With these exceptions, Aiken approved of Richards' study.

32. *Ibid.*, p. 54.

33. In using the term "aesthetic criticism," Aiken probably had in mind the essays of such impressionistic critics as Joel E. Spingarn and James Huneker, as well as Benedetto Croce; possibly also the term included such critics as Clive Bell, whom I have referred to as "formalists."

34. *ABC*, p. 56.

if art had a function, it should then be judged only in accordance with how it fulfilled that function.[35] A satisfactory definition of beauty—one that would explain its value to mankind—would have to be not metaphysical but psychological:

Let us rashly posit that the pleasurable feeling we know as "beauty" is simply, in essence, the profound satisfaction we feel when, through the medium of fantasy, we escape from imposed limitations into an aggrandized personality and a harmonized universe. This kind of satisfaction not only can be said to give rise to the feeling "beauty"— it *is* beauty . . . . It has been urged that in the daydream, or art, we do not really seek to escape from ourselves, but, precisely, to find ourselves. But what part of ourselves is it that we find? Is it not exactly that part of us which has been wounded and would be made whole; that part of us which desires wings and has none, longs for immortality and knows that it must die . . . ?[36]

In this sense, then, the main function of art was therapeutic; furthermore, this fact had been recognized in some fashion since Aristotle. "The difference between catharsis and wish-fulfillment," Aiken wrote, "is slight to the point of disappearance."[37]

Returning to the question of the relation between form and content, Aiken pursued his quarrel with the aestheticians who wanted an art "pure," free of emotional and moral "accidents." On the contrary, he argued, art not only was but must be rich in these "emotional accidents," and, perhaps, the richer the better. Criticism should of course deal with the question of form, but it must also concern itself "profoundly" with the question of material. The whole problem of form and content in art was resolved by Aiken in an interesting way. Both content *and* form, he maintained, were a product of wish-fulfillment:

For if the material of a work of art is cunningly chosen so as to give us a sense of escape, of freedom for unlimited power and experience, may we not then go further and say that a quite parallel pleasure is afforded us by the *form* of the work of art, which is cunningly chosen so as to give us the feeling of unlimited power of *expression?* If that is true . . . we can perceive at once how natural it will be for the professional artist or critic to overestimate arrangement of form or style, simply because of his own perhaps psychotic desire for skill of that kind. He is, in fact, a special case. And a sufficient degree of skill in a work of art will give him the same sort of illusion of tran-

35. *Ibid.*, p. 60.   36. *Ibid.*, pp. 61-62.   37. *Ibid.*, p. 62.

scendency that, to the layman, whose desire is for experience rather than for expression, is given rather by the narrative in which the skill is employed.[38]

In this statement, Aiken's critical relativism was carried to its logical extreme, for it was implied here that the critic, being a *special case*, was in a sense not equipped by nature to judge art. The critic's interest in form was, according to Aiken, "perhaps psychotic." The sophisticated pronouncements of the literary critic would seem, then, to have less validity than the more "normal" responses of the layman. As a critical position, this is obviously untenable; it implies that critics, as a breed, are actually worse judges of art than non-critics.

The remainder of the essay suggests that this is what Aiken had in mind. The critic, he stated, could not "with a sneer, dismiss the tastes of the vulgar," for these tastes gave us the "factor of wish-fulfillment" without which art could not exist.[39] What the common man and the sophisticated intellectual sought in the art work was essentially the same—the fulfillment, through fantasy, of the wish to be more or better than was possible within the confines of the human condition. The difference between the two was that in the intellectual, "credulity has been weakened by intelligence or self-awareness."[40] The intellectual's desire for escape was as strong as the serving maid's but he required a "greater wealth of documentation" to disguise his fantasy and make it acceptable. Familiarity dulled emotional response, and since what man craved was consolation in the primary emotional areas— those connected with "love, life, death, hope, faith, time, space"— these themes had been dealt with most frequently.[41] The result was that, historically, there had been an increasingly greater need on the part of the intellectual for greater subtlety of treatment in art, since unlike the common man, he could no longer respond emo-

38. *Ibid.*, p. 63. It should be noted that even in his discussion of the content of a work of art Aiken had significantly broadened Freud's concept of wishfulfillment so that art was conceived as fulfilling the desires of man to be more than his earthly form allowed him to be. Freud saw man's "wish" in more strictly material terms than this. Aiken's interpretation, however, although broader, was not in basic contradiction to Freud's view of the function of art as expressed in "The Relation of the Poet to Day-Dreaming" or in *A General Introduction to Psychoanalysis*.

39. *ABC*, p. 64.   40. *Ibid.*   41. *Ibid.*, p. 65.

tionally to a cliché. "Jaded by verbalism," the modern intellectual "finds the simple commonplace and flat, and must, in order to enjoy it, have it subtilized."[42] The important thing to Aiken, however, was that the impulse to art on the part of both the sophisticate and the man in the street was in essence the same. It followed from this that since the critic must inevitably view art through his own special "psychosis," he could never achieve his proper goal—an objective evaluation of literature.

Attempting some predictions about the future of criticism in the last part of the essay, Aiken repeated that criticism, if it were to avoid continuing in its present sterile course, must become "scientific," must "go into the laboratory."[43] In this fresh beginning which criticism must make, its only sure ground would be the biological. "The critic of tomorrow," he wrote, "will not be wholly unlike the critic of today. It will still be the critic of imagination, of delicate, emotional instability, the creature only less psychotic than the artist himself, who will be the most valuable—he needs only to place much of the existing machinery of criticism on its new basis"[44]—that is to say, on a scientific basis. Why the "critic of imagination" would still be valuable, Aiken did not explain; his last statement seems to be little more than a sop given the critic (and, perhaps, to Aiken himself) as a form of reassurance. The critic's role, according to this essay, would be to judge the work of art by the success with which it fulfilled its function of satisfying man's inner needs; but Aiken left unexplained why the critic was better equipped to judge this success than the average reader, and indeed, even suggested that he was ill-equipped.

Aiken's extension of Freud's wish-fulfillment concept to include the form of art as well as its content, thereby suggesting that the critic's interest in form was little more than the product of his own wish for a more subtilized disguise for his fantasies—a more intricate "fore-pleasure," to use Freud's term—may have been a result of his deep-seated suspicion of the critic's ability to transcend his own personal tastes and unconscious desires. The attempt to judge literary works according to a standard of psychological function turned out to be hopelessly relative, for the dime novel fulfills the fantasy-function for its readers as well as *The*

42. *Ibid.*, p. 66.   43. *Ibid.*, p. 67.   44. *Ibid.*, p. 68.

Brothers Karamazov does for those who need to have their fantasies presented in a more sophisticated fashion. Aiken stated this position quite explicitly in his 1927 novel, *Blue Voyage*, in which his protagonist, Demarest, urges:

A work of art is good if it is successful; that is, if it succeeds in giving the auditor or reader an *illusion*, however momentary; if it convinces him, and in convincing him, adds something to his experience both in range and coherence, both in command of feeling and command of expression. And here we come to the idea which is terribly disquieting to the purely *aesthetic* critic, who likes to believe that there are absolute standards of excellence in art. For if we take a functional view of art, as we must, then everything becomes relative; and the shilling shocker or smutty story, which captivates Bill the sailor, is giving him exactly the escape and aggrandizement, and therefore *beauty*, that *Hamlet* gives to you or me. The equation is the same. What right have you got, then to assume that *Hamlet* is "better" than *Deadeye Dick*? On absolute grounds, none whatever. They are intended for different audiences, and each succeeds.[45]

Aiken's awareness of this relativism (which, paradoxically, was intensified by his use of the "scientific" theories of Freud) made him anxious for science to step in and solve the problem; for without a scientific, objective standard, criticism was doomed to be a mere matter of opinion.

If Aiken's knowledge of psychoanalytic hypotheses about the function of art led him to an impasse in critical theory, his use of psychology in his critical practice produced some worthwhile studies. Previously discussed is his analysis of Keats, in which psychoanalytic theory lent support to some suggestive biographical interpretations. In several essays, he attempted to use psychoanalytic concepts as a means of assessing literary worth. In his review of D. H. Lawrence's *Birds, Beasts and Flowers*, for example, Aiken tried to distinguish between the "objective" and the "subjective" artist, saying that the former used themes which were universally significant and intelligible, whereas the latter's themes, in an extreme case, were intelligible only to himself. Put in another way, "The objective artist's psychosis corresponds at a maximum number of points with the 'average' of mankind, whereas the subjective artist's psychosis is peculiar to himself . . . . The ob-

45. *Blue Voyage* (New York: Charles Scribner's Sons, 1927), p. 215.

jective artist, in whom a sense of reality is relatively mature, is aware of and understands the psychotic needs of mankind, and endeavors to be as useful to his audience as to himself; but the subjective artist, in whom the sense of reality remains infantile, disregards and scorns his audience, and considers himself . . . the only true center of awareness."[46] In Aiken's view, what had been diagnosed as the "disintegration" of the arts in the twentieth century should be more properly viewed as a movement from the objective to the subjective. Ezra Pound and Gertrude Stein were examples of this movement, and even "The Waste Land" was "not untainted." Although neither objectivity nor subjectivity could be assigned an absolute value, subjective art was successful only if its creator was a genius possessing an exceptional talent for communication, and, most important, only if this personality were "unconscious partly or wholly of the extent to which it merely communicates *itself*."[47] To Aiken, Lawrence's writings failed in this respect; his "psychosis" remained unintelligible, an example of an unhealthy regressive movement toward infantilism.

In three essays on Katherine Mansfield, written between 1921 and 1927, Aiken repeated the doctrine, which was common to many critics using psychoanalytic ideas, that the greatness of a creative work was dependent to some extent on its being a product of its creator's unconscious. Such works possessed an "irridescence" or emotional resonance not found in literature which was merely consciously contrived. In the case of Katherine Mansfield, said Aiken, "One must emphasize the kinship with poetry, because it is clear that in Miss Mansfield's prose, when it is at its best, there are more subconscious compulsions at work, shaping and selecting and coloring, than we expect to find at the bottom of 'ordinary' prose: they lent it a shimmer and irridescence, a chromatic vividness (the vividness of the dream rather than the vividness of life) which apprise us that we are in the presence of work not so much 'calculated' as happily, and with the deepest of intensity, improvised."[48] In another essay on Miss Mansfield written six years later, Aiken was again to emphasize the dream-like quality of her writing, implying that its greatness and emotional power was a direct result of its unconscious roots: "Her stories

46. *ABC*, p. 258.   47. *Ibid.*, p. 260.   48. *Ibid.*, p. 292.

were poems; they were as characteristically the products of the unconscious as any poems ever written; they have the hallucinatory vividness and swiftness, the sensory magic and kaleidoscopic verbal brilliance, of dreams . . . . It is above all in her remarkable sensibility, and in the unconscious which it had so richly stored, that one seeks some explanation of her genius."[49]

Intensity and "hallucinatory vividness" alone did not render a work of art great, however. In an essay on Dostoevsky written in 1921, Aiken seems to have contradicted some of the critical beliefs he enunciated elsewhere. The issue he raised here was whether or not art works which were the product of a clearly diseased or morbid mind deserved to be taken seriously as art, despite their obvious emotional power. Attacking critics who had praised Dostoevsky as a profound seer, Aiken exhibited once more his irritation with a "mystical," non-scientific approach to criticism: "Critics of an academic cast," he wrote, "critics for whom literary values approximate the absolute, and for whom art is a kind of religion, profoundly distrust any attempt to trace aspects of a work of art to the psychic disequilibration of the artist. Dostoevsky has especially, at the hands of his admirers, come in for this kind of shielding."[50] To Aiken it was quite clear that Dostoevsky suffered from a severe mental disturbance, and that this fact could not be shrugged off as an irrelevance. Dostoevsky's works were a product of a diseased mind, and to a cetrain extent his ideas were thereby invalidated. His novels, however, deserved serious consideration, even if his ideas were rejected. They were "dreams in a Freudian sense, since they are the projection, again and again, of his own difficulties in life."[51] Rather than valuing them, as John Middleton Murry had, for their "timelessness and 'mystic terror,' " the critic should approach them as "amazing psychotic improvisations on a theme, psychological symphonies of unparalleled sensitiveness and richness . . . ."[52]

Despite the qualified approval of this conclusion, an inescapable implication of the Dostoevsky essay was that any work which had its source in a profound neurosis was suspect as a work of art: "Tuberculosis makes its victims optimistic, but we do not necessarily accept their views of life. Why, then, should we accept, as

49. *Ibid.*, pp. 297-98.   50. *Ibid.*, pp. 163-64.
51. *Ibid.*, p. 166.   52. *Ibid.*, p. 168.

something *ex cathedra*, the turbid mysticism, the febrile hypochrondria, of Dostoevsky? We might as well adore the disease that produced them."[53] This position seems inconsistent with Aiken's assumption in *Skepticisms* that great art arose from the artist's unconscious. Although accepting Freud's concept of art as essentially a wish-fulfillment fantasy of both artist and audience, Aiken seems to have denied in the essay on Dostoevsky the Freudian tenet that the impulse to artistic creation was always in some measure a product of a neurotic disturbance, or at least to have denied that art produced by a severe neurotic could be "great" art.

This appears to contradict Aiken's earlier description of art as the product of the author's "psychosis" which succeeded insofar as it corresponded to the "psychosis" of the audience. What, then, did he mean by the term "psychosis"? The word ordinarily connotes a severe mental imbalance, but apparently this was not Aiken's meaning. In his essays, the term seems to connote each individual's idiosyncratic structure of reality, a structure determined by unconscious needs and desires. In one essay, he referred to "those varieties of self-tyranny which nowadays we call psychotic."[54] In this sense, all men have a "psychosis"—which is not to say that all men are insane. Aiken nowhere defined mental health, or its opposite, but he did suggest that in the healthy man's "psychosis" (or structure of reality), the "reality principle" plays a larger role than in the "psychosis" of the disturbed individual. The great artist employed symbols which were not merely idiosyncratic but were common to mankind.[55] He was, therefore, a man who was essentially healthy but who had a more direct access to his unconscious feelings than other men.

Aiken's imprecise use of terminology is one factor which prevents him from being a critic of major stature. A certain amount of inconsistency in a critic who was primarily a reviewer of books can be expected, but Aiken's problem went deeper than this, and seems to have been as much a product of a philosophic confusion

53. *Ibid.*, p. 165.   54. *Ibid.*

55. *Ibid.*, p. 121. This position, several times enunciated in Aiken's works—as in the essay on D. H. Lawrence in which he had tried to distinguish between "objective" and "subjective" art—is almost identical to that of Herbert Read, who was also concerned with the problem of distinguishing healthy from unhealthy art. See above, p. 85.

about the nature of the unconscious as a reflection of the circumstances under which his criticism was written.

The essays in *Skepticisms* and elsewhere, however, have many merits. Despite his anguish over the inevitability of critical relativity, which psychoanalytic theory was unable to resolve, Aiken's own critical judgments of his contemporaries seem in retrospect to have been sound assessments. He reserved his highest praise for T. S. Eliot, Wallace Stevens, and Robert Frost, maintaining that the popular poets of his generation (Amy Lowell, Carl Sandburg, Vachel Lindsay, Edgar Lee Masters) were good but essentially minor poets. Throughout his criticism he paid equal attention to form and to thought, and demonstrated the sensitivity to the sensuous qualities of language which one expects from an accomplished poet. The great poem, to Aiken, was produced by two things: a conscious skill in the manipulation of language and a subject matter whose ultimate source was the deepest stratum of man's being—the subconscious mind. A critic sensitive to aesthetic values, Aiken was hampered by a lack of critical terminology, with the result that much of his criticism, in the last analysis, lacks clarity. His dissatisfaction with the state of literary criticism in his own time led him to seek in psychology—in the theories of both Kostyleff and Freud—some definitive formula whereby the critic could transcend his own bias and achieve objectivity in performing his central critical task, that of evaluation. Psychology failed him in this; and from the point of view of the present, it may seem that his belief that psychoanalysis could provide the solution to a centuries-old problem in criticism was rather naïve. Both Freud and Jung denied that their systems of thought could provide objective criteria for the evaluation of the artist's products and left the process of literary judgment specifically to the literary critic. Despite his dissatisfaction with the "subjectivity" of his own criticism, in his critical practice Aiken was both intelligent and perceptive and applied contemporary psychology to works of modern literature with knowledge, restraint, and skill.

5. *Ernest Jones*, Hamlet,
and the Oedipus Complex

It was perhaps inevitable that literary critics would use the concepts of the new psychology in an attempt to "solve" the problem of *Hamlet*, a play which T. S. Eliot once aptly called "the Mona Lisa of English literature." Because of its difficulties— and the fact that the play presents difficulties is probably the one single fact upon which critics of *Hamlet* would agree—the drama was bound to be considered fertile soil for a psychoanalytic investigation; if the Freudian approach to literature possessed any validity at all, it should be capable of clarifying the causes for Hamlet's "inexplicable delay" in avenging his father's murder and explaining the source of the play's continued emotional appeal. It is not surprising, therefore, that a psychologist interested in literature should have made a psychoanalytic examination of the most famous tragedy in the English language. What is surprising is that this examination should have achieved the dual distinction of being both the earliest and one of the best of the extended applications of psychoanalytic concepts to literature in English. Appearing first as an article in *The American Journal of Psychology* in January, 1910, Ernest Jones's "A Psychoanalytical Study of Hamlet" was extended and reprinted in *Essays in Applied Psychoanalysis* in 1923. It was then modified and extended still further and published in book form as *Hamlet and Oedipus* in 1949.[1]

1. Ernest Jones, "The Oedipus Complex as an Explanation of Hamlet's

Oddly enough, Jones's essay on *Hamlet* was the only excursion he made into the application of psychoanalysis to a literary work, although he did write several essays applying the principles of depth psychology to biography and to painting.[2] It is also unusual that this essay, one of the most influential and controversial pieces of psychoanalytic criticism to appear in America, was written by a Welshman who lived most of his life in London. Ernest Jones was born in Wales in 1879 and was educated there and in England,

Mystery: A Study in Motive," *The American Journal of Psychology*, XXI (January, 1910), 2-113; "A Psychoanalytical Study of Hamlet," *Essays in Applied Psychoanalysis* (London: The International Psychoanalytical Press, 1923); *Hamlet and Oedipus* (London: Victor Gollancz Ltd., 1949). The 1949 version expands the approximately 100 pages of the 1923 essay to 160 pages. The numbered chapters in the book correspond, with one exception, to the sectional divisions of the essay. Briefly, the major differences between the 1923 and 1949 versions are as follows: In Chapter I, "Psychology and Aesthetics," essentially the same points are made, with the inclusion of Jones's answer to such critics as J. Dover Wilson, who had accused him of the "fallacy" of treating Hamlet as a living person rather than as a created character. The second chapter, "The Problem of *Hamlet* and the Explanations Proffered," includes an examination of a greater number of critical works on the play, including T. S. Eliot's "Hamlet and His Problems." The third chapter, "The Psychoanalytical Solution," makes the same points as Section III of the essay, but in greater detail. Chapter IV, "Tragedy and the Mind of the Infant," extends the discussion of Hamlet's relation to Ophelia to explain in psychoanalytic terms Hamlet's apparent misogyny. Chapter V, "The Theme of Matricide," is the only chapter having no counterpart in the essay; here Jones discusses matricide as a special case of the Oedipal problem, and compares the Hamlet and Oedipus myths to the myth of Orestes, referring to Gilbert Murray's well-known essay, "Hamlet and Orestes." Chapter VI, "The Hamlet in Shakespeare" (Section V of the essay), is a more elaborate treatment of the difficulties of dating the play exactly, of the relationship of the play's date to the death of Shakespeare's father, and of biographical problems in connection with the identity of the Dark Lady of the sonnets. Jones here dismisses the possibility, put forward in the essay, that Mary Fitton was the woman in question, and adds the suggestion that Shakespeare was bisexual. Chapters VII and VIII, "Hamlet's Place in Mythology," and "Shakespeare's Transformation of Hamlet" (Sections VI and VII of the 1923 version), are substantially the same. An Addendum to the book makes several suggestions for performing the play. Jones did not modify his position on any essential points of interpretation between 1923 and 1949. The latter version is more sophisticated and polished, largely because Jones was able to utilize the criticism and scholarship done in the intervening years. My discussion is concerned with the 1923 essay as it appeared in *Essays in Applied Psychoanalysis*.

2. See, for example, "The Madonna's Conception through the Ear," and "Andrea del Sarto," both reprinted in *Essays in Applied Psychanalysis*.

where he received his medical degree. He became acquainted with the concepts of Freudian psychology as early as 1903, but he was unable to practice psychoanalysis in London. Because of this, he accepted a position in a mental hospital in Canada in 1908, remaining there for a period of five years. While in Canada he made frequent visits to the United States, delivering some twenty papers before various American professional societies. He was a member of the American Neurological Association and the American Psychological Association, as well as several European psychoanalytic societies. Together with A. A. Brill, Jones was in the forefront of the psychoanalytic movement in the United States. In May, 1910, he founded the American Psychopathological Association, and he helped to edit the important organ of this society, *The Journal of Abnormal Psychology,* which published some of the first papers on Freudian thought in America. Jones was also instrumental in organizing the American Psychoanalytical Association in 1911.[3] He returned to London in 1913 and spent the remainder of his life there, practicing psychoanalysis and contributing extensively to psychoanalytic journals. His three-volume biography of Freud, published in 1953, is the best treatment of the subject to date and is an invaluable aid to the historian of the psychoanalytic movement. He died in 1958.

The original inspiration for Jones's work on *Hamlet* came from Freud's discussion of the play in *The Interpretation of Dreams,* in which Freud had stated:

. . . the play is based on Hamlet's hesitation in accomplishing the task of revenge assigned to him; the text does not give the cause or the motive of this hesitation, nor have the manifold attempts at interpretation succeeded in doing so . . . . Hamlet is able to do anything but take vengeance upon the man who did away with his father and has taken his father's place with his mother—the man who shows him in realization the repressed desires of his own childhood. The loathing which should have driven him to revenge is thus replaced by self-reproach, by conscientious scruples, which tell him that he himself is no better than the murderer whom he is required to punish.[4]

3. In *Free Associations: Memories of a Psycho-Analyst* (London: Hogarth Press, 1959), he says, "There was I, a British subject, but there was nothing strange in organizing such activities in what was after all a legally foreign country. But in those days one went in and out of the United States without let or hindrance, with no passport or visa or any questions asked . . ." (p. 235).

4. Sigmund Freud, *The Interpretation of Dreams* in *The Basic Writings*

In Freud's view, all of this was unconscious in the mind of the hero, and furthermore, this unconscious conflict must also have been present in the mind of Shakespeare. Using Georg Brandes' suggestion that the play's composition took place immediately after the death of Shakespeare's father (1601), Freud concluded that the presence of the unconscious conflict described in *Hamlet* was partly due to the revival of Shakespeare's own childish feelings regarding his father. The death of Shakespeare's son, Hamnet, several years earlier (1596), may also have contributed to the theme of the play; if so, the situation was "over-determined." In concluding his remarks, Freud said: ". . . every genuine poetical creation must have proceeded from more than one motive, more than one impulse in the mind of the poet, and must admit of more than one interpretation. I have here attempted to interpret only the deepest stratum of impulses in the mind of the creative poet."[5] This last statement is worthy of note, for in it Freud suggested that the psychoanalytical interpretation was merely *one* interpretation of the play—"the deepest stratum in the mind of the creative poet." It is implied, therefore, that other interpretations are equally possible and have equal validity; in Jones's analysis, in contrast, it is implied that the psychoanalytical interpretation is the only adequate interpretation and should take precedence over all others. The result is that Jones's study, as successful as it is, is flawed,[6] for no single formula could be reasonably expected to give a final answer to a drama of the richness and complexity of *Hamlet*. In spite of this, however, Jones's examination of the play still offers a more satisfactory single answer than most, provided that one accepts the initial psychoanalytic postulates; the least that can be said of it is that it is highly provocative.

In his prefatory remarks, Jones observed that many people felt an aversion to "too searching an analysis of a thing of beauty" for fear that the beauty would be destroyed. In opposition to this, Jones argued that experience demonstrated that appreciation of a work of art was only heightened by intellectual understanding,

---

of Sigmund Freud, trans. and ed. A. A. Brill (New York: The Modern Library, 1938), p. 310.

5. *Ibid.,* pp. 310-11.

6. This tendency toward dogmatism is modified somewhat in the last version of the Hamlet essay, *Hamlet and Oedipus.*

and that to further this understanding had always been one of the recognized social functions of the critic. Too often, he wrote, art was regarded as a finished thing-in-itself, something independent of the creator's personality, whereas, on the contrary, a correlated study of the work and of the personality of the artist shed light in both directions—"on the inner nature of the composition and on the mentality of its author."[7] Many readers, he continued, wished to believe that poetic ideas "arise in their finished form, perhaps from some quasi-divine source," rather than from simple, familiar elements.[8] The artist himself had been as reluctant as his audience to trace his ideas to their source, and usually tended to dissociate them from himself. Freud, however, in such studies of creativity as his work on *Gradiva* and his essay, "On the Relation of the Poet to Daydreaming," had shown that the creative process bore a striking similarity to dream and fantasy. The application of psychoanalytic concepts to a work of art, therefore, had ample justification.

Turning specifically to the problem of *Hamlet* in the second section of his essay, Jones stated, "Some of the most competent literary authorities have freely acknowledged the inadequacy of all the solutions of the problem that have hitherto been suggested . . . . The aim of the present essay is to expound and bring into relation with other work an hypothesis suggested by Freud in a footnote to his 'Traumdeutung.' "[9] There were at least two reasons for a particular interest in this play: it was universally considered Shakespeare's masterpiece, and, according to such critics as A. C. Bradley, it "probably expresses the core of Shakespeare's philosophy and outlook on life."[10] Furthermore, the central mystery of the play—the reason for Hamlet's delay in revenging his father's murder, or, in other words, why Shakespeare did not provide a clear and sufficient reason for the delay in the text—had given rise to a flood of interpretations, none of which were wholly satisfactory.

Jones divided the various attempts at solution of this problem into three categories: (1) the view that the difficulty lay in Hamlet's peculiar temperament, which was not fitted for effective action of any kind; (2) the belief that the difficulty lay in the nature

7. "A Psychoanalytical Study," p. 2.
8. *Ibid.*, p. 3. 9. *Ibid.*, p. 5. 10. *Ibid.*, p. 6.

of the task itself, which would be impossible for anyone to perform; and (3) the view that it was some special feature of the task that made it particularly difficult for Hamlet. The first position—that of Goethe and Coleridge—Jones called the subjective view; the second, the objective. In refuting both of these positions, Jones made use of approximately thirty critical studies of *Hamlet*, evidence that he was rather thoroughly acquainted with the Shakespearean scholarship available to him, both in German and in English. His method in this section resembles that of Freud in his study of Leonardo da Vinci: close attention was paid to previous interpretations, and a specific refutation, based on internal evidence, was made of the opponent's arguments. He concluded his survey of earlier criticism with the interpretation put forth by J. M. Robertson to the effect that *Hamlet* was "not finally an intelligible drama as it stands."[11] Jones ruled out this suggestion that the mystery or "unintelligibilty" of the drama was what gave it its power: "No disconnected and intrinsically meaningless drama could have produced the effect on its audiences that 'Hamlet' has continuously done for the past three centuries. The underlying meaning of its main theme may be obscure, but that there is one, and one which touches matters of vital interest to the human heart, is empirically demonstrated by the uniform success with which the drama appeals to the most diverse audiences."[12]

Jones therefore resorted to the third possible critical category—the view that there was some peculiar feature of the task which made it repugnant to Hamlet. Previously, critics taking this general view had tried to argue that Hamlet "gravely doubted the moral legitimacy of revenge" and that he was uncertain as to what constituted his true duty under the circumstances. But, Jones reasoned, if this were true, why did Shakespeare neglect to give his audience an indication of the nature of the conflict in Hamlet's mind in his soliloquies?[13] Citing the text, he claimed that throughout the play Hamlet knows what is "right" and that where his duty and honor lie is never a subject for debate. The solution Jones proposed was that Hamlet himself was "unaware of the nature of this repugnance."[14] To the objection, "Why has the poet not put in a clearer light the mental trend we are trying to

11. *Ibid.*, p. 21.   12. *Ibid.*, pp. 21-22.
13. *Ibid.*, p. 25.   14. *Ibid.*, p. 26.

discover?" he proposed the thesis that, like Hamlet, Shakespeare was also unaware of the nature of the conflict. "So we reach the apparent paradox," he concluded, "that the hero, the poet, and the audience are all profoundly moved by feelings due to a conflict of the source of which they are unaware."[15]

To accept this, of course, one must have accepted certain basic hypotheses of psychoanalysis—particularly the hypothesis that man is moved by feelings and impulses he himself does not comprehend because, being repressed, they are inaccessible to his conscious mind. If this is true, then it would follow that our response to a work of art is largely an unconscious one. This concept is in sharp contrast to the belief that the emotional response to tragedy is a consequence of a deepened intellectual awareness of man's predicament. Most literary theorists accept in some form Aristotle's suggestion that the audience's "catharsis" or release of emotions is one of the main sources of pleasure obtained from attending the performance of a tragic drama. The Freudian critics also accept this view, but maintain that the purgative effect of tragedy is accomplished primarily by factors which operate outside of the audience's intellectual awareness.

In order to defend his thesis that the emotional power of *Hamlet* derives from its latent message, of which the audience consciously knows nothing, Jones found it necessary to "make a few observations on the prevailing views of motive and conduct in general,"[16] and to set forth the psychoanalytic view of man as "a creature only dimly conscious of the various influences that mould his thought and action."[17] If this view were correct, then Hamlet's problem could be seen in a new light: "Hamlet's advocates say he cannot do his duty, his detractors say he will not, whereas the truth is that he cannot will . . . . The deficient will-power is localised to the one question of killing his uncle; it is what may be termed a *specific aboulia.*"[18] Citing evidence from the play of the various reasons Hamlet gives himself of why "yet the thing remains to do," Jones pointed out that, as in the case of Iago, the reasons Hamlet gives for his actions could be seen as "more or less successful attempts . . . to blind himself with self-deception."[19] They were rationalizations, not reasons, and suggested

15. *Ibid.,* p. 27.   16. *Ibid.*   17. *Ibid.,* p. 28.
18. *Ibid.,* p. 29.   19. *Ibid.,* p. 30.

an emotional conflict in the prince whose full meaning he did not grasp.

Having proved to his own satisfaction that Hamlet's behavior indicated an unconscious conflict, Jones discussed the process of repression and analyzed Hamlet's relation to his uncle and to his mother, emphasizing that the really violent language in the play was directed at Gertrude rather than at Claudius. He quoted A. C. Bradley's statement that "Hamlet's melancholic disgust at life was the cause of his aversion to 'any kind of action,' "[20] which, according to Bradley, was explained by " 'the moral shock of the sudden ghastly disclosure of his mother's true nature.' " To Jones, of course, this revelation was not merely a moral shock; the revulsion was caused primarily by Hamlet's own repressed erotic feelings toward his mother which could not be admitted to consciousness:

How if . . . Hamlet had in years gone by, as a child, bitterly resented having had to share his mother's affection even with his own father, had regarded him as a rival, and had secretly wished him out of the way so that he might enjoy undisputed and undisturbed the monopoly of that affection? If such thoughts had been present in his mind in childhood days they evidently would have been "repressed," and all traces of them obliterated, by filial piety and other educative influences. The actual realisation of his early wish in the death of his father at the hands of a jealous rival would then have stimulated into activity these "repressed" memories, which would have produced, in the form of depression and other suffering, an obscure aftermath of his childhood's conflict. This is at all events the mechanism that is actually found in the real Hamlets who are investigated psychologically.[21]

It can be objected here, and elsewhere, that Jones is treating Hamlet as a real figure rather than as a created character but the last sentence in the quotation seems to indicate that he was aware of such an objection, and attempted to answer it. In defense of such treatment, it should be pointed out that this method of handling a dramatic character as a real human being had precedent in the critical writings of Bradley and others, and that Jones throughout was operating on the assumption that the created character possessed, to a certain extent, an independence of the mind of its creator. That is to say, the character, Hamlet, was ultimately

20. *Ibid.*, p. 39.   21. *Ibid.*, p. 42.

a product of Shakespeare's unconscious mind; in the act of creating him, Shakespeare, imaginatively projecting himself into Hamlet's place, must have felt that he would have acted in the same way. The poet was unaware of the reasons he chose to have his character behave in the manner he did, inasmuch as he himself was possessed of the unconscious conflict he embodied unwittingly in his character. These ideas are implied in Jones's essay, rather than stated overtly, however, and it is true that in much of it there seems to be a confusion concerning whether Hamlet is an actual man or a character who has no reality outside of the work of art.

Aware that non-psychoanalytic critics would protest that the emotions he ascribed to Hamlet were implausible, Jones supplemented his critical analysis with a discussion of the normal child's feelings of jealousy and his interpretation of death, as well as a more extended discussion of the child's erotic attraction for the mother and consequent hostility toward the father. Applying this to Hamlet, Jones cited evidence in the play of the strong attraction of the queen for her son, here interpreted as a disguised erotic attraction. Hamlet's relation to Ophelia was also analyzed. According to Jones, Ophelia, before the ghost's revelations, represented Hamlet's more or less successful attempt to wean himself from his mother and find a normal channel for his erotic drives, an attempt frustrated by the reawakening of the repressed Oedipal conflict brought about by his mother's remarriage. Hamlet's licentious behavior to Ophelia during the play scene was interpreted as a more or less spiteful attempt on Hamlet's part to arouse Gertrude's antagonism; he is conscious that she is watching him, and his replies to Ophelia are more for his mother's benefit than for her. This interpretation is one of the more interesting suggestions Jones offered of a detail of the play.

Moving to an examination of the character of Claudius, Jones emphasized the significance of the fact that Claudius was Hamlet's uncle; because of his close relation to the family, his incestuous relation with Gertrude reinforced Hamlet's own incestuous desires. And because Claudius had, in effect, carried out what Hamlet himself unconsciously wished to do, Hamlet could not accomplish the revenge with single-minded purpose: "His own evil prevents him from completely denouncing his uncle's, and in continuing to 'repress' the former he must strive to ignore, to condone, and if possible even to forget the latter; *his moral fate is bound up with his uncle's for good or ill.*"[22] Jones was usually careful to cite evidence within the play for his remarks, but here, as in a few other places, his argument is invalidated by the text itself. Nowhere does Hamlet strive to "ignore," or, worse, "condone" Claudius' actions, although the second part of the above sentence, granted Jones's thesis, is tenable. "In reality," Jones continued, "his uncle incorporates the deepest and most buried part of his own personality, so that he cannot kill him without also killing himself . . . . Only when he has made the final sacrifice and brought himself to the door of death is he free to fulfill his duty, to avenge his father, and to slay his other self—his uncle."[23] Because Hamlet's duty revived a repressed unconscious conflict, which in turn demanded further repression, action was "paralysed at its very inception, and there is thus produced the picture of apparently causeless inhibition which is so inexplicable both to Hamlet and to readers of the play."[24]

In the fifth section of his essay Jones attempted to relate Hamlet's conflict specifically to the mind of his creator: "It is here maintained that this conflict is an echo of a similar one in Shakespeare himself, as to a greater or lesser extent with all men."[25] Quoting Bradley's remark that "we do feel . . . and [Shakespeare] himself may have felt, that he could not have coped with Hamlet's problem," Jones argued that it was irrelevant to inquire into Shakespeare's conscious intention, for "the play is simply the form in which his deepest, unconscious feelings find their spontaneous expression, without any inquiry being possible on his part as to the essential nature or source of those feelings."[26] It had been suggested that Shakespeare's revulsion against adultery was derived from his revulsion against the adultery of Mary Fitton; this, according to Jones, may or may not have ultimately played a part in the emotional content of the drama. If it did, it represented another case of "over-determination": "If part of this excess arose from Shakespeare's feelings about Miss Fitton, part of it arose from a deeper source still. Behind Queen Gertrude may

22. *Ibid.*, p. 57.   23. *Ibid.*   24. *Ibid.*, pp. 58-59.
25. *Ibid.*, p. 59.   26. *Ibid.*, p. 60.

stand Mary Fitton, but behind Mary Fitton certainly stands Shakespeare's mother."[27]

Jones next examined the play's source and its date, both of these bearing on the question of the relation between Shakespeare and his created character. Accepting as the most probable date the winter of 1601-2, he followed Freud's suggestion that Shakespeare's concern with the theme of the father-son relationship was occasioned by the death of his own father in September, 1601, an event which was "usually the turning-point in the mental life of a man."[28] Although modern critics tend to accept a date for the play slightly earlier than this, the evidence is so far from being conclusive that Jones's point cannot be rejected solely on grounds of external evidence; the coincidence of the two events, to those who are psychoanalytically oriented, is rather strong corroborative evidence of Jones's thesis, and in any event is certainly suggestive.[29]

In Section VI, Janes turned to the problem of the relation of the play to the original Hamlet legend, demonstrating that the incest motif was inherent in the early myths from which the legend ultimately derived. Central to his interpretation here was the discussion of the process of "decomposition" in myths, the opposite of the process of "condensation" in the dream. Through this process, the mythical figure of the evil tyrant (ultimately, the father) gradually split off into two figures—the good father who was murdered, and the evil usurper (King Hamlet and Claudius). This, of course, further supported Jones's argument that the hostility directed by Hamlet toward Claudius in reality was unconsciously intended for the father. In an extended comparison of the play with the version of Saxo Grammaticus, Jones presented an interesting interpretation of Hamlet's relation to Polonius, another type

---

27. *Ibid.,* p. 61.   28. *Ibid.,* p. 66.

29. A point discussed in some detail, however, is far less convincing, and even tends to weaken Jones's previous argument rather than strengthen it. This is his suggestion, derived from Otto Rank, that the theme of the desire to kill the father—the incest motif—is present also in *Julius Caesar,* a play obviously written before the death of Shakespeare's father. The relation between the date of *Hamlet* and the death of Shakespeare senior, however, is not central to Jones's argument, and the discussion of the incest theme in *Julius Caesar* was apparently intended only to demonstrate Shakespeare's preoccupation with the theme in two plays written within two years.

or imago of the father, and to Laertes, who shows similarities both to Hamlet and to Claudius. This section is perhaps the most confusing one of the essay, for in the discussion of the "essences" of the various figures in the drama (i.e., of their unconscious symbolic significance), the characters seem almost interchangeable. Jones here departed most radically from the surface meaning of the play, although his central point, that "throughout the play . . . we perceive the theme of the son-father conflict recurring again and again in the most complicated interweavings," is amply demonstrated.[30]

Summarizing the legend, Jones concluded that "*the main theme of this story is a highly elaborated and disguised account of a boy's love for his mother and consequent jealousy of and hatred towards his father . . . .*"[31] On the question of Hamlet's madness, Jones contended that Shakespeare's removal of the external reasons for Hamlet's feigning insanity, present in the version by Saxo Grammaticus, was an attempt to move the tragedy from an outer to an inner realm. In contrast to the source, Shakespeare's handling of the madness was "one of the masterstrokes of the drama": "Amleth's gross acting, for a quite deliberate purpose, is converted into a delicately drawn character trait. Merciless satire, caustic irony, ruthless penetration together with the old habit of speaking in riddles; all these betray not simply the caution of a man who has to keep his secret from those around him, as with Amleth, but the poignant sufferings of a man who is being torn and tortured within his own mind, who is struggling to escape from knowing the horrors of his own heart."[32]

In the older versions, there had been no psychological problem. Whether or not Kyd's play had complicated the plot in this direction was not known. If it was Shakespeare who first introduced the psychological complications, he did so in order to transform the play "from an external struggle into an internal tragedy."[33] In doing this, Jones suggested, Shakespeare was following the dictates of his unconscious: "It is as though Shakespeare, on reading the story, had realized that had *he* been placed in a similar situation he would not have found the path of action so obvious as was supposed, but would on the contrary have been torn in a conflict

30. *Ibid.*, p. 83.   31. *Ibid.*, p. 86.
32. *Ibid.*, pp. 92-93.   33. *Ibid.*, p. 95.

which was all the more intense for the fact that he could not explain its nature . . . . His own Oedipus complex was too strong for him to be able to repudiate it . . . and he could only create a hero who was unable to escape from its toils."[34]

Shakespeare's tragedy, according to Jones, was one of a strong man struggling in vain against Fate; in this respect it accorded with the Greek tragic conception. Shakespeare, however, went beyond this in showing that the real nature of man's fate was inherent in his own soul. "It is only fitting," Jones concluded, "that the greatest work of the world-poet should have had to do with the deepest problem and the intensest conflict that have occupied the mind of man since the beginning of time—the revolt of youth and of the impulse to love against the restraint imposed by the jealous eld."[35]

Before attempting to evaluate the validity of Jones's interpretation, several points should be noted about the essay itself. First of all, it is a clear indication that psychoanalytic criticism is in a direct line of descent from historical scholarship. Jones's examination of previous studies of the play, and his extended discussion of the date and the problem of sources, are all part of the historical approach to literature. The relation of the poet's personality to his work, and the possible carry-over into the art work of events that may have concerned the poet at the time of composition also have precedent in the historical approach. Jones merely extended the area of the poet's conscious concerns into the realm of the unconscious. His treatment of Hamlet as a real person was also a common feature of historical criticism at that time—Bradley's speculations as to what Hamlet did between the acts are well-known instances. Here again Jones was extending what had already been done, this time to a consideration of events which had theoretically taken place before the play began. The justification for such a treatment rests on the psychoanalytic theory of the relationship between the poet and his creation previously discussed. Many of Jones's arguments assume a greater validity if they are translated into the subjunctive mood—that is, if his interpretation is taken *as if* Hamlet were a real person. Any speculation on the reasons for Hamlet's delay, after all, presupposes Hamlet as a man with a consciousness and will who was able to

34. *Ibid.*, p. 97.   35. *Ibid.*, p. 98.

make reasoned choices; in short, a man with a being of his own, a being which no created character actually possesses. Granting some degree of reality to fictional characters is an almost universal procedure; Jones, writing in the first decade of the twentieth century, lacked the sophistication and the critical terminology to avoid this technical "fallacy."[36]

Jones's attempt to resolve the "mystery" of *Hamlet* by exploring the hypothetical unconscious motives of the prince reveals once more a peculiar problem in assessing the validity of the psychoanalytic approach to literature. The interpretation is plausible to those who accept Freud's premises about man and about the creative process; to those who do not accept them, Jones's statements are a particularly irritating form of nonsense. Since Jones's textual "evidence" is itself interpretive (what *was* Shakespeare's intention in underscoring Hamlet's revulsion at his mother's sexual behavior?), it is not convincing proof of his thesis to critics not initially committed to psychoanalytic theory. If the premises *are* accepted, Jones's interpretation possesses a high degree of internal consistency and provides explanations for certain elements in the drama which other interpretations do not. The "problem" of Hamlet's delay is that while it does not make *logical* sense (there is no meaningful justification for his behavior provided in the text), it does make *psychological* sense (the audience accepts his behavior as explicable in terms of his character while actually witnessing the play); Jones's hypothesis illuminates this behavior and resolves the apparent contradiction.

On the other hand, his emphasis on the play's latent meaning, to the exclusion of its surface thematic preoccupations, prevents his interpretation from being in any way a definitive statement of *Hamlet's* "meaning." It is doubtful, however, that he intended it as such. As an important supplement to the long list of *Hamlet*

36. A subtler objection to Jones's treatment was made by Lionel Trilling, who saw as fallacious Jones's consideration of the play as a dream which was separable from the meaning behind it: "*Hamlet* is not merely the product of Shakespeare's thought, it is the very instrument of his thought, and if meaning is intention, then Shakespeare did not intend the Oedipus motive or anything less than *Hamlet*; if meaning is effect, then it is *Hamlet* which affects us, not the Oedipus motive." See "Freud and Literature," *Literary Opinion in America*, ed. Morton Dauwen Zabel (New York: Harper Torchbooks, 1962), II, 677-92.

interpretations, Jones's study is of major significance. His analysis of *Hamlet* was widely accepted at the time it was written, and is still highly respected by many modern critics and producers of the play. The popular film version starring Sir Lawrence Olivier, which was obviously heavily influenced by the Freudian interpretation, is a case in point.[37] Both as an important seminal work which led to a considerable re-examination of *Hamlet,* and as an example of a thorough and intelligent application of psychoanalysis to drama, Jones's essay stands as the single most important Freudian study of literature to appear in America prior to the present decade.

37. For other productions influenced by Jones's treatment, see Chapter 3, pp. 121-22. See also W. David Sievers, *Freud on Broadway* (New York: Heritage House, 1955).

6. Van Wyck Brooks's Analysis of Mark Twain

Since its appearance in 1920, Van Wyck Brooks's *The Ordeal of Mark Twain* has occasioned a great deal of controversy. Bernard De Voto's response to it and his running quarrel with Brooks, which ultimately ended in both men modifying their views so that their original positions were almost reversed, is so well known that it does not need to be repeated here. Controversial as it was, however, the *Ordeal* was a landmark in Freudian criticism and was recognized as such by Brooks's contemporaries. Four years after the book's publication, Paul Rosenfeld commented that although psychological criticism had been attempted before the publication of the *Ordeal* by critics "oriented by the new Freudian psychology to the social and subconscious background of art," no critic before Brooks had had "the depth of insight into the nature of American life . . . the erudition, the sense of the function of art, and the knowledge of psychological theory necessary to one attempting this method."[1] Similarly, Carl Van Doren predicted that the book would "take its place for a long time to come . . . pleasing the judicious by its general truthfulness and its felicitous language, even invading the textbooks

1. Paul Rosenfeld, *Port of New York* (New York: Harcourt, Brace & Co., 1924), pp. 47-48. Despite his praise of Brooks, Rosenfeld found much to criticize in *The Ordeal of Mark Twain*, particularly Brooks's tendency to "come to his subject-matter with the intention of making it prove his theory and justify his unconscious wish" (p. 54).

and becoming a classic . . . ."² Van Doren's prediction was largely accurate. For all its faults—and there are many—*The Ordeal of Mark Twain* is one of the few early Freudian studies which have survived to the present day.³

Brooks apparently first came into contact with Freudian thought while teaching at Stanford University in 1911. There he formed an acquaintance with a group of socialists—"Germans, Jews, and Russians with minds that were full of Karl Marx, Freud, Krafft-Ebing, Nietzsche, Bakumen [sic], Kropotkin."⁴ This initial introduction to Freudian ideas was strengthened by his friendship with Walter Lippmann, whom he met in London in 1913, and by his reading of Lippmann's *A Preface to Politics*.⁵ More important than either of these contacts, however, was his association with the staff members of *The Seven Arts* and particularly with Randolph Bourne, with whom he became acquainted in 1914. According to Brooks, it was "to Randolph Bourne that I owed my first knowledge of Freud and Jung, to whom *The Ordeal of Mark Twain* was indebted, and *The Seven Arts* owed its existence to these thinkers. For the editor and donor had been patients of an analyst who had advised them to start it as a therapeutic measure . . . ."⁶

Brooks's reputation as a literary critic was already established by the time of the appearance of *The Ordeal of Mark Twain* in

2. Carl Van Doren, "The Lion and the Uniform," *The Roving Critic* (New York: Alfred A. Knopf, 1923), p. 55. Van Doren also tempered his praise of the study with reservations: the work "exhibited instances of special pleading and a definite animus," and a "good many of the details of his psychoanalyzing look suspicious" (pp. 49, 50).

3. As far as I have been able to discover, the *Ordeal* represents Brooks's only attempt at psychological criticism, although traces of Freudian concepts can be found in *The Pilgrimage of Henry James*. Two chapters of the *Ordeal* were printed separately in *The Dial*: "Mark Twain's Humor," *The Dial*, LXVIII (March, 1920), 275-91, and "Mark Twain's Satire," *The Dial*, LXVIII (April, 1920), 424-43. Brooks revised *The Ordeal of Mark Twain* in 1932. The differences between these two editions, particularly as far as the psychologizing is concerned, are too slight to warrant discussion of them here; such differences as exist are largely minor changes in phraseology. All quotations here are from the 1920 edition.

4. Van Wyck Brooks, *Scenes and Portraits: Memories of Childhood and Youth* (New York: E. P. Dutton & Co., 1954), p. 214.

5. For a brief discussion of this book, see Appendix B.

6. Van Wyck Brooks, *Days of the Phoenix* (New York: E. P. Dutton & Co., 1957), pp. 22-23.

1920. In his hands, literary criticism was allied to social criticism; his first book, *America's Coming of Age*, had already expressed his thesis that the failure of the majority of American artists was a consequence of defects inherent in the nature of American society. Brooks's *The Ordeal of Mark Twain*, and his later book on Henry James, were designed partly as "case histories" demonstrating and elaborating this thesis. The ideas of psychoanalysis were quite attractive to intellectuals dissatisfied with the state of American society in the post-World War I years, inasmuch as Freud's concept of repression seemed to offer a scientific explanation for what they felt was one of the major failures of their culture—the failure to provide a climate which would encourage the free expression of man's creative impulses. Brooks's use of psychoanalytic concepts in order to attack the "Puritan" domination of American society articulated an idea dominant at the time and gave added impetus to a belief widely held by intellectuals critical of the American social scene in the decade of the 1920's.

Brooks opened his study of Mark Twain with an examination of the humorist's "despair" in the latter years of his life. Twain's previous biographers had explained this bitter pessimism as being either a consequence of old age and the many painful experiences which Twain had undergone in his lifetime or an anomaly which was not an organic part of his life. To these views Brooks opposed his own, that Twain's despair represented "some deep malady of the soul . . . a malady common to many Americans."[7] In characterizing Twain's pessimism, he relied on a concept derived from Adler: "It is an established fact . . . that these morbid feelings of sin, which have no evident cause, are the result of having transgressed some inalienable life-demand peculiar to one's nature . . . . That bitterness of his was the effect of a certain miscarriage in his creative life, a balked personality, an arrested development, of which he himself was almost wholly unaware, but which for him destroyed the meaning of life."[8]

Brooks's initial premise, then, was that Twain's pessimistic, deterministic philosophy and the bitterness of his old age were

7. Van Wyck Brooks, *The Ordeal of Mark Twain* (New York: E. P. Dutton & Co., 1920), p. 10.

8. *Ibid.*, p. 14.

signs of a "frustrated spirit"; Twain's artistic self, balked in its desire for expression, had "withered into the cynic."[9]

In his analysis of the causes of this divided self, Brooks availed himself of both psychological and "sociological" explanations; Twain's artistic failure was examined first from the standpoint of his immediate family environment and then from the standpoint of the larger social environment in which he lived, the latter reinforcing the former. The origin of Twain's neurosis, Brooks claimed, was to be found in the family situation, a situation in which Twain's mother, Jane Clemens, was the real villain.[10] On rather slender evidence, he concluded that Mrs. Clemens did not really love her husband; to round out the Freudian formula, he also concluded, again on little evidence, that the young Mark Twain had become the primary object for the blocked sexual feelings of his mother: "When an affection as intense as that is balked in its direct path and repressed it usually, as we know, finds an indirect outlet; and it is plain that the woman as well as the mother expressed itself in the passionate attachment of Jane Clemens to her son."[11]

Brooks's portrait of Mrs. Clemens was unnecessarily harsh. She was said to be "the embodiment of that old-fashioned, cast-iron Calvinism . . . which perceived the scent of the devil in any least expression of what is now known as the creative impulse."[12] Brooks's reticence in speaking of sexual matters is the source of considerable confusion in his study. It is difficult to know in this passage, for example, whether it was the "creative impulse" which Mrs. Clemens found "evil," or the procreative impulse, the distinction between the two being blurred here as in other passages in Brooks's writing. In *The Ordeal* Mrs. Clemens emerges as the repressive super-ego, the authoritarian personality, the castrating female. According to Brooks, it was the presence of Mrs. Clemens which forced Twain to think of himself as a "bad boy" and to be-

9. *Ibid.*, p. 25
10. The omission of any discussion of the influence on the young Mark Twain of his father is a serious one, as far as a psychoanalytic interpretation is concerned. For a criticism of this point, and for a general criticism of Brook's view of Twain and his handling of the biographical material, see E. Hudson Long, "Twain's Ordeal in Retrospect," *Southwest Review* (Autumn, 1963), pp. 338-48.
11. *Ordeal*, p. 33.   12. *Ibid.*, p. 35.

lieve that the creative life was "identical with sin."[13] But here he made two assumptions that can be supported by little external evidence—that Twain himself shared Mrs. Clemens' "disapproval" of the "creative" impulse, and that he had as a small boy shown distinct tendencies towards creativity which were met with disapproval by his mother.

Brooks rested much of his argument on one incident mentioned in Paine's biography of Twain, the incident in which the boy walked in his sleep one evening shortly after his father died. On the day of the elder Twain's death, "his mother led him to his father's corpse and solemnly extracted a promise from him 'to be a better boy,' and 'not to break his mother's heart.' "[14] Brooks saw this incident as the precipitating factor in his neurosis. "Who is sufficiently the master of signs and portents to read this terrible episode aright? One thing, however, we feel with irresistible certitude, that Mark Twain's fate was once for all decided there."[15] At that moment Twain became a "dual personality": "His 'wish' to be an artist, which has been so frowned upon and has encountered such an insurmountable obstacle in the disapproval of his mother, is now repressed, more or less definitely, and another wish, that of winning approval, which inclines him to conform with public opinion, has supplanted it."[16]

All this is poor psychology. Brooks postulated here an infantile "wish" to be an artist, although it is improbable that any child— and especially Mark Twain—could have any such conscious intent; and an unconscious "wish" to be an artist rests on a wholly non-Freudian view of the unconscious. If he had been following Freud strictly, he might have interpreted the sleep-walking incident as follows: Twain's somnambulism indicates some psychic disturbance, probably guilt. The most common cause of such guilt is the repressed death wish for the father, a fundamental component of the Oedipal conflict. If Twain "repressed" any emotions at this time, he would have repressed the erotic impulses which were the ultimate cause of the death wish. Instead, Brooks maintained that Mrs. Clemens' injunction to be a "better boy" caused the child to repress his "artistic" desires, an explanation which skips over the relationship between the father's death and the hy-

13. *Ibid.*, p. 37.   14. *Ibid.*, p. 40.   15. *Ibid.*   16. *Ibid.*, p. 42.

pothetical repression. Brooks's thesis would have been much clearer had he availed himself of the idea of sublimation—the concept that the creative urge is a manifestation of the more primary biological urge which is rendered acceptable to consciousness in this particular form. The incident of his father's death may have had an influence on Twain's later creative life, but stated in Brooks's terms, it is far too oversimplified to be acceptable.[17] His concept of the "dual self" is psychologically tenable not in terms of a repressed "artistic" self but in terms of repressed biological urges on the one hand—the eternally rebellious libido—and the conscious desire for social approval on the other—what Freudians would have called the "super-ego."[18]

Although his explanation of the cause of Twain's duality leaves much to be desired, Brooks's thesis that Twain's personality was a divided one is ultimately convincing.[19] Tracing the manifestations of this dual personality throughout Twain's career, Brooks hypothesized that the two "selves" of Mark Twain— the artist and the conformist—were satisfied only in his career of riverboat pilot. The reasons for this were various. Of the careers open to men on

17. Dixon Wecter has recently uncovered a more substantial reason for Twain's sleepwalking after his father's death. Apparently the young child witnessed a post-mortem performed upon his father's body, an incident which was bound to have caused considerable psychic disturbance. See Long, "Twain's Ordeal in Retrospect," p. 346.

18. Louis Fraiberg objected to Brooks's use of the term "dual self," maintaining that psychoanalytically it implies a psychotic state. (See *Psychoanalysis and American Literary Criticism* [Detroit: Wayne State University Press, 1960], pp. 124-125.) This is, I think, being too harsh on Brooks. It is true that he used the term very loosely, but it is possible that by the "unconscious self" he meant the "autonomous bundle of complexes" which, in Jung's view, could become separated from consciousness and possess a "being" of its own. More likely, he meant merely the sum of Twain's repressed unconscious desires.

19. The most recent biography of Twain, Justin Kaplan's *Mr. Clemens and Mark Twain* (New York: Simon and Schuster, 1966), accepts in essence Brooks's thesis of the dual personality, as its title implies. See, for example, the passage beginning "He was, at the very least, already a double creature" (p. 18 ff.) and Kaplan's analysis of the "dual self" theme in Twain's fiction in Chapter 16. Mr. Kaplan's agreement with Brook's thesis extends to details as well as to his over-all interpretation of Twain's character; his more sophisticated use of psychology, as well as his presentation of additional biographical evidence which has appeared since 1932, make his book more authoritative than Brooks's, but the outlines of his analysis are present in *The Ordeal*.

the frontier, only that of a pilot offered complete "moral freedom"; the profession was lucrative and widely respected; at the same time it was a highly skilled craft which satisfied a man's "instinct for craftsmanship." Whether or not Brooks succeeded in establishing the point that riverboat piloting was the only meaningful opportunity available in Twain's society for a man with artistic leanings, he did convincingly demonstrate that this period in Twain's life was one of great inspiration and constituted some sort of intellectual awakening. Unfortunately, the Civil War brought an end to this profession, just when Twain was beginning to mature as a creative personality.

From his riverboat pilot career (a "channel of inner development through a special vocation"), Twain was plunged into the Gilded Age. "With his creative instinct repressed," wrote Brooks, "the acquisitive instinct was stimulated to the highest degree."[20] In order to support his "dual-personality" thesis, Brooks made much of the fact that Twain failed in all of his money-making projects, a failure caused by the conflict between his desire to succeed and the desire to create. It could be argued against this that Twain merely lacked business sense. Of the thousands of Americans who would have liked to become millionaires, only a few succeeded; obviously not all of those who failed were "divided selves." To Brooks, however, it was quite clear that Twain failed "simply because he did not care enough about money, merely as money, to succeed. His real self, the artist, in short, could not develop, and yet, repressed as it was, it prevented him from becoming wholeheartedly anything else."[21] Twain's dilemma—the dilemma of every American writer, according to Brooks—was that his desire to be an artist "implied an assertion of individuality that was a sin in the eyes of his mother and a shame in the eyes of society . . . . Society and his mother wanted him to be a business man, and for this he could not summon up the necessary powers in himself."[22]

Brooks's view of Mark Twain's career as a humorist follows naturally from his premise of a conflict between the creative and the acquisitive elements in Twain's personality. If it was true that Twain's deepest instinct was to become a writer, he should have

20. *Ordeal*, p. 78.   21. *Ibid.*, p. 80.   22. *Ibid.*

rejoiced at the opportunity to join the staff of the *Enterprise.* "Assuming, *as we are obliged to assume,*[23] that Mark Twain was a born writer, it is natural to suppose that he would have welcomed any opportunity to exchange his uncongenial and futile life as a miner for a life of literary activities and association."[24] Twain, however, was reluctant to do so; to explain this, Brooks was led to theorize that Twain unconsciously sensed that this type of journalism was a perversion of his true literary aims. It was Brooks's thesis that Mark Twain had no desire to be a humorist, that he adopted the role unwillingly, "aware that he was selling rather than fulfilling his own soul."[25] Becoming a humorist represented a poor compromise between his literary ambitions and his acquisitive and gregarious instincts. In choosing this role, Twain exhibited "what Alfred Adler calls the 'masculine protest,' the desire to be more manly in order to escape the feeling of insecurity" which had persisted since childhood.[26]

Brooks's eclectic use of psychology is evident here. In effect, he offers the reader a choice of psychological explanations. Twain's decision to become a humorist is said to result from (1) an unconscious compromise between repressed desires to be an artist and conflicting desires to please his mother through material success (a semi-Freudian explanation); or (2) because his insecurity created a strong need for social approval (the Adlerian idea of the "inferiority complex"). Brooks's psychological machinery, at this point, is both confusing and cumbersome. In any case, for him, Twain's decision to become a humorist marked the beginning of his decline, for adopting humor as a profession was "falling back upon a line he had previously rejected, and this implied that he had ceased to be master of his own destiny."[27]

If becoming a humorist was the beginning of Mark Twain's deterioration as an artist, his marriage, in Brooks's view, hastened the process. Analyzing Twain's decision to marry in psychological terms, he wrote, "Mark Twain, who required authority as much as he required affection, could not fail now to seek in the other

23. Italics mine. Why we are "obliged" to assume this is never convincingly established.
24. *Ordeal*, p. 81.   25. *Ibid.*, p. 84.   26. *Ibid.*, p. 89.
27. *Ibid.*, p. 95.

sex some one who would take his mother's place."[28] Thus Olivia Langdon of Elmira became the new villain in Brooks's story, operating in collusion with William Dean Howells. Twain's marriage to her was represented as a "moral surrender,"[29] another instance of the artist's selling his soul to the devils of gentility, propriety, and wealth. Brooks's portrait of Livy was as harsh as his drawing of Twain's mother: "a neurotic, hysterical type . . . Mrs. Clemens was of an almost unearthly fragility, and she seems to have remained so during the greater part of her life."[30] All evidence suggests that Twain was quite happy in his marriage, but Brooks chose to disregard this, and saw in such remarks of Twain's as "I never saw a woman so hard to please about things she doesn't know anything about" a reflection of his repressed hostility to her as a substitute super-ego. "From the moment of his marriage his artistic integrity, already compromised, had . . . been irreparably destroyed."[31] Several times he quoted one of Twain's letters to his brother, wherein he had written, "When I marry, *then* I am done with literature and all other bosh—that is, literature to please the general public. I shall write to please myself then."[32] Twain's tragedy was that this dream never materialized; instead, he involved himself more and more deeply in the pursuits of "opulence and respectability."

Brooks's assumption that Twain would have been a great artist but for his "acquisitive" needs which were reinforced by his society and his friends is a dubious one. He himself admitted that intellectually Twain was little more than an adolescent; and surely one qualification for a great artist is some depth of intelligence. He sidestepped this issue, however, and interpreted Twain's indifference to art and his carelessness toward his own works as a consequence of his denial of his own artistic nature. "His original submission to the taboos of his environment had prevented him from assimilating life; consequently, he was prevented as much by his own immaturity as by fear of public opinion from ever attempting seriously to recreate it in his own imagination."[33] His odd conclusion was that Twain was "at the same time a born artist and one who never developed beyond the primitive stage."[34]

28. *Ibid.*, p. 104.   29. *Ibid.* p. 111.   30. *Ibid.*, p. 113.
31. *Ibid.*, p. 114.   32. *Ibid.*, p. 144.   33. *Ibid.*, p. 164.
34. *Ibid.*, p. 172. It could be argued against this that a good part of

On the positive side, Brooks gathered some rather suggestive evidence to support his thesis. His interpretation of Twain's love of obscene words as an "escape-valve" for his hostility towards genteel society which could not otherwise be expressed is quite plausible. So is his explanation of Twain's "laziness" and compulsive billiard-playing as a result of the frustration of the creative impulse, a restlessness resulting from dammed-up energy, for much of Mark Twain's behavior creates an impression of a strong masculine personality straining against confinement. Brooks's point, however, would have been easier to accept (and more orthodox, psychologically) if this energy were overtly identified as sexual, instead of being vaguely referred to as an "artistic" urge.

It is the evidence Brooks cited from Twain's works themselves which carries the most conviction. Twain's preoccupation with the theme of childhood, for example, was cited to demonstrate that "some central instinct [in Twain] had been blocked," causing consciousness to flow backward "until it reaches a period . . . when life still seems . . . open and fluid with possibilities."[35] His fascination with the theme of dual personalities, present in such stories as "Those Extraordinary Twins," was excellent material for Brooks's thesis; the theme was "the symbol of Mark Twain himself," in whom "two incompatible spirits [were] bound together in one flesh."[36] All of these instances of a "repressed life" escaped the notice of his contemporaries, but with the light of Freud, Brooks argued, it was possible to see the "true meaning" (that is, the unconscious content) of Twain's writings:

For is it not perfectly plain that Mark Twain's books are shot through with all sorts of unconscious revelations of this internal conflict? In the Freudian psychology the dream is an expression of a suppressed wish . . . . These mechanisms . . . of the "wish-fulfillment" and the "wish-conflict" are evident . . . in many of the phenomena of everyday life. Whenever . . . the censorship is relaxed, the censor is off guard, whenever we are day-dreaming and give way to our idle thoughts, then the unconscious bestirs itself and rises to the surface . . . . In Mark Twain's books, or rather in a certain group of them, his "fantasies," we can see this process at work. Certain

---

Twain's craftsmanship was channeled into his public speaking. To Brooks, however, this was little more than a perverted, shameful attempt to win applause from people whom Twain rightly should never have cared about.

35. *Ibid.*, p. 175. 36. *Ibid.*, p. 180.

significant obsessions reveal themselves there, certain fixed ideas; the same themes recur again and again.[37]

In such stories as "Captain Stormfield's Visit to Heaven," *Puddn'head Wilson*, "Those Extraordinary Twins," and *The American Claimant*, Twain had "conducted us unawares . . . into the penetralia of his soul."[38] In these "nightmarish" tales particularly, "the censor has so far relaxed its hold that the unconscious has risen up to the surface; the battle of the two Mark Twains takes place almost in the open, under our very eyes."[39] "Captain Stormfield" was an example of a wish-fulfillment fantasy wherein Edward J. Billings, a poet scorned on earth, was recognized as a divinity in heaven. In this and in several other satires, Brooks saw Twain's repressed desire to be a poet.

The conflict between the "good" boy who obeys the dictates of his elders and the "bad" boy who is disapproved of by society was another theme Brooks found frequent in Twain's writings, a theme which achieved its finest expression in *Huckleberry Finn*. In this book alone Twain "let himself go" and expressed his deepest, unconscious self: "His whole unconscious life, the pent-up river of his own soul, had burst its bonds and rushed forth, a joyous torrent! Do we need any other explanation of the abandon, the beauty, the eternal freshness of 'Huckleberry Finn'?"[40] It is interesting to observe here Brooks's implied criterion for greatness in art; like other psychological critics, he considered a work to be "great" art when it was derived most fully from unconscious sources. This criterion alone was deemed a sufficient explanation.

Continuing his analysis of Twain's humor, Brooks emphasized again that to Twain himself, "Mark Twain was an unworthy double to Samuel Langhorne Clemens."[41] His turning to humor as a career was caused partly by his psychological need to be loved and admired and partly by conditions existing on the frontier at that time, conditions which Brooks maintained were very "repressive." Brooks defined "repression" loosely to mean that "individuality, the whole complex of personal desires, tastes, and preferences, is inhibited from expressing itself . . ."[42] Frontier humor, as he saw it, was a disguised form of hostility; this, accord-

37. *Ibid.*, pp. 186-87.   38. *Ibid.*, p. 187.   39. *Ibid.*, p. 189.
40. *Ibid.*, p. 196.   41. *Ibid.*, p. 198.   42. *Ibid.*, p. 203.

ing to him, was particularly true of Twain's humor: "By means of ferocious jokes . . . he could vent his hatred of pioneer life and all its conditions, those conditions that were thwarting his creative life; he could, in this vicarious manner, appease the artist in him, while at the same time keeping on the safe side of public opinion, the very act of transforming his aggressions into jokes rendering them innocous."[43] Brooks derived this concept from Freud's theory of the "economy of expenditure of feeling" in *Wit and Its Relation to the Unconscious*, which viewed wit as a socially acceptable form of expressing impulses, usually hostile or sexual, which would not be acceptable if expressed directly. But if this is true of Mark Twain—that his being a humorist was essentially the result of a neurosis—it would also be true of humorists in general. Brooks indeed came very close to seeing the humorist as a neurotic, a position which greatly annoyed Bernard De Voto, who accused him, with some justice, of lacking a sense of humor.

If Twain's humor reflected conditions on the frontier, it was also a reflection of the spirit of the Gilded Age: "The acquisitive and the creative instincts," Brooks wrote, "are . . . diametrically opposed, and . . . all manifestations of the creative spirit demand, require, an emotional effort, a psychic cooperation, on the part of the reader or the spectator. This accounts for the business man's proverbial hatred of the artist . . . ."[44] The general tendency of Mark Twain's humor was "to degrade beauty, to debase distinction and thus to simplify the life of the mean with an eye single to the main chance."[45] According to Brooks, Twain could have used his talents for satire. The country was crying for a good critic, such as the British had in Arnold, Ruskin, Carlyle; but Mark Twain's attitude was "let somebody else begin." His emotional investment in the Gilded Age was too great; he was too involved with the very things he should have been attacking to be a critic of society. Having sold himself to the opposition, he had to pay the price for it in a futile pessimism, a philosophic system of rigid determinism and ultimately a childish rage against mankind. "He had so involved himself in the whole popular complex of the Gilded Age that he could not strike out in any direction without wound-

43. *Ibid.*, p. 205.   44. *Ibid.*, p. 212.   45. *Ibid.*, p. 215.

ing his wife or his friends, without contravening some loyalty that had become sacred to him, without destroying the very basis of his happiness."[46] Brooks cited Twain's own words to prove his point: "Perhaps," Twain had written in "What Is Man?" "there is something that [man] loves more than he loves peace—the approval of his neighbors and the public."[47]

The bitter pessimism of Twain's last years is perhaps the strongest evidence for Brook's thesis: Twain's frequent impulses to "confess" in an autobiography, his childish belief that his confessions would "curl the hair" of his readers, and particularly his violent denunciations of art testify to a disturbed personality. In his last works, Twain "poured vitriol promiscuously over the whole human scene";[48] the result, Brooks commented, was not satire, but pathology. Because of his failure to express his inner self, Twain's thwarted creative impulse turned back upon itself in rage. "It is not in the nature of man to desire a club so that he can pound works of art into rags and pulp unless they are the symbols of something his whole soul unconsciously desires to create and has been prevented from creating."[49]

The Ordeal of Mark Twain closes with three of Twain's dreams. "The interpretation of dreams is a very perilous enterprise," Brooks wrote. "Contemporary psychology hardly permits us to venture into it with absolute assurance. And yet we feel that without doubt our unconscious selves express through this distorting medium their hidden desires and fears."[50] The dreams, which Brooks left largely uninterpreted, if seen through Freudian eyes are excellent supports for his thesis. One of them is particularly suggestive—Twain's dream of being on the lecture platform, "trying to be funny," while the people, recognizing the falseness of his humor, leave the auditorium. Brooks commented: "On the lecture platform his prevailing self had 'revelled' in its triumphs, and, he says, 'I hate that dream worse than the other.' Had he ever wished to be a humorist? He is always 'trying to make the audience laugh'; the horror of it is that he has lost, in his nightmare, the approval for which he had made his great surrender."[51]

Brooks's final argument was that Twain symbolized the hardships of the creative life in a country where expression of individ-

46. *Ibid.*, pp. 222-23.   47. *Ibid.*, p. 233.   48. *Ibid.*, p. 244.
49. *Ibid.*, p. 259.   50. *Ibid.*, p. 264.   51. *Ibid.*, p. 266.

uality was prohibited; he was "the supreme victim of an epoch in American history, an epoch that has closed."[52] From his story Brooks drew an explicit moral, and ended with a warning to American artists: "Read, writers of America, the driven, disenchanted, anxious faces of your sensitive countrymen; remember the splendid parts your confreres have played in the human drama of other times . . . and ask yourselves whether the hour has not come to put away childish things and walk the stage as poets do."[53]

For all of Brooks's faults—the annoying, officious tone, the handfuls of unnecessary exclamation points, the (at times) false psychologizing, the overstatements of a thesis everywhere ridden too hard—*The Ordeal of Mark Twain* is a provocative and, in its broad outlines at least, an essentially sound interpretation of Mark Twain's character. The pessimism of Twain's later years and the cynicism of many of his works, indeed, much of Brooks's evidence, cannot be finally explained away. One's ultimate impression of Mark Twain is of a "divided self" (however erroneous Brooks's interpretation of the cause of this condition may be), a personality that largely wasted its talents in frustration and anger because it found no adequate expression. Overstated as it is, Brooks's thesis can be accepted only with qualifications, but his portrait of Twain still remains a stimulating interpretation of a complex and fascinating personality.

Viewing the book much later, Brooks himself had some reservations, although he maintained that basically his portrait of Twain was sound:

> My *Life of Emerson* was a sort of imputed autobiography . . . while the other two [*The Ordeal* and *The Pilgrimage of Henry James*] were psychoanalytic, more or less, and consequently bound to result in distortion. For this method reduces a person to a type, a congeries of inhibitions, complexes, and what not, in place of the individual in his concrete fullness, and, in *The Ordeal of Mark Twain*, my over-concern with psychology left no room for literary appreciation. Or, for that matter, human appreciation either . . . . Mark Twain's humor had a positive value that I had all but entirely failed to suggest . . . .
> If he was money-mad, so was Balzac; and how could one speak

52. *Ibid.*, p. 267.
53. *Ibid.* The somewhat brash quality of this concluding sentence is toned down in the 1932 edition.

of failure in connection with a writer who was the most successful of his time, if only because he had written one great book?
Later . . . I was to see all these objections clearly, yet I still felt . . .
that *The Ordeal of Mark Twain* was sufficiently just . . . . I had
not consciously invented the picture—it sprang for me out of the
evidence with almost the natural force of a revelation. I did not see
how one could shake the logic of the book.[54]

As Louis Fraiberg has pointed out, Brooks's basic point in *The
Ordeal of Mark Twain* does not depend very heavily on the psychoanalytical guise in which he surrounded it. His central idea—
that Twain's misuse of his talents and denial of his creative self
led to frustration and bitterness—can be accepted without the
psychoanalytic machinery he used as a partial explanation. Fraiberg is overly harsh in his final estimate of Brooks, however, in
concluding that his "misuse" of psychoanalytic concepts was a
"detriment [to] both psychoanalysis and criticism."[55] The psychology of *The Ordeal of Mark Twain,* to be sure, does not stand
up under a searching analysis along strict Freudian lines; many of
Brooks's ideas —particularly his concept of "repressed" artistic
urges—need considerable translation before they can be made to
fit into a Freudian framework. It is also true, as Fraiberg suggests,
that Brooks borrowed from psychoanalysis to support a preconceived thesis. In short, Brooks's psychology was largely "parlor
psychology." But it should be pointed out that Brooks was not
really attempting a strictly "scientific" study of Twain. The *Ordeal* is a *popularized* Freudian study, or, to be even more correct,
a thesis book which found corroborative evidence for its central
idea in the popular new science of its day. Throughout the volume, the writing reflects general notions of the relation of psychology and art familiar in the literary criticism of the time—the concept that art was closely related to neurosis, that art revealed
"suppressed impulses" in the same manner as did the dream, the
belief that art proceeding from the "unconscious" was better art
than any other. Brooks did not succeed in uniting all these ideas,
or his somewhat vague notions about neurosis and its causes, into
a coherent "scientific" view of the artist. But such was probably
not his intention. Like many of the psychoanalytic critics of his

54. *Days of the Phoenix*, pp. 173-74.
55. *Psychoanalysis*, p. 133.

day, he was careless in his use of psychology. It is partly for this reason that the book is a representative example of early psychoanalytic criticism, reflecting as it does a more or less typical impulse to appear scientific without actually using the methods of the scientist. With the exception of Ernest Jones, whose knowledge of psychology can hardly be disputed, few literary critics at that time had the sophisticated command of Freud's theories present in criticism of a later date. Brooks's knowledge and use of psychoanalysis was equal to other "psychoanalytic" works of its period; the superiority of *The Ordeal of Mark Twain* was the result of his far better-than-average intelligence and critical sophistication.

7. *Joseph Wood Krutch and Edgar Allan Poe*

In 1925, according to Joseph Wood Krutch, Carl Van Doren suggested that he do a study of Poe. "It seemed to me then," Krutch later wrote, "(as it still does) that if the psychoanalytical approach to literature, just then beginning to be made here and there, would work anywhere it should work on so obviously abnormal a writer as Poe."[1] The result was his *Edgar Allan Poe: A Study in Genius*, published in 1926. Like Brooks's work on Twain, Krutch's study of Poe is the only critical work he wrote that is primarily a psychoanalytic study.[2] But unlike the

1. Joseph Wood Krutch, *More Lives Than One* (New York: William Sloane Associates, 1962), p. 141.
2. Krutch wrote two essays on Poe before the book's publication. The first, "Young Poe," appearing in *The Nation*, CXXI (November 4, 1925), 518-19, briefly reviewed a new edition of Poe's letters. The second, "The Strange Case of Poe," in *The American Mercury*, VI (November, 1925), 349-56, examined Poe as a neurotic and anticipated many of the ideas developed in the book. The last chapter of *Edgar Allan Poe* was reprinted in *The Nation* in March, 1926, shortly before the book's publication, with the following headnote: "This article is an extract from *Edgar Allan Poe: A Study in Genius* to be published by Alfred A. Knopf. Mr. Krutch attempts to demonstrate that Poe's poems and stories are an imaginative adjustment to the two dominant facts of Poe's personality: a neurotic sense of inferiority and a psychic sexual incapacity. In the present section he considers Poe's critical theory in relation to these same factors and suggests the general problems which are raised by the psychological method of criticism." See "Poe's Idea of Beauty," *The Nation*, CXXII (March 17, 1926), 285-87.

Ordeal, in which psychoanalysis was used somewhat casually, Krutch's treatment of Poe was from its initial conception a psychoanalytic one. In his study Krutch identified Poe's art wholly with his neurosis, without shrinking from the implications of the Freudian concept that art is a direct result of a psychological disturbance.

One purpose of Krutch's study was to correct the over-sentimentalized versions of Poe's life current during the early part of the twentieth century. "Three quarters of a century have passed and the bibliography of writings about Poe is longer, perhaps than that devoted to any other American writer except Whitman," Krutch wrote, "and yet from this mountain of matter has emerged no solution of his mystery and no generally accepted estimate of either his work or his character."[3] Views of Poe varied from one extreme to another; he was represented either as a symbol of infamy or as the soul of honor, and, with each representation, certain facets of his personality were cited as evidence for the thesis. To Krutch, the only possible way to resolve the contradictions in Poe's personality was by recourse to psychology: ". . . we are faced by a man inexplicable by the laws of normal psychology and impossible to defend merely by reference to the difficulties of his career. Since it is impossible to imagine that disease, physical or mental, could account for the presence of goodness in a character essentially evil, we are bound to suppose that a personality so self-contradictory was essentially good; but the presence of a disease which transformed the man cannot be denied . . . ."[4]

Estimates of Poe's work had also varied extravagantly. Krutch considered it obvious that "no more completely personal writer than Poe ever existed."[5] His works were almost entirely fantasy creations having only a minimal contact with the world of reality. As such, they were wholly the result of a neurosis, and a study of them inevitably led to a study of the life which produced them: "So nearly identical are the man and his writings that to wish any difference in either the character or experiences of the first is to wish that the other had been different too; and since there is no reason to suppose that Poe would have written at all except as

3. Joseph Wood Krutch, *Edgar Allan Poe: A Study in Genius* (New York: Alfred A. Knopf, 1926), pp. 8-9.
4. *Ibid.*, p. 15.   5. *Ibid.*, p. 17.

a result of a complete maladjustment to life, that would be also to wish that he had not, as a writer, existed at all. To understand him or his works is, inevitably, to understand them together, and similarly, to accept one is to accept the other."[6] Krutch might have added, "to reject one is to reject the other," for this is his final position. His total identification of the writer's art with neurosis can be seen in his statement of his critical procedure: "Throughout the ensuing study we shall be compelled to assume that the forces which wrecked his life were those which wrote his works."[7]

Krutch did not, however, offer a specific explanation of the causes of the poet's neurosis. Indeed, he sometimes seemed to assume that Poe was a congenital neurotic, although he did not discuss his neurosis in terms of any hereditary factor. It is interesting that in his study he nowhere mentioned Freud or any specific doctrine of psychoanalysis; these were taken for granted. Essentially the book was a portrait of a neurotic rather than an analysis of the neurosis in causal terms, Krutch's main interest being to trace the evidences of a neurotic imbalance in Poe's character and in his works. It might be added that one motive behind the study seems to have been to discredit Poe both as an artist and as a man. The term "neurotic" in Krutch's hands was more than a scientific description; it had a distinctly pejorative connotation. In his portrait, Poe emerged as mean, hypocritical, envious, spiteful, inordinately quarrelsome, weak, and overwhelmingly egocentric. Krutch's judgments on Poe's creations were equally harsh: they were found to be narrow, morbid, lacking in reality, and full of specious rationalism—in short, a little more than morbid products of a morbidly neurotic individual. It is not merely that Krutch was not in sympathy with Poe; he even implied, in his discussion of Baudelaire's high estimate of Poe's work, that anyone who was sympathetic to this type of writing was so because of his own peculiar neurosis. In a sense, then, Krutch's study was in some degree a polemic against "unhealthy" art. His rejection of Poe's work on the ground that it was the product of a morbid mind is thus somewhat confusing, in view of his apparent identification of art and neurosis.[8]

6. *Ibid.*, p. 18.   7. *Ibid.*, p. 19.   8. See below, p. 199.

The suggestions he did offer to explain the origins of Poe's neurosis were relatively shallow. At one point he claimed that Poe's disturbance could be traced to his adoption by the Allans: "The true tragedy of his childhood . . . lay in the conflict between a pride constantly nourished and yet continually wounded by a sense that as the son of an outcast and as a dependent not even sure of his patron he had no right to it."[9] A deeper source of the neurosis, Krutch suggested, might have been Poe's fixation on his mother, who "exercised over his mind a baneful fascination."[10] Poe's mother died before the child was three years old. Apparently Krutch was hesitant to suggest that infantile sexuality, even in a child as precocious as Poe, could extend that far back. In any event, he was very tentative in his discussion of the effect on Poe of his mother and her early death, avoiding any implication that an unconscious necrophilia was a contributing factor in his neurosis.[11] "It was she . . . perhaps, who stood between him and any normal fruition of love. Further evidence will show how completely absent from his life and his work was anything like normal human passion, and how his inability to feel as other men in this respect increased his sense of frustrated loneliness."[12]

Poe's decision to marry the mentally defective, fourteen-year-old Virginia Clemm was made, according to Krutch, partly because of his unconscious desire to perpetuate his sexless relationship with women; his "temporary continence" was "not so much thrust upon him as deliberately chosen."[13] Partly also, Poe's decision involved securing Mrs. Clemm as a substitute mother. In his marriage, therefore, Poe satisfied several unconscious needs at the same time. Because Virginia protected Poe from the possibility of further direct sexual relationships, she played an extremely important role in maintaining his defensive neurotic system. To Krutch, she was "the means by which he sublimated his conflict, and when she was no more it drove him into actual insanity. She was, like his ex-

9. *Edgar Allan Poe*, p. 22.

10. *Ibid.*, p. 24.

11. Marie Bonaparte, a stricter Freudian, had no such hesitation. Her analysis of Poe, which is far more complete from a Freudian standpoint, postulated a strong unconscious necrophilia in the poet stemming originally from his infantile sexual desires. See Marie Bonaparte, *Edgar Poe, Étude Psychoanalytique* (Paris: Denoël et Steele, 1933).

12. *Edgar Allan Poe*, p. 24.   13. *Ibid.*, p. 53.

aggerated belief in his own greatness, a necessary part of the fiction by which he lived."[14]

Evidences of Poe's sexual conflict could be found in many of his poems, where the theme of a dead or dying woman appeared with almost obsessive regularity. After a brief analysis of "Ulalume," Krutch suggested that the recurrent figure of the dead woman could possibly represent Miss Royster or Mrs. Helen Stanard, but that behind these figures might lie the image of Poe's mother. The tentativeness with which Krutch offered this interpretation, which is a result of his shying away from the concept of infantile sexuality, is in striking contrast to the assured tone adopted by many psychoanalytic critics, especially if they themselves were psychologists. Were the figures of Ulalume and Lenore, Krutch asked, in reality

. . . the mother of dim subconscious memory who had, perhaps, reembodied herself in those other two women who held his fancy captive until he found in the unearthly Virginia some escape? To this question no final answer can be given. Psychiatrists may quarrel over the question of whether or not an inhibition such as his must actually arise from a previous experience . . . . But one thing is fairly certain. Poe could not love in the normal fashion and the reason lay . . . in the death of some woman upon whom his desire had irrevocably fixed itself. If we knew who lay behind the doors of that tomb in the ghoul-haunted woodland of Weir, we should know the answer to the greatest riddle of Poe's life.[15]

Krutch's examination of Poe's writings amounted to a catalogue of characteristics of neurotic fiction. His stories were cut off from physical nature or from any picture of the contemporary world. His characters were unreal phantasms who acted without apparent motivation and who were oppressed by an obscure sense of guilt. Thematically, the tales contained a monotonous reiteration of madness and horror, constituting "almost the complete repertory of neurotic delights from the simple sadism of . . . 'The Cask of Amontillado' . . . to the most elaborate of perversities like that described in 'Berenice' . . . ."[16] All of Poe's works were remarkably "pure," in the sense that they were free of any sexuality; this too was a symptom of a morbid personality, for, according to Krutch, "purity as conscious of itself as his was is closely akin

14. *Ibid.*, p. 57.   15. *Ibid.*, pp. 61-62.   16. *Ibid.*, p. 78.

to pruriency, and both melancholia and sadism are frequently traceable to sexual obsessions."[17] In his recurrent use of the themes of madness and sadism, Poe's tales resembled nothing so much as the obsessive fantasies of a man on the brink of madness.[18] Krutch's view that Poe's art served a "therapeutic" purpose—a commonplace in psychoanalytic criticism—differed considerably from the usual interpretation of this concept. In no sense did his tales serve as a "cure" for madness, and they functioned only slightly, if at all, to prevent the outbreak of psychosis. Their "therapeutic" value Krutch compared to the drug taken by the addict; both the drug and the neurotic's fantasies allowed a temporary escape from actuality and furnished satisfactions for needs the nature of which the neurotic was not consciously aware:

But just as the drunkard . . . prefers intoxication as something more tolerable than sobriety, so the neurotic prefers his fantasies to the actuality from which they gave an escape, since . . . they furnish him satisfactions which his conscious mind may not be able to recognize. So it was with Poe. That sense of melancholy, foreboding and horror which . . . is generally recognized as the usual accompaniment of deeply inhibited sexual desires, made his life one long misery, and a similar cloud of horror hung over his stories . . . . The world which he created was one which had, like his drunkenness, its origin in his need, and it furnished him a certain ambiguous satisfaction . . . . In it he was able both to realize what was for him perfect love and also to indulge the sadistic perversities to which his malady gave rise.[19]

Turning to an examination of Poe's character and his relationships with people, Krutch related incident after incident to demonstrate Poe's hypocrisy and his habitual distortion of truth to meet the demands of his inflated self-image. Avoiding the bald statement that Poe was a compulsive liar, Krutch attempted to mitigate his damning picture of the poet by saying that the intermingling of truth and fiction in Poe's mind was really outside his control: "The compensating sense of superiority he had to have; it was necessary for him if he was to maintain even the poor mental equilibrium which was his; and there was no choice for him save that and insanity."[20] Although Krutch frequently attempted to excuse Poe on psychological grounds in this fashion, his personal

17. *Ibid.*, p. 85.   18. *Ibid.*, p. 77.
19. *Ibid.*, pp. 86-87.   20. *Ibid.*, p. 97.

animus against the man was never entirely concealed. This ambiguous position is apparent in his treatment of Poe's "mania for
rationality," which Krutch interpreted as a defense against madness; his attitude toward the poet, however, was not quite dispassionate: "He played at being a logical genius in exactly the
same way that he played at being a scientist."[21]

The strong emphasis on logic in Poe's works and in such criticism as "The Philosophy of Composition" was interpreted by
Krutch in the same light, as a defense against the impending dis-
organization of insanity: "First reasoning in order to escape feeling and then seizing upon his idea of reason as an explanation of
the mystery of his own character, Poe invented the detective story
in order that he might not go mad."[22] The rational facade of his
criticism (criticism which Krutch felt had no value other than to
shed light on Poe's own works) was viewed in the same way; the
result was Krutch's position that Poe's critical theories were specious rationalization of his own disease. The element of rationalization was particularly obvious in Poe's philosophic treatise,
Eureka, which Krutch called "simply the product of a mind which
has been completely mastered by the fancies which it had once
been able to control and use."[23] The attempt to ward off insanity
by constructing a superstructure of logic totally failed after the
death of Virginia, when Poe broke down almost completely: "The
neurotic adjustment, however elaborate and ingenious it may be, is
at best only a makeshift. Its victim is engaged in a battle against reality which he conducts by running away, but in the end reality always wins by demanding the complete surrender of the mind . . . .
The delusions may occupy, at first, but one corner of the mind . . .
but they are never wholly adequate. They must be continually
enlarged to meet the new contingencies which constantly arise in
the course of life and . . . they finally come to dominate the
mind they served. So it was with Poe."[24]

Krutch's final evaluation of Poe's literary efforts granted that
Poe had a "gift of expression," even though it was extremely limited in range. Apparently identifying "genius" with the ability to
give form to unconscious material,[25] Krutch conceded that Poe's

21. *Ibid.*, p. 113.   22. *Ibid.*, p. 118.
23. *Ibid.*, p. 182.   24. *Ibid.*, p. 186.
25. After quoting from a wild love letter written by Poe to his fiancée,

"power of clear arrangement," added to a "neurotically deranged temperament," indicated that he was a "genius." Poe was able "to unify his obsessions and delusions into a system which serves him as a philosophy . . . by which . . . he can give to his descriptions of his world an appearance of orderliness and self-consistency which make it temporarily real to his readers."[26] The real value of Poe's works, however (and this value was to Krutch a dubious one), was that they provided his readers the opportunity to indulge temporarily their own neurotic fantasies: "If 'there is a pleasure in being mad that only madmen know' then he has at least succeeded more nearly than any other writer in revealing it to the sane. His art is essentially one which makes it possible to visualize the gloomy magnificence of which he dreamed without sharing the derangement which gave birth to the dreams, to luxuriate in the voluptuous melancholy which surrounded him without being completely its victim, and, to put it as bluntly as possible, to experience the pleasurable emotion of the sadist without of necessity being one in reality."[27]

Although in his poems and tales Poe showed a certain ingenuity in construction, his works, Krutch concluded, must finally be judged along with the whole body of the "literature of nerves" of which they were the earliest example. Krutch himself, obviously, felt that the writings of Baudelaire and his school were at the very least suspect, explicitly referring to them as "neurotic literature."[28] His final summary deserves quotation in full:

We have, then traced Poe's art to an abnormal condition of the nerves and his critical ideas to a rationalized defense of the limitations of his own taste . . . . The question whether or not the case of Poe represents an exaggerated example of the process by which all creation is performed is at least an open question. The extent to which all imaginative works are the result of the unfulfilled desires which spring from either idiosyncratic or universally human mal-adjustments to life is only beginning to be investigated, and with it is linked the related question of the extent to which all critical principles are at bottom the systematized and rationalized expression of instinctive tastes which are conditioned by causes often unknown to those whom they affect. The problem of finding an answer to these questions and

---

Krutch commented: "What we have here is the raw material of his art, madness untransmuted by genius" (*ibid.*, p. 176).

26. *Ibid.*, p. 201.　　27. *Ibid.*, p. 204.　　28. *Ibid.*, p. 212.

of determining what effect, if any, the findings in any particular case should have upon the evaluation of the works of imagination or interpretation so produced, is the one distinctly new problem which the critic of to-day is called upon to consider. He must, in a word, endeavor to find the relationship which exists between psychology and aesthetics, but since the present state of knowledge [cannot] determine that relationship, we must proceed only with the greatest caution and content ourselves with saying that the fallacy of origins, that species of false logic by which a thing is identified with its ultimate source, is nowhere more dangerous than in the realm of art, and criticism is, at times at least, much more of an art than a science.[29]

Krutch stated in this passage a central dilemma for literary critics of his day. On the one hand, criticism as a discipline felt that it should avail itself of the new science which claimed to shed light on the age-old problem of artistic creativity. On the other hand, psychoanalysis seemed to many, including Krutch, to reduce art to "unfulfilled desires which spring from maladjustments," a position which denied that art had any value other than as a compensation in both reader and writer for a biological malaise. Furthermore, the implication that all critical principles might be merely the "systematized and rationalized expression of instinctive tastes conditioned by unknown causes" seriously undermined the process of literary criticism itself. We have seen that this latter idea greatly disturbed Conrad Aiken; it also bothered Krutch. Although critics like Krutch could decry the "fallacy of origins" and warn that the Freudian view of art attempted to explain away the lily in terms of the mud, one can detect in their writings an uneasy suspicion that the Freudians might, after all, be right.

Since the publication of his study of Poe, Krutch has somewhat modified his rather extreme equation of art and neurosis, but he has not rejected his idea that Poe's works, at least, if not the works of *all* artists, were possible only because of his neurotic character. Looking back on the book years later, he wrote:

I still think . . . that my hypothetical reconstruction of the origin and character of Poe's obsessions does at least fit more aspects of his life and work into a coherent pattern than any other theory with which I am familiar . . . . What does surprise and now somewhat embarrasses me is that I seem to have been so taken by popular Freudianism as to all but equate neurosis and genius. I know that

29. *Ibid.*, pp. 234-35.

only a few years later I was myself protesting that though psychology, normal and abnormal, might often to some extent account for certain of the characteristics of a great writer's work, the very fact that neuroses are common while genius is rare is sufficient to suggest that the two are not identical . . . . In the case of Poe I seemed to be suggesting that his neurosis *was* his genius and even, I am afraid, to imply that such is always, even though not always obviously, the case.[30]

Shortly after the book's publication, Beatrice Hinkle, a psychoanalyst and the translator of many of the works of Carl Jung, had written to Krutch as follows: ". . . I cannot accept . . . that Poe's personality difficulties account for his genius . . . . I would say that Poe as well as some of his French brothers was a genius in spite of these disturbances, not because of them. I am too familiar with these individuals not to recognize and appreciate their problems, but there are few geniuses among them although practically all have artistic leanings and capacities in some degree."[31] Krutch admitted that her objections were "certainly sound," but maintained that she had gone too far in the opposite direction: "Surely Poe . . . did not write as he did merely 'in spite of' his obsessions. If they do not constitute his genius . . . they certainly influenced enormously the character and tone of his creations. He might have been a writer without them. But he would not have been the same kind of writer. He would not have been Edgar Allan Poe."[32]

Despite a certain superficiality in Krutch's use of psychoanalytic ideas in his study of Poe, his portrait, like Brooks's of Twain, is still valid in its broad outlines. The absence of dogmatism in the work is a virtue rather than a defect, and what use Krutch made of Freudian concepts was substantially correct. His confusion about the origins of art, which stemmed from an inability to define clearly the respective parts played by unconsciousness or the "id" and consciousness or the "ego" in the creative process was, as we have seen, a confusion which few if any of his contemporaries were able to resolve.[33] As a reflection of this central critical dilemma,

30. *More Lives Than One*, pp. 163-64.
31. *Ibid.*, p. 165.
32. *Ibid.*
33. Ernst Kris has only recently offered a resolution to this problem in his *Psychoanalytic Explorations in Art* (New York: International Universities Press, 1952). For a good discussion of this work, see Louis

and as an intelligent biographical appraisal of a distinctly neurotic artist, Krutch's *Edgar Allan Poe* is one of the most interesting Freudian studies of the period, and one which achieved a considerable degree of success.

Fraiberg, *Psychoanalysis and American Literary Criticism* (Detroit: Wayne State University Press, 1960), pp. 90-119.

8. D. H. Lawrence and American Literature

The early uses of the concept of the unconscious and its implications in the study of literature were far from uniform. D. H. Lawrence, one of the major British novelists and poets of his time, left behind a considerable amount of literary criticism—a long study of Thomas Hardy, many critical essays and reviews, and an influential collection of articles published in 1923 as *Studies in Classic American Literature*. Polemical, eccentric, unsystematic, profoundly unacademic, Lawrence's criticism represents a highly idiosyncratic application of the principles of depth psychology to literature, principles by no means strictly Freudian.

Lawrence disliked Freudian psychology. As Frederick J. Hoffmann has suggested, the "science" of psychoanalysis was not so much an influence on Lawrence's thought as an irritant to it, a stimulus which enabled him to clarify his own system of psychology.[1] This system, if it can be called such, is set forth most explicitly in two small books written by Lawrence between 1919 and 1921, at the same time that he was engaged in writing the *Classic American Literature* essays. *Psychoanalysis of the Un-*

1. See "Lawrence's Quarrel with Freud" in *Freudianism and the Literary Mind* (Baton Rouge: Louisiana State University Press, 1957). According to Hoffman, Lawrence first encountered the ideas of Freud through Frieda in 1912. Later he read Freud in the original and discussed it with Dr. Max Eder, one of Freud's British disciples.

conscious (1921) and *Fantasia of the Unconscious* (1922) attacked Freud's thought as being "purely mechanistic," and while betraying a considerable misunderstanding of Freud's own theories,[2] delivered some justifiable criticisms of popularized Freudianism. Lawrence's view of the unconscious was essentially religious: it was the area of man's deepest being which he equated with the "Holy Ghost," and its sacrifice to the conscious, knowing centers of the mind represented to Lawrence a great threat to the sanity and equilibrium of modern man. For this reason, psychoanalysis with its commitment to *know* the alien, unconscious self and to drag it into the area of consciousness where it could be manipulated, was essentially an immoral endeavor, one that was doomed to aggravate mankind's sickness rather than to alleviate it. Freud's descent into the world of the unconscious was, according to Lawrence, a fascinating and courageous exploration, but what he had discovered there was far from the complete truth. The true unconscious, to Lawrence, was the "well-head, the fountain of real motivity"; Freud had found nothing but a "huge slimy serpent of sex, and heaps of excrement, and a myriad repulsive little horrors spawned between sex and excrement."[3]

Psychoanalysis and the Unconscious was more outspoken in its condemnation of Freudian theory than *Fantasia of the Unconscious*, where Lawrence expressed gratitude to Freud for restoring to the sexual experience some of its importance: "We are thankful that Freud pulled us somewhat back to earth, out of our clouds of superfineness. What Freud says is always *partly* true. And half a loaf is better than no bread."[4] The half-truth, however, should not be allowed to stand uncorrected. The sexual motive for human behavior was only one of the dominant motives for man's actions: "The essentially religious or creative motive is the first

2. Lawrence most flagrantly misinterpreted Freud's view of repression, claiming that Freud argued that the inhibition of incestuous desires was unhealthy. "Any inhibition must be wrong, since inevitably in the end it causes neurosis and insanity. Therefore, the inhibition of incest-craving is wrong, and this wrong is the cause of practically all modern neuroses and insanity" (*Psychoanalysis of the Unconscious* [New York: Thomas Seltzer, 1921], p. 21). Freud was hardly an advocate of incest, which is what Lawrence makes him out to be here.

3. *Psychoanalysis of the Unconscious*, p. 15.

4. *Fantasia of the Unconscious* (New York: The Viking Press, 1960), p. 59.

motive for all human activity. The sexual motive comes second. And there is a great conflict between the interests of the two, at all times."[5] The two motives, in Lawrence's psychology, derive from a basic, two-fold division within man, which originates, he claimed, in the first horizontal division of the parent cell after conception: "In the developed child, the great horizontal division of the egg-cell, resulting in the four nuclei, this [division] remains the same. The horizontal division-wall is the diaphragm. The two upper nuclei are the two great nerve-centres, the cardiac plexus and the thoracic ganglion . . . . In the centre of the breast, the cardiac plexus acts as the great sympathetic mode of new dynamic activity, new dynamic consciousness. And near the spine . . . the thoracic ganglion acts as the powerful voluntary centre of separateness and power."[6]

Lawrence's physiological schematization of the individual becomes increasingly more complex, expanding finally into a eight-fold division, but fundamentally it was the duality in man's being which provided the cornerstone for his psychology—two centres of opposition, the sympathetic and the voluntary, the cerebral and the sensual, mental knowing and "blood consciousness." Just as Freud, living and writing in a culture which refused to recognize the importance of sexuality in human affairs, frequently gave the impression of over-emphasizing the sexual element, so Lawrence, writing at a time when truth was most frequently equated with conscious knowledge, was most insistent on the "knowledge of the blood," on truths felt by the body rather than comprehended by the mind. In consequence, there is a strong strain of anti-intellectualism in Lawrence's writing, which frequently colors his criticism. As early as 1914, in a letter to Gordon Campbell, Lawrence had written:

5. *Ibid.*, p. 60. It would seem as if Lawrence should have been temperamentally more sympathetic to the theories of Jung, with which he was also familiar (there is evidence that at this time he had at least read Jung's *Psychology of the Unconscious*). But Lawrence, oddly enough, objected to Jung's "mysticism": "Freud is with the scientists. Jung dodges from his university gown into a priest's surplice till we don't know where we are. We prefer Freud's *Sex* to Jung's *Libido* or Bergson's *Elan Vital*. Sex has at least *some* definite reference, although when Freud makes sex accountable for everything, he as good as makes it accountable for nothing" (p. 61).

6. *Ibid.*, p. 77.

I am not a Freudian and never was—Freudianism is only a branch of medical science, interesting. I believe there is no getting of a vision . . . before we get our sex right . . . . We want to realize the tremendous *non-human* quality of life—it is wonderful. It is not the emotions, nor the personal feelings and attachments that matter. These are all only expressive, and expression has become mechanical. Behind in all are the tremendous unknown forces of life, coming unseen and unperceived as out of the desert of the Egyptians, and driving us, forcing us, destroying us if we do not submit to be swept away.[7]

Lawrence's desire to escape from the area of personal feeling, (because he felt it had become mechanized) in order to experience the "tremendous unknown forces in life," became one of the major themes of his fiction and found a counterpart in his critical theories. Several of his essays reflected the view that great art originates not in the personal, biographical ego of the artist but in something deeper. The art product, a painting or a novel, was not the record of an impression of the actual world, nor was it a personal vision emerging from the artist's "unconscious." Van Gogh's sunflowers were the result of something supra-personal—the *relationship* between the artist and the perceived flower: "The vision on the canvas is a third thing, utterly intangible and inexplicable, the offspring of the sunflower itself and Van Gogh himself . . . . It exists . . . only in the much-debated fourth dimension."[8]

Refusing to separate reason and emotion, intellect and intuition in the creative process, Lawrence argued in a perceptive essay on Cezanne that "any creative act occupies the whole consciousness of a man . . . . The truly great discoveries of science and real works of art are made by the whole consciousness of man working together in unison and oneness: instinct, intuition, mind, intellect all fused into one complete consciousness, and grasping what we may call a complete truth, or complete vision, a complete revelation in sound."[9]

In his struggle to achieve the "complete vision," the artist must

7. D. H. Lawrence to Gordon Campbell, 21 September, 1914, in *The Collected Letters of D. H. Lawrence*, ed. Harry T. Moore (New York: The Viking Press, 1962), I, 291.

8. "Morality and the Novel," reprinted in *Phoenix: The Posthumous Papers of D. H. Lawrence*, ed. Edward H. McDonald (New York: The Viking Press, 1936), p. 527.

9. *Ibid.*, pp. 573-74.

continually fight the ego's tendency toward cliché. Cezanne's greatness lay in his attempt to "let the apple exist in its own separate entity, without transfusing it with personal emotion."[10] The escape from the merely personal in art (a doctrine similar to T. S. Eliot's argument that great art represents an escape from personality) is only rarely accomplished: ". . . It is a fight in a man between his own ego, which is a ready-made mental self which inhabits either a sky-blue, self-tinted heaven or a black, self-tinted hell, and his other free intuitive self. Cezanne never freed himself from his ego, in his life. He haunted the fringes of experience . . . . But at least he knew it. At least he had the greatness to feel bitter about it."[11]

The function of the critic, in Lawrence's view, was primarily to judge, not to analyze and classify like the scientist or, worse, to issue pronouncements on the nature of form. Since aesthetic judgment was finally always a matter of the critic's personal emotion, not his reason, criticism could never be scientific:

Literary criticism can be no more than a reasoned account of the feeling produced upon the critic by the book he is criticizing. Criticism can never be a science; it is, in the first place, much too personal, and in the second, it is concerned with values that science ignores. The touchstone is emotion, not reason. We judge a work of art by its effect on our sincere and vital emotion, and nothing else. All the critical twiddle-twaddle about style and form, all this pseudo-scientific classifying and analysing of books in an imitation-botanical fashion, is mere impertinence and mostly dull jargon.[12]

Critical judgments were always relative to the critic himself, but there were some criteria, Lawrence suggested, whereby one could evaluate the critic. The good critic "must be able to *feel* the impact of a work of art in all its complexity and force"; he should be "emotionally educated . . . emotionally alive in every fibre, intellectually capable and skillful in essential logic, and then morally very honest."[13]

Besides possessing these characteristics, a critic should give his readers "a few standards to go by"; in Lawrence's own criticism, the most important standard was morality, which was, in his definition, intimately related to truth. The concept that the morality of fiction lay in its "truth-seeming" is a familiar dictum of the realists,

10. *Ibid.*, p. 567.   11. *Ibid.*, p. 582.   12. *Ibid.*, p. 539.   13. *Ibid.*

but Lawrence was quick to point out that mere accuracy of report-ing, the achievement of verisimilitude, was not "truth." The re-alistic depiction in a novel of a bank clerk's purchase of a hat, for example, was not life, but mere existence, since it possessed no significance and hence no morality: "By life, we mean something that gleams, that has the fourth-dimensional quality. If the bank clerk feels really piquant about his hat . . . and goes out of the shop with the new straw on his head, a changed man, be-aureoled, then that is life."[14]

The novel, to Lawrence the greatest of all art forms, concerned itself with relationships, and it was the duty of the novelist to re-spect the relationship he portrayed and to avoid interfering in it with preconceived ideas or ethical standards. "If a novel reveals true and vivid relationships, it is a moral work, no matter what the relationships may consist in. If the novelist *honours* the rela-tionship in itself, it will be a great novel."[15] Since, Lawrence ar-gued, the novel was the greatest form of artistic communication, it had the greatest responsibility for being a genuinely moral in-strument: "The novel can help us to live, as nothing else can: no didactic Scripture, anyhow. If the novelist keeps his thumb out of the pan. But when the novelist *has* his thumb in the pan, the novel becomes an unparallelled perverter of men and women."[16] A novel accomplished its moral purpose by awakening the reader's sense of life. It could "help you not to be a dead man in life . . . . In the novel you can see, plainly, when the man goes dead, the woman goes inert. You can develop an instinct for life, if you will, instead of a theory of right and wrong, good and bad."[17]

Lawrence applied these criteria in his own critical judgments. Indeed, more often than not in his critical essays, he used the work of art he was discussing as a text for his own sermons on reality and ethics. This tendency is particularly evident in his long study of Thomas Hardy, which was concerned less with Hardy's thought than it was with Lawrence's own. His most seri-ous criticism of Hardy's tragedies was that they were not genuine: the characters were "not at war with God, only with Society." This, Lawrence argued, was the major weakness of modern trag-edy, "where transgression against the social code is made to

14. *Ibid.*, pp. 529-30.   15. *Ibid.*, p. 530.   16. *Ibid.*, p. 532.
17. *Ibid.*, p. 538.

bring destruction, as though the social code worked our irrevocable fate."[18] Hardy's world was too self-enclosed, too governed by this single moral idea, which was in itself false: ". . . every work of art adheres to some system of morality. But if it be really a work of art, it must contain the essential criticism on the morality to which it adheres. And hence the antimony, hence the conflict necessary to every tragic conception. The degree to which the system of morality . . . of any work of art is submitted to criticism within the work of art makes the lasting value and satisfaction of that work."[19]

The failure of Hardy's tragedies was a failure of moral vision. The failure of John Galsworthy's satire in *The Forsyte Saga* was a failure of courage, an unwillingness to pursue his vision honestly: "Galsworthy had not quite enough of the superb courage of his satire. He faltered, and gave in to the Forsytes. It is a thousand pities. He might have been the surgeon the modern soul needs so badly, to cut away the proud flesh of our Forsytes from the living body of men who are fully alive. Instead, he put down the knife and laid on a soft, sentimental poultice, and helped to make the corruption worse."[20]

In his criticism Lawrence only rarely commented on style and form, which was of far less importance than the art work's ultimate moral meaning, its relevance to and significance for life. Technical discussions of aesthetic form were repugnant to Lawrence; they were pseudo-scientific, snobbish, intellectualized abstractions about art, and were of little use in stimulating a more intense realization of the art work on the part of the spectator or reader: "It's all very well talking about decoration and illustration, significant form, or tactile values, or plastique, or movement, or space-composition, or colour-mass relations, afterwards. You might as well force your guest to eat the menu card, at the end of the dinner. What art has got to do, and will go on doing, is to reveal things in their different relationships."[21] The concept of art as Significant Form, preached by such men as Clive Bell and Roger Fry, was particularly anathema to Lawrence. He attacked these new apologists for art, whom he dubbed the "significant formers," as being the "primitive Methodists of art criticism," pro-

18. *Ibid.*, p. 420.
20. *Ibid.*, pp. 542-43.
19. *Ibid.*, p. 476.
21. *Ibid.*, p. 524.

claiming their message "Purify yourselves, ye who would know the aesthetic ecstacy, and be lifted up the 'white peaks of artistic inspiration.' Purify yourselves of all base hankering for a tale that is told, and of all low lust for likenesses. Purify yourselves, and know the one supreme way, the way of Significant Form!"[22]

The aestheticians, in attempting to divert the spectator's attention from content and meaning to form, were immorally attempting to turn man's mind from reality to abstraction, and were thus committing the greatest of sins in Lawrence's decalogue, the sin of transferring experience from the body and the emotions to the intellect. The penalty for this sin was death, the death of the modern spirit. Cezanne's apples were a new attempt to present reality, and this new reality hurt: "It made people shout with pain. And it was not until his followers had turned him again into an abstraction that he was ever accepted. Then the critics stepped forth and abstracted his good apple into Significant Form, and henceforth Cezanne was saved. Saved for democracy. Put safely in the tomb again, and the stone rolled back."[23]

The attitudes expressed in Lawrence's minor critical essays find their most complete expression in his most influential critical work, the *Studies in Classic American Literature*. The history of this book is complicated, each of the essays (with two exceptions) appearing separately in periodicals, then heavily revised before their final publication in book form in 1923. Recently, the earlier versions of the essays have been collected and reprinted under the title *The Symbolic Meaning*. Although less unified than in their later version, the original essays frequently were superior as literary criticism: they were more dispassionate in tone, and possessed relatively greater coherence than the more familiar version of the *Studies*. Absent there too was much of the wild humor of the later form of the book, a source both of amusement and annoyance to readers. For the *Studies in Classic American Literature* is an outrageous piece of literary criticism. Wild-eyed, polemical, deliberately shocking, it is at the opposite pole from the calmly reasoned, empirical criticism familiar to the academic world. As one contemporary critic commented, Lawrence's "ig-

22. *Ibid.*, pp. 565-66.   23. *Ibid.*, p. 570.

norance of American literature is comprehensive and profound."[24] His factual errors and radically unconventional readings of major American authors make the book difficult at times to take seriously, but despite its lack of over-all reliability, it has remained to the present day an important source of insights into our national literature and character and appears with surprising frequency in the footnotes of the more scholarly articles and books which cover the same ground.

Lawrence spent considerable time working on these essays, and considered them a major effort. Writing to his publisher in 1919, he commented: "These essays are the result of five years of persistent work. They contain a whole *Weltanschauung*—new, if old—even a new science of psychology, pure science."[25] The "new science of psychology" was not, of course, Freudian psychoanalysis, but Lawrence's own. Nevertheless, many of the assumptions common to Freudian criticism were to be found in the book; to his contemporaries, the *Studies in Classic American Literature* was simply another of the new psychoanalytically colored analyses of literature. The book achieves its originality, wrote one reviewer, "from the playing of new psychoanalytically derived methods on old familiar (and hence unknown) subjects."[26] In several respects—and this is despite Lawrence's own dislike of Jung—the *Studies* can be considered the first major example of "mythic" criticism—the analysis of fiction in terms of its latent myths, myths which revealed the unconscious beliefs and desires of an entire nation or its "national psyche." In this type of criticism, the critic takes a stance at a considerable distance from the art work, viewing its large outlines and dominant symbolic patterns. If the "New Critics" can be said to have concerned themselves with the trees, the myth critics occupied themselves with the forest, refusing to be waylaid by any single bush or twig.

In his Foreword to the *Studies*, Lawrence announced his purpose as that of finding the "new bird called the true American," claiming that the only place to look for him was "under the Amer-

24. Raymond M. Weaver, "Narcissus and Echo," *The Bookman*, LVIII (November, 1923), 327.

25. *The Collected Letters of D. H. Lawrence*, 595-96.

26. Kurt L. Daniels, "Mr. Lawrence on American Literature," *The New Republic*, XXXVI (October 24, 1923), 236.

ican bushes," in American Literature. He conceived of himself as the "midwife" to this unborn, or heretofore undefined, American personality. Since it was part of the American character, he argued, to conceal itself behind symbols, to hide there like Moses in the bullrushes, his job must be to play the part of the Egyptian princess and "lift out the swaddled infant of truth that America spawned some time back."[27]

Duplicity was a characteristic of all art, not merely American art. Hence the critic's function, according to Lawrence, was always to translate the art-communication into prose communication, even though this did violence to the art work itself: ". . . when we reduce and diminish any work of art to its didactic capacity . . . then we find that that work of art is a subtle and complex *idea* expressed in symbols . . . . For certain purposes, it is necessary to degrade a work of art into a thing of meanings and reasoned exposition. This process of reduction is part of the science of criticism."[28] The definition of art in terms of its content, the equation of its worth with its didactic message, was quite typical of Lawrence, and was one of the basic assumptions behind all of his criticism. He differed from other "moral" or humanist critics, however, is his second basic proposition—that the morality of the art work was rarely, if ever, to be identified with the *conscious* moral or didactic intention of the author: "The artist usually sets out—or used to—to point a moral and adorn a tale. The tale, however, points the other way, as a rule. Two blankly opposing morals, the artist's and the tale's. Never trust the artist. Trust the tale. The proper function of a critic is to save the tale from the artist who created it."[29]

In amplifying this idea that the ultimate statement of a fictional work was its unconscious meaning, Lawrence used the familiar psychoanalytic metaphor equating the art work and the dream and the artist and the sleepwalker: "What Hawthorne deliberately says

27. *Studies in Classic American Literature* (New York: The Viking Press, 1961), p. viii. Although it is my intention to concentrate on this later form of the essays, where occasion warrants it—either because the earlier version expresses an idea not found in the later book, or because it presents a better expression of a passage found in both versions—I shall also refer to *The Symbolic Meaning*, ed. Armin Arnold (New York: The Viking Press, 1964).

28. *Symbolic Meaning*, p. 19.   29. *Studies*, p. 2.

in *The Scarlet Letter* is on the whole a falsification of what he unconsciously says in his art-language. And this, again, is one of the outstanding qualities of American literature: that the deliberate ideas of the man veil, conceal, obscure that which the artist has to reveal . . . . The author is unconscious of this duplicity himself. He is sincere in his own intention. And yet, all the time, the artist, who writes as a somnambulist, in the spell of pure truth as in a dream, is contravened and contradicted by the wakeful man and moralist who sits at the desk."[30] Art speech, he continued, was a language of pure symbols which communicated a total experience, "emotional and passional, spiritual and perceptual, all at once." It involved a use of symbols which were "pulsations on the blood and seizures upon the nerves, and at the same time percepts of the mind and pure terms of spiritual aspiration."[31]

Because of the artist's "duplicity," Lawrence said, the reader who attempted to discover the American character in its literature had first of all to disregard what the American artist said. In fact, he should listen to Lawrence, not to the artist, who would only "tell him the lie he expects." The first American "lie" was the myth that Americans came to New England to seek freedom. On the contrary, Lawrence argued, they came to escape from themselves—a negative action which did not result in true freedom since the latter could be experienced only as the result of the ego's submission to the dictates of the "deepest self." This argument is one of the major polemical themes of the *Studies*, and partly accounts for Lawrence's antagonism toward American democracy; for his final conclusion about the American character is that racially it represented a great negative will to mechanization, a "deep lust for vindictive power over the life issue" apparent even in the

30. *Symbolic Meaning*, p. 18.
31. *Ibid.*, p. 19. Lawrence's view that the symbol was a non-rational form of communication and therefore could not be translated into prose speech without immense loss, is an early version of the "heresy of paraphrase": "Symbols are organic units of consciousness with a life of their own and you can never explain them away, because their value is dynamic, emotional, belonging to the self-consciousness of the body and soul, and not simply mental. An allegorical image has a *meaning*. Mr. Facing-both-ways has a meaning. But I defy you to lay your finger on the full meaning of Janus, who is a symbol" (*Phoenix*, p. 295). In order to "rescue the tale from the teller" the critic must try to lay his finger on Janus, however, no matter how heretical he perceives his task to be.

earliest formulation of American consciousness, American Calvinism.[32]

Lawrence's conception of the American experiment as a manifestation of an unhealthy will to mechanization that was ultimately destructive of life dominated his first analysis of an American artist, Benjamin Franklin.[33] The American drive to equality, Lawrence claimed, could only be achieved by reducing everyone to a common machine standard. In this perverted world Franklin was a natural hero; to Lawrence he was a "virtuous Frankenstein monster," living entirely from his consciousness and will rather than from the "spontaneous centres," a man who spoke of "*using* venery." Franklin's famous list of virtues was a catalogue of "strictly machine principles"; his humor always showed a "triumph of cautious, calculated, virtuous behavior." In short, Franklin was "perhaps the most admirable little automaton the world has ever seen, the invention of the human will, working according to good principles. So far as affairs went, he was admirable. So far as life goes, he is monstrous."[34]

For Franklin's contemporary, de Crèvecoeur, Lawrence had more admiration. Here, too, however, he discovered the treacherous *will to know*, the compulsion to intellectualize life. Although Crèvecoeur was capable of "opening the dark eyes of his blood to the presence of bees, birds and serpents," and longed to experience "the mystery of sensual being," he too, finally, wanted to deny this mystery and destroy it. Hence he was "divided against himself, which makes for madness."[35] Crèvecoeur "wanted to put Nature in his pocket, as Benjamin put the Human Being."[36] His desire to be an "intellectual savage" was a sign of profound dishonesty. This dishonesty finally vitiated his work in Lawrence's judgment, although he admitted that on occasion Crèvecoeur was "sometimes an artist," with a remarkable ability to capture in prose the sense of "otherness" in the animal world.

32. *Symbolic Meaning*, p. 25.
33. This is one instance in which the earlier version of the essay is preferable to the later, which is confused, badly focused, and spiteful. The thesis of Franklin as a machine is less coherently presented in the *Studies*; the only addition of any interest present in the later version is Lawrence's own catalogue of virtues to replace Franklin's. For these reasons, I have relied here on the earlier version.
34. *Symbolic Meaning*, p. 44.   35. *Ibid.*, p. 64.   36. *Studies*, p. 25.

Lawrence's two essays on Cooper contained some of his most stimulating literary insights, perhaps because of his evident affection for the man and his work. For whatever reason, these essays were less marred by the vituperation and spleen which lessened the effectiveness of some of his other interpretations. The first essay, devoted to the Effingham novels (the "white" novels, in Lawrence's phrase), served largely as a text for a Lawrentian sermon on the evils of democratic equality. Eve Effingham was "by nature" a superior being to Septimus Dodge, who should naturally have reverenced her as a higher type; it was absurd that she should be chained down, "impaled" on her belief in the equality of man.

The second essay, on the *Leatherstocking Tales*, represents the first significant appreciation of Cooper as the creator of an American myth. Before examining the novels themselves, Lawrence devoted some space to a biographical analysis of Cooper, finding that he too, like Crèvecoeur, was a divided self. Cooper "symbolized his own actual, mechanical self-determined life in the Effinghams. But in Leatherstocking he symbolizes his own last being, strange and wrought to a conclusion, seeking its consummation in the American woods and the Indian race, his pure complement in the chief Chingachgook."[37] The two selves, "Monsieur Fenimore Cooper" and Natty Bumppo, reflected the conflict in Cooper's character between actuality and wish-fulfillment, the conflict between the world of the hotel and the world of the wigwam, the desire for a wife and the desire to roam the woods with Chingachgook, "blue coat, silver buttons, buckled shoes, ruffles" and "a grizzled, uncouth old renegade, with gaps in his old teeth and a drop on the end of his nose."[38] The *Leatherstocking Tales* themselves were a mythic American legend. Viewed in their chronological order, they represented a "record of the race-individual as he moves from the present old age of the race into re-birth and the new youth which lies ahead."[39]

Lawrence's interpretation of individual characters in the *Leatherstocking Tales* could be penetrating. His usual method was to look beneath the surface actions of the character to expose a deeper layer of personality. Analyzing Harry Hutter in *The Deer-*

37. *Symbolic Meaning*, pp. 85-86.   38. *Studies*, p. 49.
39. *Symbolic Meaning*, p. 93.

slayer, Lawrence suggested that he possessed a basic cowardice which was his "deepest quality": "There is a craven deficiency in his soul, so he becomes an outward blusterer."[40] Lawrence's comments on the male-female relationships in the books reflected his own preoccupation with and philosophy of sexual relationships. He noted the light-dark dichotomy in Cooper's heroines, the "festering white lily" and the "passionate scarlet-and-black blossom," a dichotomy which later critics of American literature were to repeat with monotonous frequency. Natty's love affair with Mabel in *The Pathfinder* was dishonest, "not the love of a man for a woman, in sheer impulse [but] the uneasy ego providing for itself";[41] Cooper was perfectly right to have Mabel refuse him. Similarly, Cooper was faithful to his creation in having Deerslayer refuse to be "absorbed" by Judith, who would have destroyed him: "A race falls when men begin to worship the Great Mother, when they are enveloped within the woman, as a child in the womb."[42]

The greatest novel of the series, in Lawrence's estimation, was *The Deerslayer,* a judgment with which Cooper's later critics are in accord. It was, he wrote, "one of the most beautiful and perfect books in the world: flawless as a jewel and of gem-like concentration. From the first words we pass straight into the world of sheer creation, with so perfect a transit that we are unconscious of our translation."[43] The book celebrated a new relationship between men, symbolized by Natty and the Great Serpent, each a "crude pillar of a man, the crude living column of his own manhood."[44] The relationship between the two, the white man and the Indian, was a relationship of perfect understanding and mutual respect for the differences between them. The beauty of Deerslayer was that he knew that "there are two ways, two mysteries—the Red Man's and his own. He must remain true to his own way, his own mystery. But . . . he acknowledges perfectly and in full the opposite mystery—the mystery of the other."[45] Although

---

40. *Ibid.,* p. 100.   41. *Ibid.,* p. 97.   42. *Ibid.,* p. 101.

43. *Ibid.,* p. 98. This judgment is somewhat modified in the *Studies* to read: "It is a gem of a book. Or a bit of perfect paste. And myself, I like a bit of perfect paste in a perfect setting, so long as I am not fooled by pretense of reality" (*Studies,* 60). He later added, "But it is a myth, not a realistic tale. Read it as a lovely myth. Lake Glimmerglass."

44. *Studies,* p. 54.   45. *Symbolic Meaning,* p. 102.

Lawrence noted that the tale revealed the "collapse of the white psyche," irrevocably divided between sensuality and spirituality, his final judgment was that the novel was a true myth, concerning itself centrally with "the onward adventure of the integral soul. And this, for America, is Deerslayer. A man who turns his back on white society. A man who keeps his moral integrity hard and intact. An isolate, almost selfless, stoic, enduring man, who lives by death, by killing, but who is pure white."[46]

Lawrence's revulsion from America's unconscious self was probably strongest in his essay on Edgar Allan Poe, whom he saw as the recorder of the disintegrative process of the white soul. The beauty of Poe's works was a ghastly beauty, the "phosphorescence of decay"; Poe himself lived "in a post-mortem reality, a living dead."[47] His tales, Lawrence argued, were not art but science, demonstrating the "workings of the great inorganic forces, disruptive within the organic psyche."[48] In his "love" stories Poe revealed himself as an obsessive, forcing himself by an act of will to experience continuously the "heightening of consciousness" which results from a purely "spiritual" love, a state of being which in Lawrence's prose sounded exceedingly obscene. The great motive of Poe's lovers was to "know" the self of the beloved, an attempt which led, vampire-like, to the beloved's destruction. "Ligeia," therefore, was a "ghastly story of the assertion of the human will, the will-to-love and the will-to-consciousness, asserted against death itself."[49] Lawrence criticized the mechanical quality of Poe's prose style and the mechanical rhythms of his poetry, noting that his images, such as those of jewels and marble and statuary, were more concerned with matter than with life. Symbolically, the stories portrayed the inevitable consequence of "spiritual" love; the desire to merge into another person led to the destruction of the separate self of the love object, and hence to death. Poe's obsessive concern with being buried alive was an apt metaphor for this destruction of the passional self: "All this underground vault business in Poe only symbolizes that which takes place *beneath* the consciousness. On top, all is fair-spoken. Beneath, there is [the] awful murderous extremity of burying alive."[50]

The essay on Poe was, as usual, heavily freighted with Law-

46. *Studies*, p. 63.   47. *Symbolic Meaning*, p. 107.
48. *Ibid.*, p. 108.   49. *Studies*, p. 74.   50. *Ibid.*, p. 79.

rentian moralizing. Poe served as an excellent text for his sermon, a warning against the "terrible spirits, ghosts, in the air of America." Lawrence pitied Poe, even in a strange way admired him for "performing some of the bitterest tasks of human experience"—of consciously suffering his own disintegration, a necessary event before the new consciousness of the racial soul could be born.[51] The emphasis on the Will, in such a story as "Ligeia," made Poe an apt object lesson for Lawrence's prophecy of the doom of civilized man if he persisted in denying his "other consciousness": "[Poe] was an adventurer into vaults and cellars and horrible underground passages of the human soul. He sounded the horror and the warning of his own doom. Doomed he was. He died wanting more love, and love killed him. A ghastly disease, love. Poe telling us of his disease: trying even to make his disease fair and attractive. Even succeeding. Which is the inevitable falseness, duplicity of art. American art in particular."[52]

Probably the most irritating essay in the *Studies in Classic American Literature* was Lawrence's analysis of Hawthorne's *The Scarlet Letter*. The first version of this essay possessed greater coherence (although in both versions the actual analysis of the novel's "meaning" is rather outrageous) and moreover, contained some important statements of Lawrence's literary theory. He opened the essay with a discussion of the duality in man's consciousness, the "sensual reasoning" of the primary mind, and the "sensational" reasoning of the cerebral mind. Both processes operated simultaneously in normal consciousness, but in sleep and in art, it was the primary mind which held sway. In the highest art, the primary mind "expresses itself direct, in direct pulsating communication. But this expression is harmonious with the outer or cerebral consciousness."[53] Viewed in these terms, *The Scarlet Letter*, for all its greatness as allegory, failed to be the highest art; it was a perfect example of American duplicity, the split in the American psyche. "Hawthorne," Lawrence wrote, "is a philosopher as well as an artist. He attempts to understand as deeply as he feels. He does not succeed. There is a discrepancy between his conscious understanding and his passional understanding. To cover this discrepancy he calls his work romance."[54]

51. *Ibid.*, p. 65.   52. *Ibid.*, p. 81.   53. *Symbolic Meaning*, p. 124.
54. *Ibid.*, p. 126. On page 124, Lawrence had essayed an interesting

Like the *Leatherstocking Tales, The Scarlet Letter* was a leg-
endary myth. According to Lawrence it was the "inverse of the
Eve myth," but his meaning here is not entirely clear. The "inner
diabolism of the symbolic meaning" of this novel again involved
the sin of *knowing*; the sin of Hester and Dimmesdale finally
amounted to their self-consciousness and guilt over their passion,
not the passion itself. Dimmesdale, the "pure young man" who,
in Lawrence's view, Hawthorne secretly hated, lived by governing
his body in the interests of the spirit. Inwardly, he enjoyed fla-
gellating himself, which to Lawrence was a "form of masturbation,"
an obscene triumph of the ego over the flesh. Hester symbolized
the archetypal American female, a witch disguised as a Sister of
Mercy. Unable to achieve a genuine union with her lover, she
recoiled upon herself and became a destructive force.

The love story in *The Scarlet Letter* provided Lawrence an opportunity for one of his favorite sermons on the proper relationship between male and female, and a prophecy that a new milen-
nium would dawn only when the female would "*choose* to experience again the great submission" to the male who was secure in
his own integrity.[55] In Lawrence's psychological allegory, Pearl
represented the necessary "devil" spawned by destiny to destroy a
"rotten, false humanity."[56] Chillingworth symbolized the "black,
vengeful soul of the crippled, masterful male, still dark in his authority"; set against Dimmesdale, with his "white ghastliness of the
fallen saint," the two characters were an image of the "two halves
of manhood mutually destroying one another."[57] This "marvellous
under-meaning" of *The Scarlet Letter* made it "one of the greatest allegories in all literature," a beautiful instance of the "absolute duplicity of that blue-eyed *Wunderkind* of a Nathaniel, the

explanation of the development of modern art: "Myth, legend, romance,
drama, these forms of utterance merge off into one another by imper-
ceptible degrees. The primary or sensual mind of man expresses itself
most profoundly in myth. At the same time, myth is most repugnant to
reason. Myth is the huge, concrete expression wherein the dynamic psyche
utters its first great passional concepts of the genesis of the human cosmos,
the inception of the human species. Following myth comes legend, giving
utterance to the genesis of a race psyche. Beyond legend is romance,
where the individual psyche struggles into dynamic being, still impersonal.
When we enter the personal plane we enter the field of art proper—dramatic, lyric, emotional.

55. *Studies*, pp. 93-94.   56. *Ibid.*, p. 96.   57. *Ibid.*, p. 99.

American wonder-child with his magical allegorical insight."[58] The *Wunderkind*, needless to say, would have been exceedingly surprised to hear his own "message."

After such strenuous psychological acrobatics, which succeed in turning *The Scarlet Letter* on its head, Lawrence's essay on *The Blithedale Romance* was somewhat anti-climactic. He resumed his analysis of Pearl (playing at intolerable length upon her name) as representative of the modern female, fair outside and rotten within. She reappears, according to Lawrence, as the Black Pearl and the White Pearl, Zenobia and Priscilla, in *Blithedale*. Priscilla was denounced as a "little psychic prostitute," a "degenerate descendant of Ligeia," and Hawthorne castigated for the absurdity of his attempt to idealize work in the Brook Farm experiment, an error which resulted in his "leaving off brookfarming to take up bookfarming."[59]   Taken together, Lawrence's comments on *The Blithedale Romance* seem too scattered to possess much validity, or even clarity.

His admiration for Dana and Melville was expressed with few qualifications. In his essay on *Two Years Before the Mast*, he praised Dana's style as that of a "great tragic recorder," warmly approving his attempt at a confrontation with the "Magna Mater," the sea. In the midst of his appreciation, however, Lawrence had one quarrel to pick: he was revolted by Dana's treatment of the shipboard flogging. To Lawrence, this form of punishment was justifiable; he argued, somewhat distastefully, that there was a natural "current of interchange" between master and servant, a "reciprocity of command and obedience" which existed in a state of "unstable vital equilibrium."[60] The flogging was a "necessary storm" which served to restore the equilibrium, a natural "passional interchange" which should not have been interrupted by the busy-body sailor, John. The Captain was right to have also flogged the latter for thrusting his noxious mental-humanitarian concerns into a natural situation. This justification for sadistic brutality in the name of "nature" is an unwarranted and unpalatable intrusion into an otherwise sound assessment of a little-praised writer. For the most part, Lawrence let the book speak for itself, relying heavily on extensive quotations, and concluded that Dana's win-

58. *Ibid.*   59. *Ibid.*, p. 105.   60. *Ibid.*, p. 116.

ning through to a consciousness of the sea was a remarkable human achievement: "He has lived this great experience for us; we owe him homage."[61]

The two essays on Herman Melville in the *Studies* were among the first pieces of significant critical commentary made on this writer, whose reputation in 1923 was negligible. Beginning with *Typee* and *Omoo*, Lawrence depicted Melville as one of the "sea people," men who turn their backs on humanity and embark on a quest for the elemental. Melville's hatred of the world was not distorted, since the world *is* hateful; but he erred in his persistent search for a "paradise regained." Instinctively he himself recognized this, according to Lawrence, when he refused to accept the savage's paradise in the Marquesan islands and abandoned it for a return to the civilized world.[62] With sharp perception, Lawrence pointed out that Melville was by nature a man in revolt, one who was least comfortable when surrounded by comfort: "When he had something definite to rebel against—like the bad conditions on a whaling ship—then he was much happier in his miseries. The mills of God were grinding inside him, and he needed something to grind on."[63] Lawrence could not completely accept Melville's pessimism, however, despite his sympathy with it. Melville's problem lay, he said, in his insistence on perfect human relationships, between man and wife and between friends. When he could not find them, he blamed life, which Lawrence criticized as an unrealistic attitude.

His remarks on Melville's symbolic mode of writing were highly sensitive and reflected a temperamental affinity with his subject. "Melville at his best," he commented, "invariably wrote

61. *Ibid.*, p. 124.

62. The later version of this essay is more sympathetic to Melville's escape from the Marquesans than the version in *The Symbolic Meaning*. This may be attributable to Lawrence's own experience in Taos, which led him to the recognition that civilized man "can't go back," that there is a "gulf in time and being" between him and the savage which cannot be bridged. However false the "progress" of the civilized world might be, still "we have been living and struggling forwards along some road that is no road, and yet a great life-development. We have struggled on, and on we must still go" (*Studies*, 136-37). Lawrence further argued that we must "make a great swerve in our onward-going life-course now, to gather up the savage mysteries. But this does not mean going back on ourselves" (*Studies*, 137-38).

63. *Studies*, p. 139.

from a sort of dream-self, so that events which he relates as actual fact have indeed a far deeper reference to his own soul, his own inner life."[64] The incident narrated in *Typee* in which Melville slid down the gorge into the valley of the Typees, for example, was a "bit of birth-myth, or rebirth-myth on Melville's part—unconscious, no doubt, because his running under-consciousness was always mystical and symbolical. He wasn't aware that he was being mystical."[65]

Lawrence repeated this idea in his essay on *Moby Dick*, insisting that Melville's symbols were not consciously understood or intended, and noting the strange talent Melville displayed for transforming the concrete and immediate into the symbolic without doing violence to the physical reality: "Melville cannot always have known what his own symbols meant. He used them half-deliberately: never *quite* sure. Then again, he forgets them and moves into pure actuality. It is curious how actuality, of itself, in deep issues, becames symbolic."[66] Melville's great thematic concern, according to Lawrence, was not with personal relationships or human contacts, but with the world of the non-human: "He is more spell-bound by the strange slidings and collidings of Matter than by the things men do . . . . It is the material elements he really has to do with. He was a futurist long before futurism found paint. The sheer naked slidings of the elements. And the human soul experiencing it all. So often, it is almost over the border: psychiatry. Almost spurious. Yet so great."[67]

For all his intense admiration of Melville, amounting at times to awe, Lawrence was still annoyed by certain aspects of his prose. He disliked Melville's sententiousness, his habit of taking everything "au grand serieux." In the opening chapters of *Moby Dick*, for example, "one cannot help feeling that the author is pretentious, and an amateur, wordy and shoddy. Yet something glimmers through all this: a glimmer of genuine reality. Not a reality of real, open-air experience. Yet it is a reality of what takes place in the dark cellars of a man's soul, what the psychoanalysts call the unconscious."[68]

The symbolism of the novel itself called forth some of Lawrence's best comments. The *Pequod* was an emblem of America—

64. *Ibid.*, p. 134.   65. *Ibid.*   66. *Symbolic Meaning*, p. 218.
67. *Studies*, p. 146.   68. *Symbolic Meaning*, pp. 214-15.

"a maniac captain of the soul, and three eminently practical mates
. . . . Then such a crew. Renegades, castaways, cannibals:
Ishmael, Quakers. America!"[69] In his interpretation of *Moby
Dick*, as elsewhere, Lawrence revealed again his tendency to see
fiction solely in terms of its latent didactic import, and particularly
his tendency always to take sides, to see the cast of characters in
terms of a hero and a villain. In this case, Ahab was the villain,
the whale the hero. Ahab was the archetype of the American
will, the "maniacal fanaticism of our white mental consciousness,"
relentlessly pursuing the "deepest blood-being of the white race"—
Moby Dick, "our deepest blood nature."[70] This epic of the "last
phallic being of the white man hunted into the death of upper consciousness and the ideal will" was an unconscious prophecy of the
doom of western man. This "surpassingly beautiful book" was
all "fantastic, phantasmagoric," a strange voyage of the soul which
was "curiously, a real whaling voyage, too."[71] The greater part
of Lawrence's essay was devoted to long quotations from the novel
itself, the only other instance in the *Studies* where Lawrence si-
lenced his own voice and allowed the author's prose to stand by
itself. In his concluding comment, however, he could not resist
the old impulse to deflate any completely unqualified praise for a
writer, no matter how strong his admiration: "So ends one of the
strangest and most wonderful books in the world, closing up its
mystery and its tortured symbolism. It is an epic of the sea such
as no man has equalled; and it is a book of esoteric symbolism
of profound significance, and of considerable tiresomeness."[72]

The final essay in the *Studies*, on Walt Whitman, reveals a
curious ambivalence on Lawrence's part toward the poet he once
called "the greatest modern poet." In the earlier version of this
essay, Whitman's verse was praised as "springing sheer from the
spontaneous sources of his being . . . perfect and whole . . .
too pure for mechanical assistance of rhyme and measure. The
perfect utterance of a concentrated spontaneous soul."[73] This
early enthusiasm was changed into something similar to hatred in
the essay in the *Studies*, almost as if Lawrence felt that Whitman
had betrayed him. The same poem, for example ("I Am He That
Aches with Amorous Love") cited with approval in the first ver-

69. *Studies*, p. 150.   70. *Ibid.*, p. 160.   71. *Ibid.*, p. 148.
72. *Ibid.*, p. 159.   73. *Symbolic Meaning*, p. 240.

sion is subjected in the second to massive and tiresome ridicule. Lawrence's great quarrel with Whitman stemmed from his hatred of Whitman's generalizations and particularly his dislike of Whitman's desire to merge himself into a transcendental Oneness: to Lawrence, this desire progressed from an initial attempt to merge into a union with Woman (an impulse Lawrence had earlier attacked in his essays on Poe and Hawthorne), to a desire for a union with Man, and finally a desire to merge with Death. It was thus death which was the final outcome of Whitman's democratic program of the love of comrades.

In one of his clearest statements of the moral purpose of art, Lawrence wrote: "The essential function of art is moral. Not aesthetic, not decorative, not pastime and recreation. But moral. The essential function of art is moral. But a passionate, implicit morality, not didactic. A morality which changes the blood rather than the mind. Changes the blood first. The mind follows later, in the wake."[74] For Lawrence, Whitman's greatness lay in the fact of his being a "great changer of the blood in the veins of men." His positive contribution to morality lay in his great celebration of the body—he was the "first heroic seer to seize the soul by the scruff of her neck and plant her down among the potsherds"[75]—and in his recognition that the "great home of the Soul is the Open Road." His mistake, however, was to confound the words "sympathy" and "charity." Sympathy, in Lawrence's definition, was "the soul's judging for herself, and preserving her own integrity"; Whitman confused this with Christian love and charity, and ended with the perverted desire to violate his own innate being and merge himself into other souls, a transgression, in Lawrence's view, of man's instinctive privacy and the necessary recognition of the "otherness" of the external world. Although Lawrence tried to soften his hostility toward Whitman in the latter half of the essay, the final impression is still that of spleen, which is mitigated little by the extravagant humor of many of his comments. Altogether, the Whitman essay concludes the *Studies in Classic American Literature* on a relatively sour note.

The book itself, however, taken as a whole, represents a significant critical achievement. Although it is true that the essays

74. *Studies*, p. 171.   75. *Ibid.*, p. 172.

reflect a highly personal system of psychology—or rather, philosophy—it would be a mistake merely to reiterate the familiar cliché that this criticism reveals more about the critic than about the subject matter with which he deals. The *Studies in Classic American Literature* is indeed permeated with Lawrence's personality, which can frequently grate on the reader's sensibilities, but the essays are also a respository for some acute insights into the underlying symbolic themes in American literature. The *Studies* was a pioneering work, the first major critical reassessment of nineteenth century American writers, and it should be kept in mind that Lawrence was among the first to accord Cooper and Melville the praise now taken for granted. Moreover, Lawrence's examination of American literature as a symbolic map of the American cultural psyche was the first significant attempt at myth criticism to appear. Many of his conclusions have been accepted and elaborated by later explorers of the same territory, who have also utilized his method, the outstanding example being Leslie Fiedler's *Love and Death in the American Novel.* Lawrence's identification of the critic's principal task with the process of making moral value judgments on occasion led him into unwarranted moral pronouncements of his own which had only a tenuous connection with the content of the novel he was presumably examining; his actual grasp of the facts, biographical and textual, can be justly attacked; his prose style frequently sacrifices truth and clarity for the sake of a phrase; his psychologizing has very shaky foundations. But when the worst that can be said of the book has been said, the *Studies,* and several of Lawrence's minor pieces as well, remain a distinctive critical voice, a significant contribution to a new method, and a fertile source of fresh and original insights into the "latent truths of a tale."

9. *Retrospect*

The proliferation of Freudian analyses of literature in the years during and after the first World War reflected a remarkable degree of cross-fertilization of ideas in the disciplines of psychology and literary criticism. The appeal of psychoanalysis to American intellectuals can be explained in several ways: its apparent doctrine of sexual liberation provided a convenient stick with which the young radicals could attack the hypocrisy and repressiveness of American "Puritanism"; the pronounced individualism of psychotherapeutic technique, with its emphasis on the individual's ability to cure himself through a guided self-analysis, was easily accepted in a culture which minimized class and ethnic distinctions as important factors in man's life; the apparent hope it held out for personal salvation was assimilated to a basic cultural optimism; and, finally, psychoanalysis served to answer a deep cultural need in a society dislocated by the consequences of industrialization and urbanization coupled with the loss of a meaningful religious orientation.[1] As a discipline devoted to the study of man's mind, psychology had always been an intermediary between the humanities and the sciences. At a time when literary criticism was groping for a new methodology, the glamorous new "science" of psychoanalysis, which claimed to have demonstrated

1. For a detailed explanation of the causes for the wider American acceptance of psychoanalysis than was present elsewhere in the world, see F. H. Matthews, "The Americanization of Sigmund Freud," *Journal of American Studies*, I (April, 1967), 39-62. I am indebted to Mr. Matthews for some of my own suggestions.

empirically its theories about man's consciousness, presented a strong appeal. The relevance of this new theory to the creative process was sensed very quickly, and appears in the earliest articles on Freud's thought as well as in many of Freud's own works. Ernest Jones analyzed Hamlet in 1910; F. C. Prescott explored the analogy between art and the dream in 1912.

The absorption of the concepts of Freudian psychology into the intellectual milieu, however, presented a dilemma to the literary critic. Psychoanalytic theory was widely accepted as true; to react to it merely with a flat denial of its premises was to risk being classified as a repressive reactionary. If criticism were not to remain simply an ivory-tower exercise, it was felt, it must respond in some way to this new science of the mind and avail itself of whatever insights psychoanalysis could offer into the creative process. On the other hand, the implications of the Freudian view of the psyche were distinctly unpalatable, for if art were no more than a sublimated form of erotic desires, a fantasy of an unbalanced mind designed to protect itself from pain through the creation of an imaginary world where one's unconscious "wishes" were satisfied, it was not only unhealthy but childish, something which the adult mind should not properly concern itself with. Even if that extreme implication were avoided, the critic faced a further complication caused by his new awareness of the large part played by the irrational in the formation of judgment; was it possible that his own critical evaluations were little more than rationalizations for some unconscious need? On the practical side of the question, precisely how were the new insights Freud had given into the human mind to be used? If great art was that which drew most directly on the unconscious as a source, how was the critic to distinguish between the "unconscious" and the merely "conscious" elements in a poem? Moreover, what exactly *was* the role of the conscious intellect in the creative process? If great art differed from neurotic art by the "social validity of the symbol," what was the criterion for this "social validity"? These questions and others related to them disturbed Conrad Aiken, who, probably more than any other critic of his time, confronted all of these questions head-on. Criticism, he believed, must go into the laboratory; the new psychology was the closest science had come to being a "laboratory" of the human mind, and yet Aiken found there a host of perplexing questions rather than any single formula with which to solve age-old critical problems.

The new information about the creative process offered by the hypotheses of depth psychology raised issues which were confronted by literary critics in a variety of ways. Prescott, Thorburn, Read, Bodkin, Krutch, Aiken, Brooks, Kuttner, Burke—each of these critics responded to different aspects of psychoanalytic theory, some emphasizing one tenet, some another, no two of them being in entire agreement about the importance or application of these ideas to criticism. Many of them, rejecting the "reductive" approach of Freudian theory, which seemed to deny art its higher ethical or social function, abandoned Freud's view of the unconscious and turned to the concepts of Carl Jung, whose conception of the racial or collective unconscious allowed a view of the artist more consistent with his traditional role as prophet and articulator of universal moral truths. But this "solution" was not entirely satisfactory either, for Jung's theories, apart from the difficulties of applying them, possessed less empirical demonstrability than did Freud's and were of dubious status.

If the critics of this early period found no single solution to the problems raised by depth psychology, several of them (as, for example, Albert R. Chandler and Herbert Read) continued their attempts to resolve the dilemmas posed by a psychoanalytic view of art and produced many years later books which more closely approached a synthesis. In the most recent, and perhaps the most successful of such attempts, *The Forms of Things Unknown* (1963), Herbert Read summarized well the legacy left by psychoanalysis to the twentieth century critic:

I am anxious to protect art and the artist from misinterpretations, and there are many such misinterpretations about . . . . But in the end I think we must admit that our debt to psychoanalysis is incalculable. I would say that this new science has come to the aid of the philosophy of art in two ways . . . . The first stage was to show that art could have hidden symbolical signification, and that the power of art in a civilization was due to its expression of the deeper levels of the personality. We thus obtained a scientific justification for our belief that art was more than a representation of appearances. But the second stage was more important—psychoanalysis has proved that the significance of the symbol may be, indeed generally is, hidden; and that the symbol as such need not be representational—it can be super-real, it can be completely geometrical or "abstract" . . . . Psychoanalysis has shown that our instincts were right; that the process of symbolic transformation which is fundamental to the creative process in art is also biologically fundamental: the transformation of the archaic into the civilized, the passage from the id to the super-ego . . . . The philosopher is content to define works of art as symbols for the articulation of feeling, as patterns of sentience. The analyst has more to tell us about those feelings, and about the biological significance of the patterns we articulate. Let us welcome his contribution to our knowledge of the dynamics of the creative activity . . . .[2]

The critics who availed themselves of psychoanalytic concepts in the decades between 1910 and 1930 did not constitute a definite critical "school." The criticism appearing in psychology journals was written largely by men whose interest in literary theory and practice was incidental to their other concerns. The psychoanalysts were mostly amateurs in the field of literature, and their frequently highly reductive interpretations were offensive to many literary critics, who objected to their lack of sensitivity to the aesthetic dimensions of a work of art. Moreover, even in the case of the most successful of them, Ernest Jones, the contribution made to literary criticism represented one single effort, and reflected more an interest in one specific literary work than in the problem of creativity or criticism in general. On the other hand, the essays written by men of letters were also, for the most part, solitary ventures into psychoanalytic criticism. *The Ordeal of Mark Twain* and *Edgar Allan Poe* were the only studies in which Brooks and Krutch approached their material primarily through psychoanalytic tenets; D. H. Lawrence's foray into American literature was his only major effort in this direction and represented a highly personal system of psychology; Conrad Aiken used the concepts of depth psychology only sporadically; and even Prescott, perhaps the only major critic here considered who could properly be classified as a "psychoanalytic critic," discarded Freudian ideas in his last major work, *Poetry and Myth*. Psychological critics at this time had no single periodical or outlet for the publication of their essays; furthermore, there was no single articula-

2. Herbert Read, *The Forms of Things Unknown* (New York: Horizon Press, 1963), pp. 92-93.

tion of a psychoanalytic theory of literature available for any potential disciples. Such discussions of theory as existed were themselves unclear on several major points, and no two of these discussions agreed on any basic points of methodology. This absence of a formulated method for applying psychoanalytic ideas to the examination of individual works of literature resulted in the idiosyncratic use of such ideas by individual critics, who frequently differed both from Freud himself and from other practitioners of psychological criticism.

To group the authors of the works examined here as a school of "psychoanalytic critics," therefore, would be a partial falsification. Literary criticism during this time was a rather confused affair. The major critics were men as diverse as James Huneker, Joel Spingarn, H. L. Mencken, and Paul Elmer More. More than anything else, their work, considered as a body, reflects a conscious groping after critical values. To many literary theorists Freudian psychology represented one attempt to introduce into literary criticism the discipline and order of science. The same search for discipline and coherence led also to an intensified interest in formal literary history, particularly in the field of American literature, as illustrated by V. L. Parrington's *Main Currents in American Thought*, published in 1927.

During the 1930's, four main streams of criticism emerged in America: social criticism based on or influenced by Karl Marx; "aesthetic" criticism, stemming from T. S. Eliot, Ezra Pound, I. A. Richards and (more indirectly) Benedetto Croce; historical scholarship; and Freudian criticism. By this time Freudianism had been assimilated into the academic world as one of several standard critical approaches. Such reputable critics as Kenneth Burke, Lionel Trilling, and Edmund Wilson used psychoanalytic concepts frequently in their writings, although certainly not to the exclusion of other approaches. Criticism based exclusively on the psychoanalytic method remained relatively minor, although numerically the number of essays and books in which Freudian and Jungian ideas were used continued to increase. That psychoanalytic criticism was not a major "school" before the decade of the 1930's is reflected by the fact that no essay representing this approach appeared in any of the numerous anthologies of criticism published during the early 1920's. Not until 1930 was the use of psycho-analytic concepts recognized as a distinctive type of criticism and represented as such in E. B. Burgum's collection of critical essays, *The New Criticism.*

The application of Freud's theories to the study of literature represented one response to a widespread feeling of dissatisfaction with the existing state of literary criticism in the years following World War I. It was also a reflection of the intense interest in the new view of man offered by depth psychology, an interest which was at its height during those years. The questions raised by Freud's hypotheses concerning the nature of man had to be taken into consideration by the intelligentsia of the day. These questions still remain, although the passage of time has rendered them less pressing to the modern critic. At the time of the publication of *The Origin of Species,* there were those who felt that the Christian religion had been irreparably damaged, but as the shock wore off, Darwin's ideas were gradually absorbed and eventually became harmless commonplaces. Something similar has occurred with the theories of Sigmund Freud. They have become part of the background of twentieth-century consciousness, compartmentalized by some minds and in others modified and integrated into larger systems of thought. One no longer has to take a stand on Freudian psychology in quite the same way that one did fifty years ago.

The use of depth psychology in literary criticism continues to flourish, and seems to have experienced something of a renaissance during the 1960's, despite the apparent decline in the acceptance of Freudian thought in the field of psychology itself. The past decade has seen the publication of such psychoanalytic studies as William Phillips' *Art and Psychoanalysis,* Daniel Schneider's *The Psychoanalyst and the Artist,* and Simon O. Lesser's *Fiction and the Unconscious,* as well as innumerable single studies of individual artists. Moreover, two journals now exist which devote themselves exclusively to psychoanalytic criticism—*Literature and Psychology,* published by the Modern Language Association, and *American Imago.* Many of the same problems encountered by the earliest writers of psychoanalytic criticism are still being confronted today; as in the first quarter of this century, the value of such criticism is still far from uniform. As a single approach to the work of art, the psychoanalytic method of analysis will probably never yield completely satisfactory results, but taken in conjunction with other approaches, it can enormously increase our knowledge of the creative process and can yield stimulating insights into the nature of an individual writer and his work. One criterion for the success of any critical approach is the extent to which it enlarges our understanding of the art work and increases our appreciation of it. Through their exploration of the unconscious roots of the creative process and their introduction of a new vocabulary by means of which the literary critic could articulate previously un-noticed aspects of literature which contribute to our total aesthetic response, the early practitioners of psychoanalytic criticism pioneered an approach which continues to illuminate the persistent mystery of the nature and effect of art.

Appendix A

A chronological outline of events relevant to the acceptance of Freud's ideas in the United States, including dates of publication of Freud's own works, popularizations of psychoanalytic theory, and major works of psychoanalytic criticism:

1899-1900   Publication of Freud's *Die Traumdeutung* (second edition, 1910)

1902   Smith Ely Jelliffe and William A. White assume the editorship of *The Journal of Nervous and Mental Disease*

1904   Freud's *The Psychopathology of Everyday Life* (English translation, 1913)

1905   Freud's *Three Essays on the Theory of Sex* (English translation, 1910) and *Wit and Its Relation to the Unconscious* (English translation, 1916)

1906   Founding of *The Journal of Abnormal Psychology*
Boris Sidis' article on Freud in *The Journal of Abnormal Psychology*

1907   William A. White's *Outlines of Psychiatry* (Nervous and and Mental Disease Monograph No. 1)
Jung's *Psychology of Dementia Praecox* (English translation, 1908)
Freud's *Delusion and Dream in Jensen's "Gradiva"*
Otto Rank, *Der Künstler*

1908   Formation of the International Psychoanalytic Society, with Freud as its President
Freud's "On the Relation of the Poet to Day-Dreaming"

1909   Freud founds *Jahrbuch der Psychoanalyse*

Freud's *Selected Papers on Hysteria and Other Psycho-neuroses* published in English
Freud lectures at Clark University
Karl Abraham, *Dreams and Myths* (English translation, 1913)
Otto Rank, *The Myth of the Birth of the Hero* (English translation, 1914)

1910   James J. Putnam's "Personal Impressions of Freud and His Work" in *The Journal of Abnormal Psychology*
Publication of the Clark lectures in *The American Journal of Psychology* (April, 1910)
A. A. Brill's translation of *Three Contributions to the Sexual Theory*
Freud's *Leonardo da Vinci*
Ernest Jones, "The Oedipus Complex and Hamlet" in *The American Journal of Psychology*
Isador Coriat, *Abnormal Psychology*
Albert R. Chandler, "Tragic Effect in Sophocles"

1911   A. A. Brill organizes the New York Psychoanalytic Society
Ernest Jones organizes the American Psychoanalytic Society with James J. Putnam as its first President
Freud's "Formulations on the Two Principles of Mental Functioning"

1912   Founding of *Imago*
Allen Starr's attack on Freud at the New York Academy of Medicine
Jung visits Fordham College at the request of Smith Ely Jelliffe
Jung's *Psychology of the Unconscious* (English translation, 1916)
Ernest Jones, *Papers on Psychoanalysis* (first full-length book on psychoanalysis published in English)
Otto Rank, *Das Inzestmotiv in Dichtung und Sage*
Isador Coriat, *The Hysteria of Lady Macbeth*
F. C. Prescott, *Poetry and Dreams*

1913   A. A. Brill's translation of *The Interpretation of Dreams*
Freud's *Totem and Taboo* (English translation, 1916), and "The Theme of the Three Caskets"
Eduard Hitschmann, *Freud's Theories of the Neuroses*
White and Jelliffe establish *The Psychoanalytic Review*
Smith Ely Jelliffe, *The Technique of Psychoanalysis*
Jung's break with Freud

1914   A. A. Brill's translation of *The Psychopathology of Everyday Life*

Freud's *The History of the Psychoanalytical Movement*
Walter Lippmann, *A Preface to Politics*

1915   Freud's "Some Character Types Met With in Psychoanalytic Work"
A. A. Brill, *Psychoanalysis, Its Scope and Limitations*
Isador Coriat, *The Meaning of Dreams*
Edwin B. Holt, *The Freudian Wish and Its Place in Ethics*
Jung's *Theory of Psychoanalysis*
Franz Ricklin, *Wishfulfillment and Symbolism in Fairytales*
Susan Glaspell's *Suppressed Desires* produced at the Provincetown Playhouse
James J. Putnam, *Human Motives*
Max Eastman's articles on Freud in *Everybody's Magazine*

1916   A. A. Brill's translation of *Wit and Its Relation to the Unconscious*
Beatrice M. Hinkle's translation of Jung's *Psychology of the Unconscious*, and the resulting controversy in *The Nation* and *The New Republic*
Poul Bjerre, *The History and Practice of Psychoanalysis* (original German publication, 1913)
Sandor Ferenczi, *Contributions to Psychoanalysis*
Otto Rank and Hanns Sachs, *The Significance of Psychoanalysis for the Mental Sciences*

1917   English translation of Adler's *The Neurotic Constitution*
Jung's *Analytic Psychology*
Helen M. Downey's translation of Freud's *Delusion and Dream*
Isador H. Coriat, *What Is Psychoanalysis?*
Alfred Booth Kuttner, "The Artist"
Freud's *Introductory Lectures on Psychoanalysis*

1918   Albert Mordell, *The Erotic Motive in Literature*

1919   Eugene C. Taylor, "Shelley as Myth-Maker"
Conrad Aiken, *Skepticisms*
Jung, "On the Relation of Analytic Psychology to Poetic Art" (English translation, 1923)

1920   English translation of Freud's *A General Introduction to Psychoanalysis*
Axel John Uppvall, *August Strindberg*
Jung, *Psychological Types* (English translation, 1923)
Adler, *The Practice and Theory of Individual Psychology* (English translation, 1924)
Freud's *Beyond the Pleasure Principle* (English translation, 1924)

Lucile Dooley, "Psychoanalysis of Charlotte Bronte"
Van Wyck Brooks, *The Ordeal of Mark Twain*

1921   Katherine Anthony, *Margaret Fuller*
Freud's *Group Psychology and the Analysis of the Ego*
(English translation, 1924)

1922   F. C. Prescott, *The Poetic Mind*
Robert Graves, *On English Poetry*
Louise Brink and Smith Ely Jelliffe, *Psychoanalysis and
the Drama*

1923   Ernest Jones, *Essays in Applied Psychoanalysis*
Wilhelm Stekel, "Poetry and Neurosis"
English translation of Jung's "On the Relation of Analyt-
ical Psychology to Poetic Art"

1924   Roger Fry, *The Artist and Psychoanalysis*
Charles Baudoin, *Psychoanalysis and Aesthetics*
Clive Bell, "Dr. Freud on Art"

1925   John M. Thorburn, *Art and the Unconscious*
Robert Graves, *Poetic Unreason*
Freud's "Autobiography" (English translation, 1933)
Kenneth Burke, "Psychology and Form"
Edward Carpenter and George Barnefield, *The Psychology
of the Poet Shelley*

1926   Joseph Wood Krutch, *Edgar Allan Poe*
Herbert Read, *Reason and Romanticism*
Sandor Ferenczi, *Further Contributions to Psychoanalysis*

1927   F. C. Prescott, *Poetry and Myth*
Maud Bodkin, "Literary Criticism and the Study of the
Unconscious"

Appendix B

An annotated list of selected early works on psychoanalysis, including some of the major works applying psychoanalysis to literature:

ABRAHAM, KARL. *Dreams and Myths: A Study in Race Psychology* (1909).

The early application of Freud's principles of the dream to the world of mythology, in which Abraham formulated the concept that "the myth is a fragment of the repressed life of the infantile psyche of the race. It contains (in disguised form) the wishes of the childhood of the race." Through an examination of the Prometheus myth, Abraham attempted to demonstrate that the mechanisms discovered by Freud to be operative in the dream (condensation, displacement, secondary elaboration) are also applicable to myth. His central thesis is the oft-quoted statement that "myth is a retained fragment from the infantile psychic life of the race and the dream is the myth of the individual." An English edition was published in 1913.

ADLER, ALFRED. *The Neurotic Constitution* (1917).

In this book Adler set forth his theories of neurosis, which revolved around the idea that the neurotic character was determined by an unconscious life plan or "fiction," the most common example of which was the "masculine protest." The necessity for this "life fiction" arose in response to a general feeling of inferiority experienced during childhood ("the inferiority complex") or for some particular malfunction, real or imagined, of some part of the individual's body ("organ inferiority"). Adler departed from Freud's theories on the question of sexuality, maintaining that Freud's conception of infantile sexuality and his emphasis on this as an etiological factor in the neuroses was the result of his having misconstrued the neurotic's attempts at maintaining the "life fiction"; the female child's attraction to the father, for example, was in Adler's view not a manifestation of an unconscious incestuous desire, but part of the wish to identify with the father and be herself a man (one form of the "masculine protest"). Adler's system found wide acceptance in this early period; certain of his concepts, particularly the idea of the "inferiority complex," frequently appeared in explanations of the artist's personality. The book was available in an English edition in 1917.

————. *The Practice and Theory of Individual Psychology* (1924).
A collection of papers on various subjects, dealing in a more expanded form with problems of neuroses according to the theory of "organ inferiority" and the "masculine protest."

BJERRE, POUL. *The History and Practice of Psychoanalysis* (1913).
A historical account of the origin of Freud's theories and a critical examination of them. Although he found Freud's hypotheses very fruitful, Bjerre was disturbed at his "occasional brutal disregard of the importance of the conscious life" which he felt resulted from Freud's intense fascination with the new world of the unconscious he had discovered. Bjerre himself had a personal preference for Adlerian psychology, which he also discussed at some length. A balanced and well-written critique of psychoanalytic theory as it existed at the time. In 1916, an English edition was published.

CORIAT, ISADOR H. *Abnormal psychology* (1910).
One of the earliest books in which Freud was mentioned and his theories discussed in some detail. In this volume, Coriat relied mainly on the *Studies in Hysteria* and the Clark lectures for his knowledge of Freud. Jones's study of *Hamlet* was also commented on favorably. Freud was treated in this book with respect, but was not considered revolutionary or in any way superior to Charcot and Janet, with whom he was associated.

————. *What Is Psychoanalysis?* (1917).
This book is typical of the popularized, simplified versions of Freud's theories which appeared after 1915. Coriat used the question and answer format, and included a short bibliography, which is a useful reference for books on psychoanalysis current at that time.

FREUD, SIGMUND. *Delusion and Dream in Jensen's "Gradiva"* (1907).
In this original example of the application of psychoanalysis to a literary work, Freud examined a short novel, *Gradiva*, by Wilhelm Jensen, which had been published in 1903. The story involves an archaeologist who falls in love with a marble relief of a woman he calls Gradiva; in a dream, he sees this girl in Pompeii; he then goes there and discovers that the dream figure is in reality his forgotten childhood sweetheart. Freud interpreted the tale as a corroboration of

psychoanalytic theory. Postulating that the artist intuitively understood the workings of the unconscious even though he was not clearly
aware of its laws, Freud concluded that "either both of us, the writer
and the doctor, have misunderstood the unconscious in the same way,
or we have both understood it correctly." Freud's examination, then,
was primarily written as evidence for support of his own ideas, rather
than as a contribution to aesthetics or to an understanding of the
creative process. In his analysis, he showed remarkable restraint;
he analyzed two dreams in the novel without referring to unconscious
childhood wishes or to the Oedipus triangle or even to unconscious
sexual symbolism—an obvious lizard in the dream, for example, was
ignored. His study closed with the words, "but we must stop here,
before we forget that Hanold and Gradiva are only creatures of their
author's mind." Like his study of Leonardo, Freud's *Delusion and
Dream* established a pattern for later psychoanalytic criticism; unfortunately, few of the later works had as much success as this. The
book was translated into English in 1917 by Helen M. Downey.

———. "The Relation of the Poet to Day-Dreaming" (1908).
    Although brief, this is an extremely important essay for psycho-
analytic criticism, for in it Freud set forth his concept of the function
of art. Relating the artist's creation to the play of the child and to the
fantasies of the adult, Freud discussed art as a controlled day-dream.
For this examination he deliberately chose "less pretentious writers of
romances, novels and stories," thus omitting "great" art. In such art
he found behind the person of the hero "His Majesty the Ego." The
formula at which he arrived for approaching literature in a way
"which might not be unfruitful" was the following: "Some actual experience which made a strong impression on the writer had stirred up
a memory of an earlier experience, generally belonging to childhood,
which then arouses a wish that finds a fulfillment in the work in question, and in which elements of the recent event and the old memory
should be discernible." The writer's day-dream was made palatable
by his art; he softened its egotistical character "by changes and disguises" and "bribed us by the offer of a purely formal, that is, aesthetic pleasure in the presentation of his fantasies." Aesthetic pleasure
Freud here called "fore-pleasure" and maintained that the real enjoyment of a work of art proceeded from "the release of tensions in
our minds." This treatment of form in art as a "bribe" to the conscious mind was one of the most objectionable of Freud's hypotheses
concerning creativity and aroused the most protest. Together with
the passage on the artist in *A General Introduction to Psychoanalysis*,
this essay contains Freud's central aesthetic position; as such it was
widely used by early psychoanalytical critics.

———. *Leonardo da Vinci: A Study in Psychosexuality* (1910).
    The first example of a psychoanalytic biography, or "psychography,"

of an artistic personality, Freud's object was to "explain the inhibitions in Leonardo's sexual life and in his artistic activity." Through the investigation of one of Leonardo's childhood memories, the fantasy of a vulture, Freud reconstructed the artist's psychosexual development, concluding that Leonardo suffered from a strong latent homosexuality, and that the smile that recurred in several of his great paintings was ultimately derived from a memory of his mother. He specifically denied in this work that psychoanalysis could explain the nature of artistic achievement: "As artistic talent and productive ability are intimately connected with sublimation, we have to admit also that the nature of artistic attainment is psychoanalytically inaccessible to us." He also explicitly stated that psychoanalysis "could not possibly furnish a definite view that the individual would turn out only so and not different." The study is a remarkable exercise in Freudian deduction from little external evidence, and is also an excellent example of Freud's own restraint, a restraint frequently in sharp contrast to the works of his followers. As far as I have been able to discover, the book was not translated into English before 1926, but was frequently referred to with respect by psychoanalytic critics and biographers.

————. "The Theme of the Three Caskets" (1913).

Beginning with Bassanio's choice of the three caskets in *The Merchant of Venice*, Freud analyzed this theme and its connection with the myths of Aphrodite, Cinderella, and Psyche. The "three caskets," in dream symbolism, are representations of three women; these "three sisters," are ultimately representations of the Three Fates, the third sister being Atropos, or Death. In all of these myths, and in Shakespeare's *King Lear*, this figure of death was replaced by its "wish-opposite," with the result that the third sister was presented as a goddess of life and fertility. Her real nature, however, was still present; in Freud's reading, Lear's reconciliation with Cordelia becomes the aged man's succumbing to inevitable death. This essay is rather involved and is less convincing as a piece of literary criticism than Freud's analysis of *Gradiva*, *Macbeth*, or *Rosmersholm*. It is an excellent example, however, of his method and logic, neither of which would be acceptable to many critics. It is also a fine example of Freudian "myth" criticism and a reminder that this type of approach was not solely confined to Carl Jung and members of his school.

————. "Some Character Types Met With in Psychoanalytic Work" (1915-1916).

In this essay, Freud examined three dramas, ostensibly as illustrations of certain types of patients he had encountered. The briefest examination was that of the character of Richard III, followed by a stimulating but inconclusive analysis of Lady Macbeth involving the theme of childlessness. The remainder of the essay largely involved a brilliant and extensive analysis of Ibsen's *Rosmersholm*. Examining the play from the standpoint of a typical female fantasy deriving from the Oedipal conflict, Freud concluded that *Rosmersholm* was "the greatest work of art among those which treat of this common girlish phantasy." Together with the analysis of *Gradiva*, this essay represents the best piece of psychoanalytic literary criticism Freud ever attempted, and it probably surpasses the former in its consideration of the play as drama rather than as supporting evidence for Freud's own ideas.

HITSCHMANN, EDUARD. *Freud's Theory of the Neuroses* (1913).
The most detailed early outline of Freud's theories, Hitschmann's book is striking in the extraordinarily heavy emphasis it placed on sexuality in the human personality. Taking with great seriousness Freud's somewhat casual remark that there could be no neurosis with a normal sex life, Hitschmann advocated legalized abortion and legalized prophylactics as a step towards national mental health. The book was favorably received in psychology journals of the time and appeared frequently in the "sexology" advertisements in little magazines. It is typical of the dogmatic writing of the popularizers of Freud's ideas and of their tendency to reduce a complex structure of thought to one single principle.

HOLT, EDWIN B. *The Freudian Wish and Its Place in Ethics* (1915).
Taking the "wish" as the "basic unit" of Freudian psychology, Holt applied this concept to the field of ethics. He defined "wish" as a motive for action, whether carried out or not. Therefore, he argued, morality consisted of actions which satisfied all wishes at the same time. This, of course, implied an obligation on man's part to be consciously aware of his wishes and his ambivalent attitudes toward some situations. Holt made very little use of Freud outside of the initial concept of the wish, relying more heavily upon behavioristic psychology. His ethical scheme seems to ignore repressed wishes, which, according to Freudian theory, were inaccessible to consciousness except through psychoanalysis, an omission which would seem to invalidate his theory. Despite this rather serious reservation, the book is an interesting attempt to connect Freud's name with morality and to make Freudian psychology a "usable truth" in the realm of ethics.

JUNG, CARL G. *Psychology of the Unconscious* (1912).
A long, digressive work which takes as its starting point an examination of some poems of a Miss Frank Miller, an American woman "who has given to the world some poetical unconsciously formed phantasies under the title, 'Quelque faits d'imagination creatrice subconsciente.'" In a sense, this is the original piece of Jungian literary criticism, for it ostensibly is an examination of these poems. In actuality, the poems and their images merely serve as a point of or-

ganization for Jung's examination of universal symbols and motifs as expressed in world mythology, ancient and modern, and a discussion of their psychological significance. The material examined here is the basis for Jung's concept of the "collective unconscious" and "primordial images." The book is difficult to read both because of its style and the enormous range of material covered. Two qualities of Jung's thought—vagueness and a tendency toward a mystical expansiveness—also contribute to the difficulty. The latter are emphasized by critics of Jung; his adherents stress the tentativeness of his generalizations and the impressive erudition he displayed. A "seminal" work, the book marked the obvious divergence of Jung from Freud and was of great influence upon those literary critics and social theorists opposed to the "reductive" nature of Freudian theory. The 1916 English edition contained a good exposition of Jung's position (in contrast to Freud's) in Beatrice M. Hinkle's introduction.

————. *Psychological Types* (1920).

An important work, in which Jung discusses personalities as falling into certain loosely defined categories, the major two being "introversion" and "extroversion." The book was of importance to students and critics of literature because of its concern with the creative aspect of the unconscious. It is here that Jung took up the problem of symbolism, the "primordial image," and the "collective unconscious," the latter term first fully defined here. The volume was available in an English translation in 1923.

————. "On the Relation of Analytical Psychology to Poetic Art" (1919).

In this important article Jung set forth his fundamental propositions about the nature of the artistic process and presented an excellent case against the Freudian approach. Limiting psychology to an explanation of "only that aspect of art which consists in the process of artistic form," Jung denied that it could shed any light on the problem of "what is art in itself." He also emphatically denied that art and neurosis belonged in the same category, except insofar as they were both manifestations of the human psyche. The origin of a work of art, he maintained, shared "similar psychological pre-conditions" with neurosis, but that was all. Freud's "reductive" method erroneously explained art in terms of these preconditions, which were universal for all human activity; the result was the "indescribable monotony" of Freudian studies of the artist. Jung also differed from Freud on the nature of the symbol, which he defined as "the expression of an intuitive perception which can, as yet, neither be apprehended better, nor expressed differently." Psychological criticism, according to Jung, should concern itself with the meaning of the work of art and should be "concerned with its preconditions only in so far as they are necessary for an understanding of its meaning." The work was "supra-personal" and had its roots not in the "personal unconscious" but in the racial or "collective" unconscious. Creativity, in this view, was an "autonomous complex," possessing an energy system of its own, and a being and will of its own. This autonomous complex sometimes possessed the artist completely ("introverted" art) or might be the motive impulse behind his conscious artistic intention ("extroverted" art). In symbolical art of the former kind, there occurred an "unconscious animation of the archetype"; the artist drew upon the collective unconscious to produce an image which was "best fitted to compensate the . . . onesidedness of the spirit of the age." By bringing this image into relation with conscious powers the artist served mankind, for he revealed to man the "deepest springs of life which would otherwise remain closed to him." This, according to Jung, was the social value of art and explained its power. Although this essay contained many ideas which differed from Freud's, the basic divergence was in Jung's postulate of a "collective" unconscious, of which he spoke at times as if it were a "world-soul," and his insistence that the work of art proceeded from supra-personal forces. The essay was much longer than any comparable work of Freud's on the same subject and is complex and penetrating. It exerted and continues to exert a considerable influence on psychological criticism. It was reprinted in *Contributions to Analytical Psychology* in 1928, and was published in English in *The British Journal of Medical Psychology* in 1923.

LIPPMANN, WALTER. *A Preface to Politics* (1914).

This extended inquiry into the nature of politics and government was not primarily a "Freudian" study, but Lippmann contributed to the popularization of psychoanalytic ideas through his frequent references to Freud and to his suggestion that psychoanalysis could help resolve many of society's problems. Although the effects of the new science had been felt in education, morals, and religion, Lippmann argued, it had not yet been applied to politics: "The impetus of Freud is perhaps the greatest advance ever made toward the understanding and control of human character. But for the complexities of politics it is not yet ready. It will take time and endless labor for a detailed study of social problems in the light of this growing knowledge." The book is an interesting testimony to the influence of psychoanalytic concepts on other disciplines as early as 1914 and as a reflection of the feeling that even at that time Freud's ideas were a matter of common knowledge.

RANK, OTTO. *The Myth of the Birth of the Hero* (1909).

Subtitled "A Psychological Interpretation of Mythology," this book presented psychoanalytic studies of fifteen related myths of the hero, including Moses, Sargon, Paris, Oedipus, Tristan, Romulus, Hercules,

Perseus, Jesus, Siegfried, and Lohengrin. The heroes shared in common a wonderful infancy: Rank's thesis was that these hero myths were the productions of adults who drew upon their unconscious childhood fantasies, and that the universality of these fantasies accounted for the similarity of myths in widely scattered countries. The mythical hero was the ego itself, endowed with the powers that the child wished to have. Rank stressed particularly two elements in these fantasies: the revolt against the father and the presence of what he termed "the family romance." The book was important because it was the first one in which the concepts of psychoanalysis were applied to myth formation and in which myth was treated as an unconscious childhood fantasy. An English translation by D. F. Robbins and Smith Ely Jelliffe appeared in 1914.

RICKLIN, FRANZ. *Wishfulfillment and Symbolism in Fairy Tales* (1915).
In this study, which was intended as further evidence in support of psychoanalytic theory, Ricklin examined fairy tales from German, Norse, and Russian mythology in terms of their "wish-fulfillment" structure. Citing Freud's hypotheses about art, Ricklin wrote: "The poet, whose longings reality cannot still, creates for himself quite unconsciously, in phantasy, what life has denied to him." He thought this was particularly true of such primitive poetic productions as fairy tales. Ricklin studied the tales with reference to their sexual symbolism, which was similar to that found in dreams, and in terms of recurrent themes such as the Oedipal situation, sexual rivalry, impregnations by eating, and the disguise of the handsome prince as an ugly (phallic) animal. An interesting early study, the book was similar to the work of Abraham and Rank on myths as supporting evidence for psychoanalytic concepts of man in general and of artistic production in particular. William A. White's English translation (1915) is unfortunately very bad.

Index

A

Abraham, Karl, 45, 59, 237, 244
Adler, Alfred, 38, 83, 84, 103, 109, 111, 117, 142, 183, 237-38
Aiken, Conrad, review of *The Poetic Mind*, 70-71; review of *The Erotic Motive in Literature*, 75-76; on John Keats, 105-6; use of Freudian thought in *Skepticisms*, 142-60; mentioned, 200, 227-28, 229
Albrecht, Adelbert, 9-10
Anderson, Sherwood, 41, 42, 137
Angell, James R., 5
Anthony, Katherine, 113-16
Austen, Jane, 110

B

Bailey, Pearce, 20
Barnefield, George, 104-5
Barrie, James M., 123
Baudelaire, Charles, 199
Bell, Clive, 77-79, 80, 86, 92, 95, 96, 150, 209
Beowulf, 130
Beresford, J. D., 41
Bergson, Henri, 22, 23, 29
Birdwood, Wilbur P., 42-43
Bjerre, Poul, 238
Blake, William, 127-28
Bodenheim, Maxwell, 41

Bodkin, Maud, 86, 92-95, 228
Bonaparte, Marie, 195n
Bourne, Randolph, 177
Bradley, A. C., 165, 168, 170
Braithwaite, William Stanley, 157
Brandes, Georg, 164
Brewster, Edwin T., 16-17
Brill, A. A., 6, 7, 18, 22n, 24, 25, 51n, 163; translations of Freud, 19, 24, 25, 35, 142
Brink, Louise, 122-23
Brontë, Charlotte, 106-11, 114, 118, 139
Brontë family, the, 109-10
Brooks, Van Wyck, 176-91, 192, 229
Broom, 40
Browning, Robert, 129-30
Bruce, H. Addington, 12
Burgum, E. B., 231
Burke, Kenneth, 95-96, 228, 230
Byron, George Gordon, Lord, 68, 102

C

Campbell, C. M., 22
Carlyle, Thomas, 64
Carpenter, Edward, 104
Carus, Paul, 19
Cassity, John H., 102
Cazamian, Louis, 73-74

Cezanne, Paul, 206-7, 210
Chandler, Albert R., 19, 36, 119-20, 228
Chase, H. W., 14
Clark University lectures, 6-8, 9, 10, 11, 13n, 238
Clarke, Mitchell, 5
Coleridge, Samuel Taylor, 61-62, 68, 166
Collier, John, 25
Cooper, James Fenimore, 215-17, 225
Coriat, Isadore H., 124-25, 238
Cowley, Malcolm, 40
Cowper, William, 73
Craven, Thomas Jewell, 69-70
Crawford, Nelson A., 135-36
Crèvecoeur, St. John de, 214
Criterion, The, 39, 76, 82
Croce, Benedetto, 151, 152n, 230
Cuchulain, 130-31
Current Literature (Current Opinion), 12, 16, 23

D

Dana, Richard Henry, 220-21
Darwin, Charles, 231
Dell, Floyd, 24, 136-37
De Voto, Bernard, 176, 187
Dickens, Charles, 73
Dooley, Lucille, 106-9
Dostoevsky, Fyodor, 138, 158-59
Dreiser, Theodore, 41

E

Eastman, Max, 23, 24, 27
Eder, Max, 203n
Edes, Robert, 5
Eliot, Thomas Stearnes, 149, 157, 160, 161, 162n, 230
Ellis, Havelock, 5, 13, 14, 23, 34
Emerson, Ralph Waldo, 56, 112-13, 189

F

Ferenczi, Sandor, 7, 45, 142
Fiedler, Leslie, 225
Fite, Warner, 30-31
Fletcher, John Gould, 147
Fraiberg, Louis, vii, 181, 190, 201n

Frank, Florence K., 38-39
Frank, Waldo, 40, 41
Franklin, Benjamin, 112, 214
Freud, Sigmund, spread of psychoanalytic theory in U.S., 3-36; *The Interpretation of Dreams,* 17, 19-23, 28, 119, 142; views on art, 44-45, 78-79, 80, 137, 165, 238-41; interest in drama, 119, 124
Frost, Robert, 160
Fry, Roger, 77, 79-82, 86, 92, 95, 96, 97, 209
Fuller, Margaret, 112-16

G

Galsworthy, John, 209
Goethe, 94, 166
Graves, Robert, 74-76

H

Hall, G. Stanley, 6-7, 9, 29, 116
Hamlet, 119, 121-22, 126, 156, 161-75, 227
Hardy, Thomas, 203, 208-9
Hawthorne, Nathaniel, 212-13, 218-20, 224
Haywood, William, 25
Heine, Heinrich, 49
Hinkle, Beatrice, 201, 242
Hitschmann, Eduard, 37, 241
Hoch, August, 6
Hoffman, Frederick J., vii, 143, 203
Holt, Edwin B., 7, 26, 241
Howells, William Dean, 184
Huneker, James, 152n, 230

I

Ibsen, Henrik, 94, 123n, 131n, 131-32, 241

J

Jacob, Cary F., 69
Jacobsen, Arthur, 101-2
James, Henry, 149, 177n, 178, 189
James, William, 5, 7, 10, 59
Jane Eyre, 108-9
Janet, Pierre, 12, 238
Jastrow, Joseph, 7
Jean Christophe, 138
Jeffreys, Harold, 131-32

Jelliffe, Smith Ely, 18, 24, 35n, 122-23, 244
Jensen, Wilhelm, 238
Jones, Ernest, mentioned, viii, 6, 7, 11, 16, 45, 74, 84, 85, 227, 229; as biographer of Freud, 3; as literary critic, 36, 161-75, 238
Josephson, Matthew, 40
Journal of Abnormal Psychology, The, founding, 6, 163; receptive to Freudian theory, 8, 11; early critiques of Freudian theory, 14; publishes *Poetry and Dreams,* 51
Jung, Carl, mentioned, 6, 7-8, 14, 34, 37, 38, 57, 59, 66-67, 83, 84, 86, 87, 90-91, 103, 109, 111, 122-23, 128, 129, 130, 134, 135, 140, 160, 201, 211, 228, 230, 240, 241-43; association test, 8; reception of *Psychology of the Unconscious,* 28-32

K

Kallen, Horace, 21
Kanner, Leo, 131
Kaplan, Justin, 181n
Kaplan, Leo, 124, 137
Keats, John, 72, 73, 105-6
Keble, John, 52-53, 65
Kostyleff, Nicholas, 145-47, 160
Kris, Ernst, 201n
Krutch, Joseph Wood, 192-202, 228, 229
Kuttner, Alfred Booth, 23, 24-27, 37, 45-48, 55, 138-39, 228

L

Lamb, Charles, 73
Lawrence, D. H., ix, 40, 41, 42, 137, 138-39, 148, 150, 156, 159n, 203-25, 229
Lay, Wilfrid, 33
Lesser, Simon O., 231
Lewissohn, Samuel, 25
Lindsay, Vachel, 160
Lippmann, Walter, 23, 24, 25, 27-29, 177, 243
Lombroso [Cesare], 100, 103
London, Jack, 33

Long, E. Hudson, 179n
Longfellow, Henry Wadsworth, 73, 112
Lowell, Amy, 105, 160
Lucas, F. L., 75-76
Luhan, Mable Dodge, 24, 25

M

Mansfield, Katherine, 157-58
Marlowe, Christopher, 94
Martin, Jay, 142
Marx, Karl, 136, 177, 230
Masters, Edgar Lee, 149-50, 160
McComb, Samuel, 17
Melville, Herman, 220, 221-23, 225
Mencken, H. L., 39, 230
Meyer, Adolf, 6, 8
Moore, Thomas V., 128-29
Mordell, Albert, 71-73
More, Paul Elmer, 230
Münsterberg, Hugo, 12
Murray, Gilbert, 162n
Murray, Henry A., 143
Myers, F. W. H., 4, 11

O

Oberndorf, Clarence P., 1n, 11
Oedipus complex, 16, 30, 34, 42, 98, 102, 114, 117, 118, 134, 139, 161-75
O'Higgins, Harvey, 112, 113
Oppenheim, James, 29, 46-47

P

Paine, Albert, 180
Parrington, V. L., 230
Peterson, Fred, 6, 10-11
Pfister, Oscar, 34, 38, 81, 142
Phillips, William, 231
Poe, Edgar Allan, 56, 73, 102-4, 192-202, 217-18, 224
Pound, Ezra, 150, 157, 230
Praz, Mario, 99-100
Preger, J. W., 127-28
Prescott, Frederick Clarke, mentioned, 36, 77, 81, 92, 93, 96, 97, 120, 227, 229; *Poetry and Dreams,* 51-57; *The Poetic Mind,* 57-69; *Poetry and Myth,* 37, 67;

reviews of *The Poetic Mind,* 69-71, 150-51
Prince, Morton, 11-12, 21
Pruette, Lorine, 103-4
Putnam, James J., 7, 18

R

Rank, Otto, 26, 45, 48, 142, 243-44
Ransom, John Crowe, 42
Read, Herbert, mentioned ix, 92, 95, 159n; review of *The Artist and Psychoanalysis,* 82; "Psycho-Analysis and the Critic," 82-86; study of the Brontës, 106, 109-11, 228
Reade, Edward H., 112, 113n
Reed, Raoul, 41
Renan, Ernest, 73
Richards, I. A., 151, 230
Ricklin, Franz, 31, 33-34, 244
Rivers, W. H. R., 74
Rivière, Jacques, 39-40
Robertson, J. M., 166
Rosenfeld, Paul, 176

S

Sachs, Hanns, 45, 125
Sandburg, Carl, 160
Schneider, Daniel, 231
Seeger, Alan, 150
Seven Arts, The, 45-48, 177
Shakespeare, William, 120-22, 124-26, 150, 161-75, 240
Sharpe, Ella Freeman, 111-12
Shaw, George Bernard, 89
Shelley, Percy Bysshe, 56, 72, 89, 104-5, 132-35
Sidis, Boris, 4, 12
Sinclair, May, 41
Sophocles, 119
Spingarn, Joel E., 152n, 230
Starr, Allen, 17-18
Steffens, Lincoln, 24, 25
Stein, Gertrude, 157
Stekel, Wilhelm, 45, 48-51
Stevens, Wallace, 160

Stevenson, Robert Louis, 56
Stragnell, Gregory, 138
Strindberg, August, 116-18, 124, 139
Strong, Margaret K., 128
Swift, Jonathan, 101-2
Swisher, Walter S., 129-30

T

Tannenbaum, Samuel A., 31, 120-22
Taylor, Eugene C., 132-35
Tennyson, Alfred Lord, 73, 128
Thompson, Francis, 111, 128
Thorburn, John M., 86-92, 95, 97, 228
Titchener, E. B., 7, 8
Towne, Jackson E., 125
Trilling, Lionel, 174n, 230
Trotter, Wilfrid, 6
Turgenev, Ivan, 138, 150
Twain, Mark, 112-13, 176-91, 192

U

Uppvall, Axel, 116-18

V

Van Doren, Carl, 176-77, 192
Van Doren, Mark, 70
Vivante, Leone, 76-77

W

Watson, James B., 5
Wecter, Dixon, 181n
Weinberg, Albert K., 130-31, 138
West, Rebecca, 42
Wells, F. L., 21-22
Weyer, Edward M., 15
White, William A., 18, 244
Whitman, Walt, 223-24
Wilde, Oscar, 124, 137-38
Wilson, Edmund, 230
Wilson, J. Dover, 162n
Woodworth, Robert S., 31
Wordsworth, William, 56, 61, 62, 68, 73